COUNSELING AND
GUIDANCE IN SCHOOLS

COUNSELING AND GUIDANCE IN SCHOOLS:
A First Course

C. H. PATTERSON
University of Illinois

Harper & Row, Publishers
New York, Evanston, and London

"Really effective counseling is the keystone of the arch of a widespread educational system dedicated to the principle of equality of opportunity."

James B. Conant, *Education in a Divided World.* Cambridge, Mass.: Harvard University Press, 1948. P. 204.

CONTENTS

PREFACE

This book was written because, in spite of the existence of so many other introductory texts in counseling and guidance, the writer feels there is a place and need for a book which differs from the standard or conventional text in several respects. The book thus represents a relatively new, or at least a relatively rare, approach to the introductory course in counseling and guidance. It emphasizes principles and problems, or issues, rather than procedures and techniques.

Critics of texts and teaching in counseling and guidance, in pointing out the preoccupation of books in this field with techniques and methods of the how-to-do-it variety, have indicated a need for a consideration of fundamental purposes and philosophy, for the presentation of a consistent point of view having a theoretical basis. The present book attempts to meet these criticisms, to some extent at least, although it is not possible to provide all that the critics might desire. There is a chapter on the educational setting in which counseling and guidance services operate, and a chapter concerned with the philosophy of guidance.

The point of view, or theoretical position, adopted is that which is variously known as the self-theory, the self-actualizing or the client-centered approach to counseling and human relationships. While many might regard this as a limited point of view, it is nevertheless one which might be defended upon various grounds. First, it appears to be the most adequately developed point of view, with practical applicability in a variety of situations, including the school. There are a limited number of theoretical positions, of which the most widely known is perhaps the psychoanalytic; this point of view does not seem to offer much to the school counselor in his everyday activities with students. Second, the client-centered point of view appears to the writer to be most consistent with the democratic philosophy which permeates all of our social institutions, including the school. Third, the point of view has become widely accepted and incorporated into much of the graduate training in counseling. The beginning student should therefore be introduced to it early. The instructor is at liberty to supplement the presentation of one point of view with others, or with the more traditional—or so-called eclectic—approach as he desires.

Many introductory texts include consideration of developmental or child psychology, personality theory and adjustment, and learning. These topics, in the opinion of the writer, should be covered in separate courses, and no attempt is made to include them here.

Beginning texts also, it seems to the writer, attempt to cover too much in terms of the details of the areas of counseling services in the schools. Much of this discussion of specific counseling techniques and practices should be postponed until the second course in counseling. This book, therefore, does not attempt to cover in detail specific counseling procedures and practices.

Again, many introductory texts spend a large proportion of space on methods and procedures of collecting information about students, and the recording, filing, and storage of this information. Critics have referred to "anecdotal records that fill filing cabinets and keep the instructional staff more than well occupied, but which serve little purpose in terms of what is actually done to help youngsters or to enlarge the scope of knowledge basic to the facilitation of personal development. Yet more than one school points with pride to the fact that an anecdotal record is available on each child enrolled without reference to the meaningfulness of this technological accomplishment."[1] It almost appears that the goodness of a counseling and guidance program is judged by the weight of records in the files per student. Because of the overemphasis on this area and its adequate coverage

---

[1] Shoben, E. J., Jr. Student personnel work: a worry and a vision. *Personnel Guid. J.*, 1954, 33, 152–153.

in other sources, little attention is given to the routine procedures of information collection in this book.

The book is intended for an introductory course which is offered to nonprofessional as well as professional students, and is designed as a comprehensive survey of the field. The nonprofessional student does not need a detailed treatment of services, but he should have a broad view of counseling and guidance in the schools. At the same time, the aim was to make the treatment detailed enough to serve as a good foundation for the professional student in counseling and guidance.

A matter which is troublesome in almost all areas of counseling is that of terminology. The word *guidance* has been long and widely used. With developments in counseling philosophy and practice which emphasize the self-determination and decision-making of the client, guidance has certain connotations which make it not quite appropriate. It has declined in usage in many areas in recent years.

The Division of Counseling and Guidance of the American Psychological Association has become the Division of Counseling Psychology. The Veterans Administration has abandoned the term *advisement and guidance* for *counseling*. At the college level, services to students are student personnel services, not guidance services. Yet the word persists in the public-school programs.

In addition to the force of habit of usage, it may persist partly because there seems to be no other word to replace it. In attempting to find a more suitable term, the writer considered substituting *counseling*. Counseling is, however, not broad enough to cover the services provided to students in the schools. Another term considered was *student* (or *pupil*) *personnel services*. This is the standard term at the college level, so that it might appear to be appropriate to use it also at the elementary- and secondary-school levels. It is so used by some writers.

But it appears to the author that this term is too broad for what is generally subsumed under counseling and guidance services. Personnel services include medical, nursing, psychological, social, and other services, as well as counseling and guidance services. There thus appears to be a need for a term to cover only these latter services, including counseling (educational, vocational, personal), test administration, occupational information services, group counseling, etc. The major service is counseling, but counseling appears to be too narrow to cover all of them.

Since no adequate substitute appeared, and since the writer does not favor using *guidance*, at least alone, the compromise of using the term *counseling and guidance* has been adopted. On the other hand, rather than referring to *counseling and guidance personnel*, the word *counselor* is used when referring to individuals performing these services on a professional level. In the case of other staff members who provide certain guidance services, in addition to teaching or administration, but who are not qualified as counselors, the term *guidance workers* is preferred.

The basic assumption of the book is that counseling and guidance services are specialized services provided by professionally trained persons. There is another point of view, the view that guidance is the function of the teacher. There seems to be confusion as to just what services are necessary or desirable in counseling and guidance. It is true that teachers have some guidance functions (see Chapter 6) and it is also true that the curriculum, indeed the entire school program, should be guidance-oriented. But this does not mean that teachers and administrators provide all, or even the major part of, the guidance services. There are many services which can only be provided by persons who have specialized professional training. And these services are not minor, not merely frills, but are necessary for the highest functioning and adequate education of all students. A school psychologist cannot substitute for the services of a trained counselor.

This is true at the elementary-school level as well as in the secondary school. It is often claimed that there is less need for counselors in elementary schools, except as consultants to teachers who provide individual counseling services to the children. While elementary-school children do not need individual educational-vocational counseling, they are in need of more help with individual personal-social-emotional problems than the untrained teacher can provide. The availability of psychological or psychiatric services in a clinic or child-study center is not adequate, and does little if anything to help the average child with his average, everyday problems. Here is where a professionally trained counselor can contribute directly to the child. There is, or should be, no question but that there is a place for the specialist in counseling and guidance in our schools, and that such specialists require professional preparation beyond that required of the teacher.

I wish to express my appreciation to Dr. Ralph H. Johnson, Consultant in Counseling, Minneapolis Public Schools, who read the manuscript and made a number of useful suggestions. My wife, Frances, also contributed to improving the clarity and smoothness of the exposition. I am indebted to Cynthia Schleef, Martha McDuffee, and Barbara Reher for the typing. And again, Julia Snyder, in supervising the typing, improved the writing by her questions and suggestions.

C. H. PATTERSON

Urbana, Illinois
July, 1961

PART I

INTRODUCTION

CHAPTER 1

THE EDUCATIONAL
SETTING FOR COUNSELING
AND GUIDANCE

The philosophy of education on which American schools operate is the basis for the philosophy of the counseling and guidance program of the schools. The nature of counseling and personnel services in the schools is thus closely related to the kind of educational system which we have. The goals and purposes of the schools influence the nature of the personnel services which are seen as being desirable or necessary.

An adequate consideration of educational philosophies is not possible in a brief chapter. Nevertheless, it is necessary to begin here if we are to understand the basis for personnel services in the schools, and if we are to develop a rationale for the kinds of services which should be included in a counseling and guidance program. In this chapter, therefore, we shall briefly present two philosophies of education which are not, however, mutually exclusive, and indicate the philosophy underlying the approach to counseling and guidance services adopted in this book.

Public education has come under strong criticism, even bitter attack, in the last few years. The specific criticisms are many, and the issues and problems complex. The controversy cannot be detailed, but the basic issue must be examined, since its solution determines the nature of personnel and counseling services in our schools. The problem reduces essentially to two conflicting concepts of the functions of the school. One point of view would limit the functions of the school to concern with the intellectual development of the individual. Although there is no commonly accepted designation for this point of view, its supporters were known as "essentialists" in the 1930s. The other concept of the function of education has become commonly known as "life-adjustment" education. We shall consider these two concepts of education briefly because of their differing implications for counseling and guidance.

Education as Intellectual Development

American education has traditionally been concerned with the inculcation of knowledge. Emphasis has been placed on the acquisition of the accumulated knowledge of the human race. The ability to acquire and to transmit knowledge requires a mastery of the skills of reading, writing, and arithmetic—the "three R's" of American education. The curriculum has been organized to teach these skills and the content of the major fields of knowledge, or the subject matter areas.

This point of view does not necessarily limit itself to the acquisition of knowledge for its own sake. The ultimate purpose of education is to develop the power to think, to provide disciplined intellectual training. It recognizes the need for citizens who are "highly literate, accurately informed, and rigorously trained in the processes of rational and critical thought."[1] Indeed, this point of view has often argued for the retention of courses whose content is no longer pertinent or useful on the basis that the process of learning the material contributes to disciplining the mind.

Hutchins has been one of the strongest advocates of this point of view. He has attempted to implement it in his concept of a liberal education at the college level. But he has also advocated it in public education. "The basis of education is to know how to read, write, and figure."[2] While recognizing that ". . . men are rational, moral, and spiritual beings and that the improvement of men [which is the purpose of education] means the fullest development of their rational, moral, and spiritual powers,

[1] A. E. Bestor. *Educational wastelands*. Urbana, Ill.: University of Illinois Press, 1953. P. 12.

[2] R. M. Hutchins. *The conflict in education in a democratic society*. New York: Harper, 1953. P. 93.

. . . education deals with the development of the intellectual powers of men. Their moral and spiritual powers are the sphere of the family and the church."[3] He recognizes that society must have some system that attempts to adapt the young to their social environment, but feels that this is not the function of education. "What belongs in education is what helps the student to learn to think for himself, to form an independent judgment, and to take his part as a responsible citizen."[4]

Criticisms of "Essentialist" Point of View

This last statement of Hutchins, including responsible citizenship as one of the goals of education, is the basis for a major criticism of the "essentialist" point of view. Responsible citizenship requires more than a developed intellect. Society needs citizens who not only have knowledge and skills and who know how to think but who also are prepared to be socially responsible. We need not only intelligent men, but men who have personal integrity—the attitudes and dispositions of social justice—and who are able to exercise cooperation, understanding, and skill in human relations, as well as skill in reading, writing, mathematics, and science. We need statesmen as well as atomic scientists. We need men who know themselves and other human beings as well as the physical environment.

A second criticism which has been leveled against the intellectual concept of education is that it is subject-centered, and ignores many of the important psychological factors in learning. Kelley lists several assumptions of this approach:

We assume that the child goes to school to acquire knowledge, and that knowledge is something that has existed for a long time and is handed down on authority. . . . We assume that subject matter taken on authority is educative in itself. . . . We assume that the best way to set out subject matter is in unassociated fragments or parcels. . . . We assume that a fragment or parcel of subject matter is the same to the learner as to the teacher. . . . We assume that education is supplementary to and preparatory to life, not life itself. . . . We assume that since education is not present living, it has no social aspects. . . . We assume that the teacher can and should fur-

[3] *Ibid.*, pp. 69–70.
[4] *Ibid.*, p. 13.

nish the purpose needed for the acquisition of knowledge. . . . We assume that working on tasks devoid of purpose or intrinsic interest is good discipline. . . ."[5]

While these criticisms are not entirely applicable to the best programs of education as intellectual development, it does appear that this approach tends to overlook many psychological principles of learning, and tends to give little attention to individual differences. With the development of free, democratic public education, our public schools now include almost 90 percent of the school-age population, compared to about 50 percent a hundred years ago. It would appear obvious that with this increase in numbers has come an increase in the range of individual differences in intelligence, interest, motivation, attitudes toward education, and life aims and goals. While it is true, as Hutchins and Bestor point out, that a liberal education is desirable for all, and that there is no evidence that it cannot be absorbed by all, it should be apparent that it cannot be provided to all, or absorbed by all, in the same form.

A third criticism of education as intellectual training is that it ignores the fact that learning is not a purely intellectual process. Learning is affected by the total state of the individual—physical, mental, and emotional.

Although it is now trite to say so, the child brings more than his mind to school; he brings everything that he is. If he is physically sick, emotionally disturbed, or socially maladjusted, optimum learning cannot occur. So the schools, even if their goal is the training of the intellect, must be concerned about the rest of the child's being.

Education for Living

These criticisms are the basis for the development in the 1940s of what is labeled, sometimes derogatively, as "life-adjustment" education. To some extent, education for living has been part of American education for some time. It is represented in the increasing development of professional and vocational training in our schools and colleges. This has been objected to

[5] E. C. Kelley. *Education for what is real.* New York: Harper, 1947. Pp. 15–20.

by many of those who are concerned with liberal education, although some, including Bestor, agree that the schools can contribute to vocational training as long as they do not neglect their main job of intellectual training. But "Intellectual effort must be the central, inspiring ideal of the school's life."[6]

Also, early American education to some extent automatically included the development of social skills. Small schools, in small communities, were often the center of social life, and the teachers informally, if not formally in some cases, taught social skills, as well as attitudes of personal and social responsibility. Early apprenticeship training, for those who had little schooling, included training in social skills.

It is also true that in early America, and perhaps even up to the present century, the family and the church were more active or more influential than at present in inculcating social attitudes and responsibility, and, together with the small community with its wider area of primary relationships, provided training in interpersonal relationships. With the decline of the close, large family, with increasing urbanization and its corresponding decrease in primary relations, and with the increasing complexity of social and political life in general, the family and the church are no longer adequate to assume the entire responsibility for training in life-adjustment.

So although it may seem to be logical to divide responsibility for education and training between the school, the family, and the church, with the school being concerned only with intellectual training, it appears to many to be an inadequate, if not an unwise, solution to the problem of society's responsibility for the development and improvement of men—to use Hutchins' term.

Life-adjustment education has been concerned with the whole individual, and with the whole range of life problems which he must face. It recognizes that emotional problems and attitudes can interfere with learning and intellectual development, and is therefore concerned with the child's personal and social adjustment. It recognizes that adequate preparation for responsible citizenship goes beyond the training of the intellect, and is therefore concerned with the personal and social development of the student.

[6] Bestor, *op. cit.*, p. 36.

Realizing the importance of interest and motivation in learning, life-adjustment education programs are concerned with the development of a curriculum that will be intrinsically interesting and motivating. Knowing that life is not compartmentalized into subject-matter areas, the curriculum is modified to be more representative of life.[7] These curriculum developments have been designated by the terms *core curriculum,* and *common learnings.*

Criticisms of Education for Living

Life-adjustment education has been subjected to criticism by those who favor education for intellectual development. Much of this criticism has been sincere and reasoned; some of it has been highly emotional.

A major point of criticism has already been mentioned: It is that personal and social development is not the business or responsibility of the schools; it is the responsibility of other social institutions, such as the family and the church. The purpose of education is the cultivation of the mind. ". . . Whatever can be learned outside the educational system should be learned outside it,"[8] no matter how valuable it is.

It has been indicated above that it has become apparent that life-adjustment training cannot be left entirely to other institutions. Whether it wants to or not, the school teaches the child more than how to use his intellect. The child learns much more than the subject matter he is sent to learn. He learns, whether we will it or not, or whether we plan it or not, how to adjust to many kinds of people or situations, how to compete or cooperate, how to be honest or to cheat. He acquires attitudes and beliefs, ethics and morals. The school has the child for more of his life than any other institution except the family, and it handles the child in even more of a learning situation than does the family. It would seem to be only reasonable that the school

---

[7] (1) Florence B. Stratemeyer, H. L. Forkner, Margaret G. McKim, & A. H. Passow. *Developing a curriculum for modern living* (2nd ed., rev.). New York: Bureau of Publications, Teachers College, Columbia University, 1957. (2) Educational Policies Commission. *Education for all American youth, a further look* (rev. ed.). Washington, D.C.: National Education Association and the American Association of School Administrators, 1952.

[8] Hutchins, *op. cit.,* p. 29.

recognize its influence, and that it use that influence in a conscious, rational, and planned manner.

It is further argued, however, that, even though the needs of youth and society are not adequately met by other agencies or institutions, the school is limited in capabilities and resources. This is of course true. The school is limited in many respects. It nevertheless can contribute, and its resources can be improved and increased.

There is of course nothing ordained about the purposes of the school. They are whatever society wants to make them. To say that the school should limit itself to the training of the mind is the expression of an opinion, a preference, a value. It does not mean that society, or the public, cannot think otherwise and delegate other functions to the schools.

A second major criticism of life-adjustment education is that it is producing graduates who are inferior in academic achievement to those trained when education was supposedly concerned only with intellectual development. It is claimed that the curriculum is emasculated and watered down. In Bestor's phrase, life-adjustment training is "a parody of education,"[9] and progressive education is "regressive education."[10] Certain curriculum materials and subjects are cited as examples of the childish trivialities with which life-adjustment education is concerned. It is implied that life-adjustment education is anti-intellectual, and that it neglects academic subjects. Life-adjustment is characterized as a ". . . concept of the educational system as a gigantic play-pen in which the young are to amuse themselves until we are ready to have them do something serious."[11]

While there no doubt have been instances of these extremes, they are probably not representative of the life-adjustment oriented schools. There is no good evidence that students today are inferior to those of fifty years ago. In fact, the evidence suggests that they are superior academically.[12]

[9] Bestor, op. cit., in title of Chapter 6.
[10] Ibid., in title of Chapter 4.
[11] Hutchins, op. cit., p. 93.
[12] (1) A. W. Anderson. The charges against American education: what is the evidence? Prog. Educ., 1952, 39, 94–96.   (2) E. H. Hanson. Today's schools are better, too—the facts are on their side. N.E.A.J., 1951, 40, 619–621.

Education in a Democracy

The two points of view outlined above are not necessarily incompatible or irreconcilable. It has been indicated that the essentialists do not insist that the schools should not offer courses in vocational training, physical education, or similar nonacademic subjects, nor do they insist that the schools should not provide certain health and welfare services. "The school should pay attention to certain non-educational needs of youth, provided the effort does not interfere with its fundamental task of intellectual training . . . So far as the school is able to do so without interfering with its essential programs of study, it should make its facilities available for these services."[13] The danger, which some claim has materialized, is that these courses and services will be overemphasized at the expense of intellectual training.

On the other side, it has been pointed out that, with few extreme exceptions, the schools actually have not gone very far in the area of personal and social adjustment and development. There appears to be a real need for more concern with this aspect of education, for reasons enumerated above. With the recent emphasis on scientific and technical training, it must be remembered that great achievements are more likely to be accomplished by individuals who are personally effective, occupationally and socially adjusted, relatively happy and not highly frustrated, and physically and emotionally healthy.

Life-adjustment education is not unconcerned about intellectual development. Knowledge, skill, and competence are necessary. Academic subjects and intellectual training have not been eliminated from life-adjustment curriculums, nor is there any apparent intention to do so. The methods by which they are presented, or how they are taught, have been revised and improved along lines suggested by psychological knowledge about the optimum conditions for learning.

Buswell has pointed out some areas of general agreement which appear to be acceptable to most of those concerned about education. These include the following: that the child is an organic whole; that learning by doing, based on experience, is essential; that real problems are more stimulating than artificial

13 Bestor, *op. cit.*, pp. 8, 73.

ones; that personality development is an obligation of education; that the activity of the learner must be free rather than dictated by authoritarian control; that education must have content; that the culture must be transmitted to each generation; that content must be organized, logically as well as psychologically; that intellectual discipline and effort are necessary.[14]

It would appear that education in a democracy must be concerned about the development of personally and socially responsible, as well as intelligent, citizens. Individuals must be prepared for social and community leadership responsibilities. Education, as Conant emphasizes, has three major objectives: education for citizenship, education for the good life, and education for a career or vocation.[15] These objectives were expressed over twenty years ago as education for self-realization, education for good human relationships, education for economic efficiency, and education for civic responsibility.[16] Even earlier, the report of the Commission on the Reorganization of Secondary Education suggested similar objectives for education.[17]

Education must be for all the citizenry, providing for each the opportunity for the fullest intellectual and personal development of which he is capable. A system of education which is to achieve this must recognize, and deal with, the following factors:

1. *The presence of a wide range of individual differences.* Although each individual must have the opportunity to absorb all the academic education of which he is capable, abilities vary greatly, and not all can absorb the same amount. Nevertheless, all should have the opportunity to learn the basic fundamentals. Teaching, and the curriculum, must be adapted to the abilities of the students. While all youth should have a public secondary education, the nature of this education will vary, depending upon the aptitudes and abilities of the student. The problems

[14] G. T. Buswell. Educational change and opportunity [Editorial]. *Elem. Sch. J.*, 1946, **46**, 239–241.

[15] J. B. Conant. *Education in a divided world.* Cambridge, Mass.: Harvard University Press, 1948.

[16] Educational Policies Commission. *The purposes of education in American democracy.* Washington, D.C.: National Education Association and American Association of School Administrators, 1938.

[17] Commission on the Reorganization of Secondary Education. *Cardinal principles of secondary education.* U.S. Bureau of Education, Bull. 35. Washington, D.C.: Government Printing Office, 1918.

of providing such education are great, and are presently receiving considerable attention.

2. *The nature and conditions of learning.* Learning does not occur automatically, or in a vacuum. It is dependent not only on the intellectual ability of the learner but it involves numerous nonintellective characteristics of the learner, as well as environmental conditions, including the atmosphere of the classroom and the method of instruction. Education must recognize these factors, and incorporate favorable conditions into the teaching-learning process.

3. *The unity of the individual.* As has been pointed out, the student brings his total self to the learning situation. He is not a disembodied mind or intellect. His attitudes, feelings, emotions, and physical state affect his capacity to learn or to profit from instruction. We cannot achieve the best results in terms of intellectual training if we ignore these influences. The school must be concerned with the child as a whole, and provide assistance in resolving problems and conflicts and remedying unfavorable attitudes and other conditions which impede learning.

4. *Intellectual and personal-social development cannot be separated.* In addition to the implications for intellectual development of the concept of organismic unity, there is an implication for the function and purposes of the school. The school does, whether it desires to or not, have an influence on the personal-social development of the individual. It should therefore assume a responsibility in this area, rather than allowing its influence to operate without awareness, concern, or plan.

While the school is not the only institution with responsibility in this area, it does have considerable responsibility by virtue of the amount of time which it has the child under its influence. Society, or the public, therefore has the right to ask that the school accept and discharge responsibility in this area as adequately as it can with the resources with which it is provided.

Summary

In this chapter we have attempted to sketch the background for counseling and guidance in schools. Two rather different conceptions of the function of the school have been outlined. While there are perhaps few who would take the extreme positions, there is nevertheless a basic difference in the concepts of education represented by the two points of view. One sees the function of the school as being limited to the development of the intellect. The other supports a broader purpose of education, suggesting that the school has an obligation to prepare its students for life in general, with its economic, social and personal problems and responsibilities.

While the extremes are in conflict, most people would take a middle point of view, and recognize that our schools should not, and actually cannot, narrowly restrict themselves to the three R's. The functions of the school have increased with the demands of the public for more attention to the varying and individual needs of all the students. This concern for the individual as a total or whole person is the soil in which personnel services have developed.

SUGGESTED READINGS

Bestor, A. E. *Educational wastelands.* Urbana, Ill.: University of Illinois Press, 1953. One of the strongest critics of life-adjustment education, a professor of history at the University of Illinois, details the criticisms. Although often intemperate, the points and issues raised are important and deserve consideration.

Conant, J. B. *Education in a divided world.* Cambridge, Mass.: Harvard University Press, 1948. Discusses the goals of education as a social process, making the case for education for citizenship and a vocation, as well as for the good life. A good rebuttal to Bestor and Hutchins.

Conant, J. B. *The American high school today.* New York: McGraw-Hill, 1959. Known as "The Conant Report," this book presents the results of an analysis of the needs and problems of the high school, with recommendations for the improvement of the American secondary school.

Henry, N. B. (Ed.) *The psychology of learning.* Forty-first Yearbook of the National Society for the Study of Education, Part II. Chicago: University of Chicago Press, 1942. This is still an excellent presentation, by various authors, of theories of learning and their implications for education, with chapters on motivation in learning and the relation of emotional behavior to learning.

Hutchins, R. M. *The conflict in education in a democratic society.* New York: Harper, 1953. Dr. Hutchins, former president of the University of Chicago, and author of several books on higher education, discusses the conflicts in educational philosophies and advocates that a liberal education must be concerned with the development of the intellect.

Kelley, E. C. *Education for what is real.* New York: Harper, 1947. Dr. Kelley, on the basis of the Hanover Institute experiments in perception, elaborates their implications for education. "The only reality is a perception, located somewhere between the eyes" (p. 35).

Mathewson, R. H. *A strategy for American education: an inquiry into the feasibility of education for individual and social development.* New York: Harper, 1957. The most fundamental objective of education is the development of individual potentiality, personal effectiveness, or personal-social maturity. We must educate the individual to know who he is, what he is doing, and why. The implications of this goal for the schools are developed.

Pediwell, J. A. (Foreword by Harold Benjamin.) *The saber-tooth curriculum.* New York: McGraw-Hill, 1939. A delightful satire on American education, in which stone-age schools continue to teach the paleolithic curriculum, although it is no longer applicable to the environment. Eventually, "progressive educators" revolt against the traditional curriculum.

CHAPTER 2

THE NATURE OF
PERSONNEL AND
GUIDANCE SERVICES

It should be apparent that the kind and extent of student personnel services provided in the schools are closely related to the educational setting. The philosophy and goals of the educational system determine the philosophy of student personnel services.

Definition of Student Personnel Services

The point of view taken toward education in the preceding chapter has, as was indicated there, certain implications regarding the functions of the school. The school, if it is concerned with the intellectual, personal, and social development of students, must provide more than classroom instruction in academic subjects. It will go beyond this to provide services which contribute to the physical, mental, personal, and social development of the individual student. These services constitute what is broadly designated as pupil personnel, or student personnel, services.

Personnel services are usually considered to be those which are provided outside the classroom, which are noninstructional in nature, and which are provided to the individual student on an individual basis. These services are usually provided by specialized personnel, professionally trained in various fields, rather than by the teacher.

However, it is often difficult to draw a line between instruction and personnel services. On the one hand, teachers perform many activities which can be broadly termed personnel services. The good teacher is interested in the individual student as a unique person. She adapts her instruction to the individual students in her class. She provides individual instruction in some instances. On the other hand, student personnel workers may give instruction in certain areas, such as courses or units in health and safety or occupational information. They also engage in specialized or remedial instruction in many instances. They may engage in other activities, such as extracurricular clubs or group counseling, with groups of students.

Nevertheless, it is desirable to make a distinction between those activities of the school which are mainly instructional in nature—even though these are, or should be, pervaded by a student personnel (or guidance) point of view—and those activities which are primarily noninstructional, and concerned mainly with the personal and social, rather than directly with the intellectual, development of students. Student personnel services are, therefore, essentially concerned with the life-adjustment or nonsubject-matter aspects of education.

It is also desirable to make a distinction between those services which are or can be provided by the teacher, or other staff members without special training, and those which should be performed by specially trained professional personnel.

Ordinarily, even those who would de-emphasize life-adjustment education would retain certain personnel services. But these would be rather limited in nature, consisting mainly of diagnostic medical services. Possibly certain remedial teaching services would be included. In some cases perhaps other personnel services, mainly of a psychological nature, might be provided, in order to enable students to progress in intellectual development to the limits of their potentialities. Psychological or guidance services might be utilized for the evaluation of students for assignment to special classes or curriculums.

An educational system which is concerned with the broader problems and goals outlined in the preceding chapter would go farther than this. It would, of course, provide those services which would assist students in intellectually achieving up to their capacities. But it would also be concerned with the student's personal and social development as a goal in itself, not only as it contributes to his intellectual functioning and development.

The kinds of personnel services provided in the schools vary greatly, depending on the resources of the schools, as well as the concept of education which is held. Student personnel services include general medical and dental examinations, as well as simple vision and hearing tests, the latter usually being performed by the school nurse or the teacher. A visiting teacher or school social worker may be provided. Special teachers for students having disabilities which require exceptional methods of instruction may be considered as rendering a personnel service, as can teachers engaged in remedial instruction. The school psychologist would be included in the personnel services of the school. Finally, the counselor or guidance specialist or director and his staff are part of the personnel services of the school. In elementary and secondary schools the counseling staff is the center or major part of a student personnel program. In colleges and universities, the student personnel services are usually more extensive and varied, and may include additional medical, psychological and psychiatric staff and facilities.

We shall be concerned in this book with the student personnel services provided by the counseling and guidance staff. Other personnel services will be considered only as they relate to counseling and guidance. The personnel services performed by the counseling and guidance staff are varied in nature, and warrant such separate consideration. Although counseling is, or should be, the main function of the counselor, he engages in many other activities of a personnel nature, including some specialized teaching, testing, placement, and consulting with and assisting teachers in performing particular personnel services. Since counseling is considered to be the main function, we shall use the term counselor to refer to staff members engaged in these various activities, rather than the alternative designations of guidance worker, guidance director, guidance specialist, guidance counselor, pupil personnel worker, or student personnel worker.

A Philosophy of Counseling and Guidance Services

The assumptions underlying counseling services are implicit in our earlier discussion in this and the preceding chapter. They may be stated here explicitly in summary form.

We have alluded to the fact that our present society is highly complex in nature. This complexity presents problems to every individual in the process of his personal and social development. One of the purposes of life-adjustment education is to assist the individual in this process of development during the earlier stages of childhood, adolescence, and youth. This is attempted through the curriculum, in which efforts are made to develop realistic understanding of the complexities of society. Instead of discrete subject-matter approaches, content is integrated in terms of problems as they are presented in life itself.

This is excellent, as far as it goes. The individual, however, faces his own unique problems in his development. A basic assumption of counseling and guidance services is that all individuals, from time to time, require specific individual or personalized help of a professional nature in understanding the world, and themselves in relationship to the world, and in dealing with the problems with which they are continually faced.

To be sure, every individual receives assistance of various kinds from others—from parents, relatives, friends, teachers, etc. This help is often useful; it may sometimes be harmful, even though well-intentioned, because such help in many instances requires professional skill, competence, and responsibility.

This recognition of the need for assistance does not contain any assumption that all individuals are inadequate, helpless, or maladjusted. Some are, of course, and these can be helped by counseling. But even those who are essentially normal individuals need, and can benefit from, counseling, because most counseling and guidance services are not directed toward normalizing the abnormal. Certain specific counseling services may, of course, be directed to this end. But counseling and guidance services are provided mainly for the more or less normal individual—to assist him in functioning optimally, in developing his potentialities, and in achieving to his capacity. The goal is to increase the individual's achievement and his contribution to society through the use of all his abilities and capacity. The terms self-realization and self-actualization have been used by some to designate this goal. Dugan succinctly states the nature of guidance services as follows: "Guidance during the last two decades has been inter-

portunity for the development of responsible independence. Counseling accepts the existence of individual differences and the uniqueness of the individual and recognizes that these lead to diverse personalities and diverse choices. Not only is it believed that freedom of choice enables each individual to make his greatest unique contribution to society, but it is assumed that in any event, in a democratic society, no one, not even a professionally trained counselor, should determine the decisions and choices of another. Counseling itself, moreover, while available or offered to all, is not imposed, but is provided to those who desire it. Certain other personnel services may be provided to those who do not desire or ask for them, but counseling is not one of these.

A third basic assumption of counseling and guidance services is confidence in the individual's capacities to resolve his own problems, and to make adequate choices, when given the opportunity. More than respecting the right of the individual to make his own choices, the counselor also has confidence in his ability to do so. The counselor facilitates the solution of problems and the making of adequate choices by providing a situation conducive to these results, and in some cases, where necessary, by assisting the individual in obtaining essential information.

Counseling and guidance, then, is not a means or method of control or discipline. It is not to be used by the administration to impose its wishes and decisions upon students. It cannot be used to persuade students to do what someone else desires them to do. Of course, there are students who present problems of discipline, or problems in other areas of antisocial behavior, and who may reject counseling help in resolving their problems. These students must be dealt with; however, they cannot be "given counseling" as if it were a medicine. Counseling is effective only when it is accepted by the individual client.

Guidance in a Democracy

The title of a recent article[5] raises an important issue in counseling and guidance. With the advent of man-made satellites and the resulting realization of the importance of scientific and

[5] D. E. Super. Guidance: Manpower utilization or human development. *Personnel Guid. J.*, 1954, 33, 8–14.

preted as encouragement of youth's development in terms of
basic concern about individual differences and as active assistan
to youth in making appropriate adjustments to personal, educ
tional, and vocational needs and problems. In short, guidan
services have aimed primarily at self-realization of the ind
vidual."[1]

Some have been concerned about the possibility that emphasi
upon the individual and his development might lead to self-cen
tered, selfish, or antisocial individuals. The question of the
individual versus society is frequently posed.[2] To the presen
writer this is an unwarranted fear. The issue of the individua
versus society, in this context, is a pseudoproblem. It is assumed
that the state exists for the individual, not the individual for the
state. What is good and desirable for individuals is therefore
good for society. Of course, there are individuals whose conception of what is good for themselves is at variance with the concepts of others. But most individuals include, in their concepts
of their personal welfare and good, adequate relationships with
others. The attitudes of others toward them are important, and
self-realization requires the development of adequate social relationships.

Thus, the goal of personal and social development includes the
concept of personal responsibility. Mathewson uses the term
"personal-social maturity."[3] The present author has called it
"responsible independence," recognizing the social, as well as
the individual, aspects of self-actualization.[4]

A second major assumption of counseling and guidance services
should now be apparent. This is that the individual is self-autonomous, and as such must be allowed self-determination of his
behavior. His freedom of choice must be recognized and respected. Without self-autonomy and freedom of choice, there
would be no individual responsibility for behavior, and no op

[1] W. E. Dugan. The organization and administration of guidance servic
Rev. educ. Res., 1960, 30, 105–114.
[2] R. H. Mathewson. *Guidance policy and practice* (rev. ed). New Y
Harper, 1955. This contains a thorough discussion of the problem.
[3] *Ibid.*, pp. 12, 82, 100.
[4] C. H. Patterson. *Counseling and psychotherapy: theory and pra*
New York: Harper, 1959. Pp. 61–62.

technical manpower, the issue has been sharpened.[6] The question is, do the needs of society for particular talents and skills in specific occupations dominate educational and vocational counseling, or are the interests, desires, and abilities of the individual recognized as primary? The discussion so far would favor the latter, but there have been suggestions that the former should be the case. Super[7] cites evidence that in other countries manpower needs dominate counseling. It is conceivable that a trend in this direction could develop in this country, with pressure being exerted on counselors to influence students in their educational and vocational choices. There have been suggestions that counselors recruit students for certain fields or professions. If national security should be seriously threatened, the welfare and freedom of the individual might be subordinated to the presumed needs of society. Under the emergency of actual warfare, this freedom of the individual is surrendered, and the armed forces assign manpower where it is needed, without regard for individual preferences or desires, and sometimes without consideration of an individual's abilities or talents.

The concern about the manpower shortage in scientific and technical fields has resulted in increased attention to guidance and counseling. While it is desirable to focus upon the need for more and better counseling services, it appears that the concept of counseling and guidance which is held by some who look to this field for help are not the concepts held by professional people in the field itself. To these persons guidance seems to be synonymous with selection and classification. There is emphasis upon identification of the talented, with the implication, if not the explicit suggestion, that after identification the talented will automatically be routed into special educational programs in preparation for scientific or technical careers. This concept of

---

[6] This emphasis upon the utilization of manpower for industrial production and military strength was present before *sputnik* focused public attention on the issue, as evidenced in the reports of the National Manpower Council: (1) National Manpower Council. *A policy for scientific and professional manpower.* New York: Columbia University Press, 1953. (2) National Manpower Council. *A policy for skilled manpower.* New York: Columbia University Press, 1954. (3) National Manpower Council. *Improving the work skills of the nation.* New York: Columbia University Press, 1955.

[7] *Op. cit.*

guidance appears to be present in a recent article on the nature of guidance, as is pointed out by Williamson in his comments on the article.[8]

But while guidance may resemble selection and classification in certain respects, such as in the use of the same or similar tests, there is a basic difference. This is essentially the difference between a primary concern for the individual and a primary concern for society, or a group. Selection and classification is the process utilized in the personnel services of the armed services and industry for the recruitment and assignment of personnel. Vocational counseling and guidance is the process by which the individual makes his own free choice of an occupation or career. It is therefore important that there be no misunderstanding or confusion regarding the functions and goals of guidance counselors (see Chapter 10, p. 181).

Conant, in some of his writing, appears to conceive of guidance as selection and classification.[9] However, in referring to effective counseling as "the keystone of the arch of a widespread educational system dedicated to the principle of equality of opportunity," he notes that "a democracy, unlike a totalitarian state, cannot force its youth into what the authorities consider the appropriate groove of advanced education. In this republic of free men, no official can decree what line of study must be pursued."[10]

The report of the Educational Policies Commission points out that "In dealing with manpower data it is essential to keep in mind that one is considering the lives and destinies of people. . . . Dignity and worth for the individual is a cornerstone of American philosophy. To forget this or to deny it even temporarily under the pressures and demands of a manpower dilemma is to violate the nation's ideal and to move toward the calculated regulations of an autocratic state."[11] The Commission later states that "the objectives of guidance lie in the individual's welfare

[8] F. H. Bowles. The nature of guidance. *Personnel Guid. J.*, 1959, **38**, 112–120 [Comment by E. G. Williamson].

[9] J. B. Conant. *Education in a divided world.* Cambridge, Mass.: Harvard University Press, 1948. Pp. 136–143.

[10] *Ibid.*, p. 204.

[11] Educational Policies Commission. *Manpower and education.* Washington, D.C.: National Education Association and the American Association of School Administrators, 1956. Pp. 61–62.

and growth, even when the interests of manpower needs are considered."[12]

Concern about this problem led the American Personnel and Guidance Association, the national organization of personnel and guidance workers, to prepare a statement of policy concerning the nation's human resources problems. The statement reads, in part, as follows:

This generation has been called upon to make a decision that will shape the destinies of many future generations. At the heart of this decision lies one of this nation's basic freedoms—*freedom of choice*.

Faced by a tragic shortage of scientists and technologists, we are strongly tempted to solve the manpower problem by channeling outstanding high school and college students into scientific and technical careers. Here lies the danger of tampering with freedom of choice. If the top academic potentiality of this nation were to be forced into a single, selected career pattern, generations of youth would lose their privilege of freely choosing their life careers—a privilege cherished by youth throughout the history of this nation. Such a course of action might not solve even part of the problem, for a lack of educated talent persists in all areas of our national life. The solution, therefore, must be viewed from a broader perspective, and we must aim toward utilizing *every* available talent. Only then will the demand for scientists and technologists be met, along with the demand for educated talent in all fields.

Utilization of human potentialities depends upon two factors: one, the nation's decisions to turn needed educated talent to national uses; two, the maximum growth of human talent through our educational processes. This statement concerns only the latter.

Through education, it is possible to alleviate the present manpower shortage without damaging freedom of choice.

Counselors have a profound obligation to individuals and to our society to assist students in making their career and educational plans in terms of their potentialities, as well as in terms of the uses to which these potentialities can be placed in our society. Students whose future contributions and prospects of self-fulfillment can be greater in fields other than science and technology should be encouraged to develop in these fields.[13]

[12] *Ibid.*, p. 87.
[13] American Personnel and Guidance Association. A statement of policy concerning the nation's human resources problems. *Personnel Guid. J.*, 1958, **36**, 454–455.

What Super refers to as "the increasing recognition of the needs and potentialities of the individual, the awareness of the dangers inherent in the imposition of the counselor's conception of social need upon the planning of an individual's career, and the realization that individual and social welfare can both be achieved by truly democratic counseling processes"[14] must be manifested in counseling and guidance programs in a democracy. Guidance, as Super states it, is a "process of guiding individual growth in order that the person may develop to the fullest of his potentialities," and is thus "a means of assuring to society the availability of all possible talents, with its manpower so oriented to itself and to social needs that it readily assumes the responsibilities which accompany ability."[15]

Breadth of Counseling and Guidance

In addition to the danger discussed above, the current interest in guidance in relation to manpower poses another possibility for a narrow concept of counseling and guidance. This is the limitation of counseling to the educational-vocational area. The National Manpower Council, for example, has recommended that "school officials use their guidance staff primarily for vocational guidance purposes and when expanded resources of staff and funds permit, also for counseling students with personal adjustment problems."[16]

By limiting guidance services to a narrow area even on a temporary basis, a pattern may be set which it will be difficult to break. It is only relatively recently that counseling and guidance in our schools has progressed from concern with educational-vocational guidance to the concept of counseling as a service to the total individual. The extension of this concept has been slow in some school systems. There is in addition another facet of this attempt to limit counseling and guidance—the impossibility of compartmentalizing the various aspects or problems of the individual. In the preceding chapter we have pointed out the necessity, in education, of considering the individual as a whole,

14 Super, *op. cit.*
15 *Ibid.*
16 National Manpower Council. *A policy for skilled manpower.* New York: Columbia University Press, 1954. P. 27.

and this is also necessary in counseling and guidance. Vocational or occupational problems and choices cannot be divorced from personal problems. As the Educational Policies Commission points out, "Analysis of career situations emphasizes the importance of personal traits and qualities to occupational success. The manpower situation calls for people with mental and emotional health, skilled in cooperation with others, capable of adjustment to new conditions. . . . Technical skills and manual skills are best utilized only where other skills of wholesome living are also present. . . . One's aptitudes and interests, his attitudes and habits and skills, indeed his whole life philosophy, are pertinent to career possibilities."[17] It is well known that personality difficulties are the most common cause for discharge from employment.[18]

It therefore seems apparent that, as personal and social development must be the concern of education, even if the major objective of education be the development of the intellect, so must they be the concern of counseling and guidance, even if the major interest is in vocational and occupational guidance. As personal and social adjustment are important for good citizenship, so are they important for good workers.

But there is also the concern for the individual as a person, not only as a worker. The satisfaction, happiness, and efficiency of the individual in his personal and social life are legitimate goals of counseling and guidance. As these are included in the goals of education, so they are included in the goals of student personnel and guidance services. The responsibility for individual or personal assistance to students in the development of self-understanding, self-acceptance, and self-respect, which are basic for good mental health and sound personal and social adjustment, falls upon the counseling and guidance staff.

Summary

Student personnel services are those services concerned with the individual needs of students which are provided in general

---

[17] *Op. cit.,* pp. 70–72.
[18] See, for example: H. C. Hunt. Why people lose their jobs or aren't promoted. *Personnel J.,* 1936, **14,** 227.

outside the classroom, and which are noninstructional in nature. They are usually provided by specialized professional personnel. The provision of student personnel services is based on the recognition of the need of the student for individual assistance in facing the complexities of modern life.

Counseling and guidance services are a part of a broader program of personnel services. The assumption behind these services is that all individuals, from time to time, can benefit from individual assistance in understanding themselves and the world in which they live, as a basis for making choices and dealing with problems with which they are confronted. A second assumption of counseling and guidance services is that the individual is self-autonomous and must be allowed freedom of choice. This is related to a third, that the individual, when given the opportunity, is capable of making adequate choices and resolving his own problems. Counseling and guidance, then, is not a means of controlling, manipulating, or disciplining students. Nor is the counselor an instrument of society in the sense that he recruits or directs students into areas in which there is a shortage of manpower. His focus and dedication is to free the individual to develop his potentialities and talents for their exercise in a free society.

SUGGESTED READINGS

American Council on Education. *The student personnel point of view.* Washington, D.C.: The Council, 1949. A succinct statement of the central place of the individual student and his needs in student personnel work.

Educational Policies Commission. *Manpower and education.* Washington, D.C.: National Education Association and American Association of School Administrators, 1956. This brief publication (128 pages) is an excellent discussion of the relation of manpower needs to education. The chapter on guidance and personnel services outlines the functions of educational and vocational guidance.

Mathewson, R. H. *Guidance policy and practice* (rev. ed.). New York: Harper, 1955. A development of the implications for counseling and guidance of the educational point of view outlined in the preceding chapter. While somewhat repetitious, possibly because of its organization, it is still the only guidance text whose major concern is with the philosophy underlying guidance policy and practice.

Moynihan, J. F. The philosophical aspects of guidance. *Rev. educ. Res.*, 1957, 27, 186–191.

Wilkins, D. W., & Perlmutter, Barbara J. The philosophical foundations of guidance and personnel work. *Rev. educ. Res.*, 1960, 30, 97–104. This and the reference above are brief reviews of the literature concerning the philosophy of guidance and counseling services from 1953 to 1959.

Wrenn, C. G. Philosophical and psychological bases of personnel services. In Henry, N. B. (Ed.) *Personnel services in education.* Fifty-eighth Yearbook of the National Society for the Study of Education. Part II. Chicago: University of Chicago Press, 1959. This is a rather advanced and highly condensed discussion of philosophies and psychological theories as related to personnel work in education.

CHAPTER 3

ORGANIZATION AND ADMINISTRATION OF COUNSELING AND GUIDANCE SERVICES

Guidance is often described as a point of view, and one which should permeate the entire program of the school. Thus guidance is sometimes considered to be synonymous with instruction. While there is some merit in this way of looking at guidance, and while guidance services are provided by the entire staff, it is also true that the point of view must be specifically implemented in order to provide a total program of planned, balanced services. A guidance program, to be complete and adequate, must include specialized noninstructional services provided by special staff members. These services must be organized, as well as coordinated with the other guidance services provided by the instructional staff, and all guidance services should be integrated into the total school program. The guidance program contributes to the entire school program, and thus, as indicated in the last chapter, is related to the philosophy and objectives of the school. In the kind of educational setting which has been described, guidance services are designed to supplement the instructional program in its efforts to develop personal and social maturity in its students. The purpose of organization and administration is to provide adequate services in the most effective manner for maximum value to the school and its individual students.

This chapter will consider some of the many problems in the

organization and administration of a program of guidance services. We shall discuss the initiating or activating of such services, the organizational structure of the services, and administrative responsibility for the support of the services. Since we are concerned with the guidance program from the point of view of the counselor or specialized guidance staff, we shall consider organization within the school, rather than a school system. We shall be concerned with guidance services, rather than with the organization of the entire program of pupil personnel services, although the latter term is sometimes applied to guidance services alone. The integration of guidance services with other pupil personnel services will be dealt with later (Chapter 16).

Not only is the organization of guidance services related to the philosophy and objectives of the school, but it is also influenced by many other factors or conditions, such as the views of the administrator (principal or superintendent), the size of the school, and the attitudes and resources of the community. It is therefore impossible to define a pattern of organization which would apply to all schools. Nevertheless, there are certain general principles which should be applicable, at least in most situations.

Preparation for a Guidance Program

While many schools have existing guidance programs, so that trained counselors are increasingly going into an established program—whether joining a counseling staff or replacing a counselor—there are still schools which do not have such programs. It is therefore desirable to consider the procedure for establishing a program in such schools.

The provision of guidance services is the responsibility of the school administrator. Nevertheless, a program of guidance services should not, and cannot, be imposed upon the staff of a school. The development of a program on a broad, democratic basis not only will lead to a better program, but one which will be supported by the faculty.

The administrator, of course, must provide leadership and support. Without this, no program can get started. But it is also true that without the support of the faculty, as well as of students and parents, no program can be successful. The entire staff must participate in the planning and developing of a program which will serve the needs of the faculty and students of that particular school. Some suggestions regarding procedures for planning a program follow.[1]

Prior to initiating formal consideration of a guidance program, certain conditions must be present. The administrator must be concerned about guidance services. He must be prepared to interpret and show support for a program before the school board, or to the superintendent, and to the community. The faculty also must be interested, and be willing to spend time in studying and planning for a program. Consultative help may be necessary or desirable, and its availability should be determined. Finally, financial resources for a program must be present or potentially available.

Some of the specific steps in preparation for a program are as follows:

1. A guidance council, or committee, appointed by the principal, who may serve as the chairman, should be assigned the task of developing a program. The council may be assisted by subcommittees in various areas, the chairmen being members of the council. Faculty members may be appointed to committees on the basis of stated preferences. It may be desirable to have student representation, as well as parent or general community representation, on the council.

2. The council, or its committees, conducts studies of guidance needs and resources. (a) A survey should be made of existing guidance services, with identification of strengths and weaknesses. This may take the form of an inventory or review of facilities, equipment, and staff guidance functions. (b) A study of the unmet needs of students and staff in the guidance area should be undertaken. (c) There should be a survey of the resources and facilities, in the school and the community, which are, or might be made, available to fill the gaps in the services. (d) Finally, a survey of the attitudes of staff, pupils, and perhaps

---

[1] Detailed consideration of the suggestions given here and in the following sections of this chapter will be found in books devoted to organizing and administering guidance services. Several are listed at the end of this chapter.

parents and the community toward the establishment or expansion of a program of guidance services is desirable.

3. On the basis of these studies, the council prepares a report, with recommendations and a plan for providing or expanding guidance services.

4. The faculty considers the recommendations and, together with the administration, reaches a decision regarding action to be taken.

5. The plan is approved by higher administrative authority or by the school board.

Initiating the Program

Once a plan has been developed, and its execution approved or authorized, action is required to get the program started. The administrator, by reason of his position and function, is the central figure here, at least at the beginning. However, it is important that the participation of the faculty continue, or the program may fail to develop to its fullest. There are several important steps to be taken by the administrator.

1. The guidance council, or committee, is retained and appointed on a continuing basis. The committee serves to continue the interest and participation of the faculty in the program, and is a means of communication between the counseling and guidance staff and the instructional staff. The committee may exercise either a policy-determining function, or only an advisory one, depending on the nature of the situation and the wishes of those involved. It might be that the committee would be reconstituted at this time, dropping parent and community representation.

2. The administrator designates or appoints a guidance staff, including a head, director, or coordinator. This step involves the definitions of the functions of the program in terms of job descriptions and qualifications. Certain administrative functions and responsibilities are delegated to the head of the program. The director becomes a member of the council if not already a member. Salary scales and differential pay for special guidance services must be determined.

3. If the guidance staff, or part of it, consists of persons who

are carrying other assignments, including teaching, the administrator provides for time to be devoted to their guidance functions.

4. The administrator has a responsibility for providing adequate space and supplies for the successful functioning of the
program. This includes individual, private offices for each counselor, as well as space for a conference room, for a reception
area, for clerical staff, for individual and group testing, for test
and occupational information files, and for files for the cumulative records. Adequate space is a continuing problem in most
guidance programs.[2]

The administrator must also provide an adequate budget for
test supplies, occupational information materials, and other
equipment, including recording machines. Adequate secretarial
assistance must not be omitted, or the program may bog down
because staff members are too busy with clerical tasks to function
as counselors.

Developing the Program

Once an administrative head for the program is appointed,
he becomes an important factor in the further development of
the program. He must perform certain functions in the organizing of actual services to students and staff. The actions which
he takes may be in consultation with the guidance council, or
under general policies which they set up. Insofar as staff assignments are concerned, the school administrator or principal is involved also.

1. Staff assignments are made in terms of special interests and
specialized training and skills. Recruitment of new staff involves
consideration of needs for specialized services and skills and
for the general needs of the program. Decisions must be made
regarding the assignment of counselors to groups of students,
e.g., whether women counselors are assigned to girls and men

[2] (1) J. A. Bedard. Physical facilities for guidance. *Occup.*, 1951, **29**,
354–357.   (2) R. N. Hatch. & B. Stefflre. *Administration of guidance
services.* Englewood Cliffs, N.J.: Prentice-Hall, 1958. Pp. 233–244.   (3) R.
O. Stripling. How about physical facilities—are we selling student personnel
services short on space? *Personnel Guid. J.*, 1954, **33**, 170–171.

counselors to boys, whether there are separate counselors for each class, or whether counselors are responsible for certain groups of students throughout their school careers.

2. Personnel policies are set up with provisions for evaluation of the effectiveness of staff activities and for promotions and pay increases.

3. Provisions are made for advanced academic training for staff who lack the training necessary for the most effective functioning. In addition, a program of in-service training is planned and made a part of the total program (see Chapter 18).

4. Schedules are set up which provide for allocation of staff time to the various services, including individual counseling and consultation with the instructional staff. Procedures for scheduling appointments are developed. It is important that adequate time be provided for the counseling function. Erickson and Smith point out that "Many guidance programs have failed because the importance of the counseling service was not recognized, or if it was, because inadequate provision was made for counseling time in the school program."[3]

5. If, as is likely at the beginning of a new program, there is inadequate staff to provide all the services, or services to all students, decisions must be made regarding the services which are given, and to whom. Frequently the freshman class is provided counseling, and counselors are added for each new freshman class until a sufficient number are available. On the other hand, it might be decided that the seniors are more in need of counseling, and services are begun here, and extended downward with the addition of staff.

6. Procedures of referral from the teaching staff are set up, as well as procedures for consultation with teachers. The specialized guidance services must be coordinated with the guidance services performed by the instructional staff. In addition, guidance services must be coordinated with other personnel services, and procedures worked out for referral to these other services, as well as to out-of-school or community services (see Chapters 16 and 17).

[3] C. E. Erickson & G. E. Smith. *Organization and administration of guidance services.* New York: McGraw-Hill, 1957. P. 8.

Some Problems Related to Administration

Specialized services are professional services. They involve certain professional responsibilities and relationships with students which differ from those of a teacher or administrator. These differences result in some problems—in conflicts of roles and responsibilities. These problems have not been adequately resolved, and in some instances or in some situations perhaps they cannot be. It is important that the student of counseling be aware of them, however.

Utilization of professional skills. It would appear to be desirable that individuals with special professional training and experience, or even those without complete professional preparation, but assigned to professional guidance duties, should spend their time in the performance of such duties rather than in other activities which untrained individuals can perform. Counseling services are greatly needed, and counselors are in great demand. Few schools have adequate counseling services. Only the most fortunate schools are able to provide one full-time counselor for every 250 to 300 students, which is the recommended ratio.[4]

Yet in spite of this shortage, in all too many instances counselors are performing duties which bear little if any relationship to their training, or to counseling and guidance activities. Not only are they performing clerical and administrative duties, because of lack of clerical assistance, but they are often assigned many other nonguidance functions. These include disciplinary functions, keeping attendance and tardiness records, sponsoring student activities, proctoring halls and lunchrooms, etc.[5] Because they do not have a full class-teaching schedule, counselors are often considered fair game for all kinds of extra miscellaneous assignments.

[4] See, for example: J. B. Conant. *The American high school today.* New York: McGraw-Hill. P. 44.

[5] (1) D. L. Arnold. Time spent by counselors and deans in various activities. *Occup.*, 1949, **27**, 391–393. (2) *Counseling services in the secondary schools of Illinois.* Allerton House Conference on Education. Urbana, Ill.: College of Education, University of Illinois, 1958. (3) K. A. Martyn. We are wasting the counselor's time. *Calif. J. second. Educ.*, 1957, **32**, 439–441. (4) Florence E. Purcell. Counseling assignments and efficiency. *Voc. Guid. Quart.*, 1957, **5**, 111–113. (5) C. C. Stewart. A bill of rights for school counselors. *Personnel Guid. J.*, 1959, **37**, 500–503.

Now it may not be desirable that the guidance staff be exempt from certain general responsibilities of the school staff, such as committee assignments and sponsoring certain student activities, although it is possible that some of these duties may not be entirely consistent with the individual counseling relationship with students. But the guidance staff should not be specifically assigned these functions to relieve teachers of them. It sometimes happens that certain duties, such as attendance reports and disciplinary functions, are assigned to guidance personnel because no one else is available, or willing to take them on, and it is felt that the guidance staff has the time to perform them.

It is inefficient and poor economy to use professionally trained staff for clerical work, even such clerical activity as keeping the cumulative records up to date, which can be done by less highly trained personnel. In addition, all duties of guidance personnel must be examined in terms of their effects on the performance of the counseling function. Aspects of this problem will be considered below.

Authority and the counseling relationship. An important factor to consider in providing counseling services is the influence of administrative authority on counselor-student relationships. Many counselors feel that authority and the counseling role do not mix, and that one cannot counsel a student when one has disciplinary authority over him, for example. Others feel that it is possible to combine the two.[6] There does seem to be a real problem here, at least in terms of some kinds of counseling relationships.

A counselor may be able to develop a counseling relationship with a student guilty of an infraction of rules and subject to discipline, as long as the counselor is not charged with judging the case and meting out the punishment. But it is more difficult, and

---

[6] See, e.g., the following: (1) Kate H. Mueller. Theory for campus discipline. *Personnel Guid. J.*, 1958, **36**, 302–309. (2) H. C. Peiffer, Jr. & D. E. Walker. The disciplinary interview. *Personnel Guid. J.*, 1957, **35**, 347–350. (3) E. G. Williamson & J. D. Foley. *Counseling and discipline.* New York: McGraw-Hill, 1949. (4) E. G. Williamson. Discipline and counseling. *Education*, 1954, **74**, 512–518. (5) E. G. Williamson. The fusion of discipline and counseling in the educational process. *Personnel Guid. J.*, 1955, **34**, 74–79. Reprinted in H. B. McDaniel, *et al.* (Eds.). *Readings in guidance.* New York: Holt, 1959. Pp. 236–242. Also reprinted in G. F. Farwell & H. J. Peters. (Eds.). *Guidance readings for counselors.* Chicago: Rand McNally, 1960. Pp. 378–386.

perhaps unlikely, that he can be judge and counselor at the same time. This does not mean that many guidance functions cannot be performed by a staff member who holds authority over the student, but that certain counseling functions are at least hampered by a position of authority. Erickson and Smith note that "once the guidance program identifies itself with administrative authority, it is likely to become a tool for the administrator and the nemesis of pupils."[7]

Guidance services are, or should be, professional services, and thus should be performed by personnel with staff, as contrasted with line, positions. Line positions, such as principal, assistant or vice principal, dean or assistant dean, are those which carry administrative authority. But line officers may, and often do, have staff functions. A mixture of roles is thus created, with the possibility of conflict of roles, or impairment of performance of certain staff functions. In many schools, the person responsible for guidance services may be the assistant or vice principal, or dean. If there is a large guidance staff, and the responsible person is an administrator, without actually performing individual counseling functions, there may be no problem. It is possible, however, that even here the matter of confidentiality—to be discussed later—may pose a problem. But in many instances, the only guidance staff member, except for teachers, may be the assistant or vice principal, or dean. It would appear to be better, where possible, to avoid the use of these titles for staff members who are actually doing individual counseling. The title "director of guidance" may offer as much prestige. Such a position, while involving some administrative authority, does not, or if possible should not, involve authority over students, but over a program, or a staff of professional personnel. Hatch and Stefflre suggest that, even though the title of director of guidance is becoming increasingly popular, "it is extremely doubtful that such a position is necessary to the development of the guidance program."[8] The administrative, or line, functions of the director of guidance are performed by the assistant principal for pupil personnel services. This has the advantage of avoiding confusion of staff responsibilities with a line title and responsibilities. At the system level,

---

[7] *Op. cit.,* p. 5.
[8] Hatch & Stefflre, *op. cit.,* p. 134.

however, there might be a director of guidance on the staff of the assistant superintendent for pupil personnel.

Teaching and counseling. As in the case of administrative authority, there are some who feel that teaching is not entirely consistent with an individual counseling relationship. Others feel that every member of the counseling staff should carry some regular classes, not merely special classes in group guidance or occupational information. Some suggest that it is valuable for a counselor to have his students in one of his classes. Teaching is also felt to be desirable as a means of assuring that the counselor keep in close touch with the teaching staff and their problems. Curiously, this is not advocated for other staff members in the personnel area, such as the school nurse, the psychologist, or even the visiting teacher. It might be suggested that a nonteaching counselor who lost touch with the situation in which he was working, or one who would do so if he did not teach, was not a good counselor.

The extent to which teaching is incompatible with counseling is not known, and, as suggested above, is the subject of widely differing opinions. In a survey of 308 guidance specialists, 67 percent agreed, though in some cases with reservations, that the counselor should be freed of all classroom activity, or should teach one class closely related to guidance activities, such as occupations.[9] To some extent it depends on the nature of the counseling services performed, and the personality and preferences of the counselor. In any event, there are many situations where the counselor must also teach, because the school does not need a full-time counselor. On the other hand, where there is a relatively large staff of counselors, it should be possible for some, at least, to devote full time to counseling and guidance activities. Conant recommends that counselors should devote "virtually full time to the counseling work."[10] The question of counselors being teachers will be considered again in connection with the training of counselors in the next chapter.

Confidentiality of information. Many of the things which a student discusses with a counselor are highly personal in nature.

[9] G. L. Keppers. Organizing guidance services—specialists speak. *Clearing House,* 1956, 31, 216–220.
[10] *Op. cit.,* p. 44.

The counseling relationship is a professional relationship in which the counselor is ethically bound to confidentiality.[11] Yet, "too many principals and teachers expect the counselor to break confidences and discuss confidential information with them."[12] In a study of 50 public high schools in Illinois, 67 percent of the principals and 76 percent of the counselors stated that information given the counselor was available to the principal on his request. On the other hand, only 24 percent of the students believed that such information should be released to the principal.[13]

Arbuckle reports that at a meeting of top administrators of teacher-training institutions in Massachusetts "a significant number of them apparently felt that a counselor should be expected to reveal any information that he might have on a student to a dean or other administrative officer."[14]

This situation constitutes a real problem in many schools, and will continue to do so until administrators understand the professional nature of counseling. We shall consider further the implications of lack of confidentiality in counseling in Chapter 13.

A frequent problem which appears to be related to confidentiality, and to a lack of understanding of counseling on the part of the administrator, is inadequacy of counseling space. The need for an individual office, and for complete privacy, is not recognized, or accepted, in many instances. While counseling *can* take place in many situations, under many conditions, this does not mean that optimum conditions should not be provided if possible. It is not likely that students will reveal their deepest, most personal problems within hearing of other staff members or students.

Administrative understanding and support of the program. The matter of confidentiality is illustrative of the problems arising from lack of, or inadequate, understanding of counseling and guidance services by administrators. Administrators sometimes

---

[11] For an extended discussion of the ethics of counseling, including confidentiality, see Chapter 3 of the writer's *Counseling and psychotherapy: theory and practice.* New York: Harper, 1959.

[12] *Counseling services in the secondary schools of Illinois, op cit.,* p. 18.

[13] *Ibid.,* p. 17.

[14] D. S. Arbuckle. Five philosophical issues in counseling. *J. Counsel. Psychol.,* 1958, **5**, 211–215.

see counseling services as a means of controlling or disciplining students. Counseling is often conceived of as something that can be imposed upon a reluctant or unwilling student, much as a shot of an antibiotic may be given. Unless an administrator accepts the philosophy of education and guidance services outlined in the two preceding chapters, he will have difficulty understanding the goals and procedures of modern counseling and guidance programs. The prime consideration of counseling and guidance is the individual student, rather than the convenience of the administrator or the smooth running of the school.

It is important, even necessary, that school administrators be exposed in their training to some work in counseling and guidance to enable them to appreciate the procedures and goals of a counseling and guidance service. Beyond this, the administrator must respect the professionally trained counselor, and have confidence in his work. If an administrator does not understand a problem, he should not contradict or discredit the counselor. Incidents such as the following would not occur if administrators had some training in counseling and guidance and/or respect for the training of the counselor. In a staff meeting a counselor suggested that a score on a test was not necessarily accurate, that tests were not perfect, and that any test score could be in error. After the meeting, his principal rebuked him for questioning the infallibility of tests, suggesting that he was discrediting testing and counseling and destroying the confidence of teachers in tests. Olsen comments on the importance of administrative understanding. He states that "possibly the most overlooked and neglected area in the field of guidance today is the role of the administrator in the school system. . . . Adequate programs exist only where the administrator has the guidance point of view. . . . Administrators with the guidance point of view are usually those with some guidance training."[15]

Other problems. There are numerous other problems associated with the organization and administration of a program of guidance services. They cannot all be dealt with here; many of

[15] L. Olsen. A neglected area in guidance. [Letter to the Editor.] *Personnel Guid. J.,* 1960, 38, 509.

them have unique aspects. The general principles implicit in the guidance point of view may be applied to such problems.

The location of the counseling offices is sometimes a problem. On the one hand, it may appear to be desirable to have the counseling staff close to the administration offices. Some feel that they should share the same space, with a common waiting room and clerical staff. On the other hand, it has been suggested that the guidance area should be in a separate part of the building. This latter suggestion is favored by those who are concerned about counseling as a professional activity, divorced from administration and requiring privacy. A study of the opinions of counselor-trainers, counselors, and principals found that 74 and 62 percent respectively of the first two groups preferred offices separated from the administration, while 67 percent of the principals preferred guidance offices wholly or partially integrated with the administrative offices. Principals who had had counseling experience, however, were more likely to favor separation of offices. Almost three-fourths of both principals and counselors in the study were dissatisfied with their present facilities for guidance.[16]

It is sometimes argued that since counselors frequently use cumulative records, and such records are usually maintained in the administrative offices, counselors' offices should be adjacent to the administrative offices. On the other hand, if there are good reasons for separating the counseling and administrative offices, the fact that counselors use the cumulative records more frequently than the rest of the staff would be a good reason for moving the files from the administrative to the counseling offices.

Another area in which problems frequently arise is that of providing guidance services to all students, and yet at the same time recognizing that services or assistance cannot, and should not, be imposed upon students. Teachers and administrators frequently desire to refer their problem cases to the counselor, and

[16] K. H. Parker. Location of guidance facilities within the physical plant. *Personnel Guid. J.*, 1957, **36**, 251–254. Reprinted in G. F. Farwell & H. J. Peters (Eds.). *Guidance readings for counselors.* Chicago: Rand McNally, 1960. Pp. 461–467.

expect the counselor to "straighten them out." This is particularly likely to be the case in the early stages of a guidance program. Now while a counselor is willing to see a student who is a forced referral (although it might be better in some cases to work with the teacher rather than with a resistant student), there is no way in which the counselor can counsel a student who refuses to enter a counseling relationship. Sometimes other things can be done to help the student, or to help those involved with the student at least to understand him better. But counseling cannot be "administered" or applied; it must be accepted and utilized by the student.

Nevertheless, while counseling cannot be administered, other guidance services such as testing can be. An organized program of testing, and of routinely obtaining and assembling other information about students, is a standard and legitimate function of a guidance program. Such information is gathered for two different purposes. It is useful in the classification and the assignment of students, which is an administrative function. It is also useful in the individual counseling of the student. Too often the first is the only, or the major, use of test results.

The philosophy of guidance outlined in this book does not preclude the scheduling of routine interviews with students. It is desirable that each student be seen by a counselor each semester. This should be more than the making out or signing of a program card. It should include offering the student an opportunity to discuss educational and vocational choices or plans, or any other problems he might have, and thus provide the opportunity for the initiation of a counseling relationship if the student so desires.

It is one of the assumptions of a guidance program that every student in every school could at some time benefit from the services of such a program. Some of these services are provided to the student indirectly, through the school or its administration, or through the teaching staff; others are provided to students in groups. Counseling services are provided to individual pupils (even group counseling is individually entered into by the student), and on a voluntary basis. Thus the individual's integrity is protected, as is his right to privacy, if he desires to exercise such right. In a democracy, counseling services are available and offered, but they cannot be imposed or required.[17]

Summary

To be effective, counseling and guidance services must be organized and administered in a manner which is consistent with the principles outlined in the preceding chapter. The understanding and support of an enlightened administrator are essential. Acceptance by the faculty is also necessary. In this chapter we have outlined a procedure for preparing for and developing a program of guidance services in a school which does not have such a program.

Some of the problems of providing counseling and guidance services which require administrative understanding and support are discussed. These include the recognition and utilization of the professional skills of the counselor, the avoidance of assigning conflicting responsibilities and duties to the counselor, the importance of privacy for counseling and respect for the confidentiality of the counseling relationship, and the provision of adequate physical facilities, equipment, and tools for the program. The importance of understanding and effective administrative support for a counseling program cannot be overemphasized. Without it no program can succeed, but with it a school can develop a program of high-level professional services which will contribute to the welfare of all students.

SUGGESTED READINGS

Andrew, D. C., & Willey, R. DeV. *Administration and organization of the guidance program.* New York: Harper, 1958. A discussion of the general principles of organization and administration, with chapters on administering the various specialized activities of the guidance program.

Coleman, W. Basic steps in developing a guidance program. *Clearing House,* 1952, **26,** 474–479. Reprinted in Farwell, G. F. & Peters, H. J. (Eds.) *Guidance readings for counselors.* Chicago: Rand Mc-

---

[17] An exception to this may be the prescribing of "exposure" to counseling or psychotherapy in instances where the individual is dangerous or harmful to society. Amplification of the counseling point of view proposed here will be found in Part III.

Nally, 1960. Pp. 445–453. A brief discussion of the procedure of initiating a guidance program; directed to the school principal.

Dugan, W. E. The organization and administration of guidance and personnel work. *Rev. educ. Res.*, 1960, **30**, 105–114. A summary of the literature from 1956 to 1959.

Erikson, C. E., & Hatch, R. N. Principles for programming personnel services. In Henry, N. B. (Ed.) *Personnel services in education.* Fifty-eighth Yearbook of the National Society for the Study of Education. Part II. Chicago: University of Chicago Press, 1959. This is a highly condensed summary, or outline, of the steps and procedures in planning and organizing a program.

Hatch, R. N., & Stefflre, B. *Administration of guidance services.* Englewood Cliffs, N.J.: Prentice-Hall, 1958. Part I deals with the principles and techniques of organization and administration, while Part II contains case studies of three school districts to illustrate the application of the principles.

Roeber, E. C., Smith, G. E., & Erikson, C. E. *Organization and administration of guidance services.* (2nd ed.) New York: McGraw-Hill, 1955. A revision of a basic text. There is consideration of the functions of school personnel and the selection and training of guidance workers, as well as chapters on organizing the various guidance services (counseling, individual inventory, information, and placement and follow-up).

Shear, B. Physical facilities for pupil personnel services. *Amer. Sch. Bd. J.*, 1950, **120**, 24–27. Reprinted in Farwell, G. F., & Peters, H. J. (Eds.) *Guidance readings for counselors.* Chicago: Rand McNally, 1960. Pp. 454–461. A report of a survey of school plans, indicating that less than half included guidance space. Suggestions and typical plans for guidance space are given.

Twiford, D. D. (Ed.) *Physical facilities for school guidance services.* Washington, D.C.: Department of Health, Education and Welfare, Office of Education [no date]. A statement of suggestions to assist in planning and improving physical facilities for guidance, prepared by the Office of Education and the National Association of Guidance Supervisors and Counselor Trainers.

Weitz, H. Creating a climate for accepting guidance services. *Personnel Guid. J.*, 1959, **38**, 190–194. Discusses the relation of philosophies and concepts of guidance to the kind of program which is developed, and suggests how to involve the staff and community in the development of a program whose goal is to provide the child with the opportunity to acquire skills in making self-directed, rational decisions.

PART II

QUALIFICATIONS FOR COUNSELING AND GUIDANCE

CHAPTER 4

SELECTION FOR

COUNSELING AND

GUIDANCE

Although there has been some consideration of specialization in terms of preparation and training, as well as of function, among counseling and guidance personnel, it is generally agreed that all such personnel should have the same basic training. The titles by which guidance staff workers are designated are varied; they include guidance worker, pupil personnel worker, guidance specialist, counselor, guidance counselor, and others. But there seems to be no difference of opinion regarding the primary responsibility of such staff members. Counseling is, or should be, the major duty of guidance personnel. It is therefore necessary that they be thoroughly trained as counselors. Because of this, we shall refer to them as counselors, and this chapter will deal with the selection of students for counselor-training programs.

The qualifications or requirements for counselors depend upon a number of factors. These include the relation of demand to supply, the preferences and beliefs of employers, and the sources of recruitment. This chapter will briefly consider these factors.

The Need for Counselors

Counseling services were established in public schools early in this century, following the founding of the Vocation Bureau in Boston by Frank Parsons in 1908. Interest developed during the next ten years and showed a spurt following World War I. However, there was a lag during the late 1920s. Interest was revived again during the next decade, and was stimulated following World War II. The history of vocational guidance during the years prior to World War II is told by Brewer.[1]

The growth of counseling and guidance services has been great in the last ten years. Accurate statistics are difficult to obtain, however. There are many more counselors devoting half-time or less, down to one hour a week, to counseling than there are working half-time or more. The number of counselors doubled between 1945 and 1952, with 8153 counselors employed half-time or more and 11,000 employed less than half-time. Nevertheless, in 1952 formal guidance services were available in only 17 percent of the public secondary schools, although these schools included 50 percent of the pupils enrolled in public secondary education. The ratio of full-time counselors to students in these schools was 1 to 524.[2] In 1956, 44,000 individuals were estimated to be engaged in counseling—a 120 percent increase—but only 10,000 were full-time counselors, while another 8000 spent half-time or more, but less than full time, in counseling. The remaining 26,000 spent less than half-time in counseling activities. In 1958, the American Personnel and Guidance Association, on the basis of a survey, estimated that there were 13,000 full-time equivalent counselors. One half of the schools had no counselors, and the counselor-student ratio in schools having counselors was 1 to 550.[3] It appears that, although the number of counselors has increased, and the number of schools having counseling services has grown, the increase has just about kept pace with the expanding school population.

Even though there has been a rapid growth in counseling services, the demand for counselors exceeds the supply. This leads to a situation where untrained personnel are employed as

[1] J. M. Brewer. *History of vocational guidance.* New York: Harper, 1942. See also C. H. Miller. *Foundations of guidance.* New York: Harper, 1961. A broader historical treatment of the social foundations of guidance services.

[2] A. J. Jones & L. M. Miller. The national picture of pupil personnel and guidance services in 1953. *Bull. Nat. Assoc. Secondary-School Principals,* 1954, 38, (200), 103–159.

[3] A. A. Hitchcock. By what means can the quality and quantity of guidance services, particularly in high schools, be increased? *Current issues in higher education,* 1958. Washington, D.C.: Association for Higher Education, National Education Association, 1958.

counselors, or are assigned to counseling duties. This is particularly true for part-time counselors, who are frequently teachers or administrators with little, if any, training in counseling. In Illinois in 1959–1960, there were 1491 individuals performing guidance services at least 5 hours per week in the 627 schools reporting to the office of the Superintendent of Public Instruction. Of these, 1094 were designated as counselors, the rest being deans, administrators, advisers, attendance directors, etc. About 12 percent of those designated as counselors had no training in counseling and guidance; another 35 percent had no more than one semester of training; and only about 35 percent had more than 24 semester hours of training.[4] Forty-five percent of the counselors were devoting less than half-time to counseling.

There is no reason to believe that this situation is not typical. A study of counselors in Ohio in 1955 found that less than half had taken at least one graduate course in principles of guidance.[5]

This situation has led Hitchcock, the Executive Director of the American Personnel and Guidance Association, to make the following statement: "Our great problem in years ahead . . . will be to make sure that those persons who are designated as counselors . . . are actually well-qualified persons. The crisis cannot be met by adding on persons who are not equipped to perform a guidance job."[6] In a survey of 308 guidance specialists, Keppers found that 91 percent agreed (none actually disagreed) that "for the successful functioning of the program it was essential to have qualified personnel."[7]

The selection and training of individuals for counseling and guidance are thus important factors in providing adequate guidance services in our schools.

[4] *Development of guidance services, 1959–1960.* Springfield, Ill.: State of Illinois, Office of the Superintendent of Public Instruction, Board of Vocational Education, Occupational Information and Guidance Service, 1961 [mimeo].

[5] R. A. Wendorf. Qualifications of guidance counselors in Ohio high schools. *Personnel Guid. J.,* 1956, 34, 569–571.

[6] A. A. Hitchcock. From the executive director. *Personnel Guid. J.,* 1959, 37, 472.

[7] G. L. Keppers. Organizing guidance services—specialists speak. *Clearing House,* 1956, 31, 216–220.

Problems of Selection

While it may no longer be generally true that "appointment as a guidance counselor comes as a kind of reward for faithful years of classroom teaching,"[8] it is still the case that counselors are almost invariably appointed from the teaching staff by the principal or administrator. Hitchcock describes the usual path to becoming a counselor as follows: a teacher who appears to have the personal qualifications is asked by the principal to assume a period or two of counseling the next year. The teacher enters upon this with no preparation or training, and finds during the year that there is more to counseling than was expected. He or she then begins graduate work in counseling the next summer, and over a period of years devotes more time to counseling and continues with more education. Eventually certification may be achieved, perhaps only on a provisional or temporary basis.[9] As Hitchcock points out, the result may or may not be a good counselor. Wendorf's study indicates that, although such counselors usually have considerable educational experience, they acquire little professional training. In his study, only 14.3 percent achieved certification, and only about 12 percent intended to do so.[10]

This traditional method of entrance into counseling constitutes a problem. It not only means that most part-time counselors are inadequately trained, but it means that the selection of counselors is mainly in the hands of principals and administrators. While there may be a sincere effort to select those who have an interest in the work and who have personal qualities which appear to be desirable in a counselor, it takes more than teaching experience, an interest in students, a desire to help them, and good intentions to be a good counselor. Wrenn notes that a de-

---

[8] L. L. Lerner. The academic approach to vocational guidance. *Sch. and Soc.*, 1951, 74, 54–57.

[9] Hitchcock: from the executive director, *op. cit.*

[10] Wendorf, *op. cit.* The comments of Cutts about school psychologists are equally applicable to counselors: "The teacher considering such a change, however, must be helped to understand the extent and variety of training which he must undertake. Any belief that the change of profession can be effected by a few scattered courses obtained in odd moments must be dispelled." Norma E. Cutts (Ed.) *School psychologists at mid-century.* Washington, D.C.: American Psychological Association, 1955. P. 116.

sire "to do good" and a liking for people, are not adequate for counseling.[11] Yet these appear to be the criteria for the selection of counselors by some school administrators.

Such counselors then present themselves for graduate work at our colleges and universities, and sometimes create a problem regarding admission. As Wrenn points out, "Graduate institutions should accept the responsibility for admitting to special training programs only those for whom there is some evidence that they will succeed in the graduate program and on the job."[12]

The criteria which such institutions should use are difficult to determine, however. This may be a reason for the fact that many graduate schools do little if any selection, and for the existence of wide diversity among those which do utilize selection procedures.[13] Some schools practice progressive selection rather than, or along with, initial selection on academic ability.

Most institutions apply some selection on the basis of academic achievement and aptitude. Undergraduate grades are most widely used. Tests such as the Miller Analogies Test, the Ohio State Psychological Examination, the American Council on Education Psychological Examination, and the Graduate Record Examination are frequently used as measures of academic aptitude.

The personal qualities desirable for training and performance in counseling are more difficult to define and evaluate than the intellectual qualifications. The writer has summarized the prob-

[11] C. G. Wrenn. The selection and education of student personnel workers. *Personnel Guid. J.*, 1952, **31**, 9–14.

[12] *Ibid.*

[13] (1) American College Personnel Association, Professional Standards Committee. American College Personnel Association Professional Standards Committee studies graduate student selection and admission. *Personnel Guid. J.*, 1954, **32**, 362–366. (2) American Psychological Association, Division of Counseling Psychology, Counselor Training Committee, Subcommittee on Counselor Trainee Selection. An analysis of practices in counselor trainee selection. *J. counsel. Psychol.*, 1954, **1**, 174–179. (3) P. MacMinn & R. G. Ross. *Status of preparation programs for guidance and student personnel workers.* Department of Health, Education and Welfare, Office of Education. Bull. 1959, No. 7, Washington, D.C.: Government Printing Office, 1959. (4) G. E. Hill & D. Green. The selection, preparation, and professionalization of guidance and personnel workers. *Rev. educ. Res.*, 1960, **30**, 115–130. (5) R. W. Stoughton. The preparation of counselors and personnel workers. *Rev. educ. Res.*, 1957, **27**, 174–185.

lems in this area elsewhere.[14] The list of desirable qualities suggested is long; however, there is little evidence regarding the relation of the qualities to successful counseling, and there are no adequate methods of measuring them. They tend in general to be based on common sense, and to include qualities desirable in almost any professional person, or in all individuals working with other people. The duties of guidance workers vary, and it is possible that varying personalities may be effective in various functions, even in the same functions. There appears to be some basis, however, for believing that a genuine interest in and understanding of people, respect for others, and emotional stability and maturity would be important characteristics in a successful counselor.

The American College and Personnel Association's Professional Standards Committee, on the basis of a survey of twenty-one institutions offering graduate training in counseling, made the following recommendations regarding the selection of students for graduate training in counseling:

1. Selection must be exercised by the training institutions.
2. Superior academic ability and achievement, and a scientific attitude are necessary.
3. Knowledge of other fields than a single major is desirable.
4. There should be a demonstrated interest in the field, evidenced by previous activities and measured interests.
5. The student must possess emotional stability and personality adjustment.
6. The following personal qualities should be present, judged on the basis of references from teachers and employers and tests:
    a. Social sensitivity.
    b. Leadership ability.
    c. Ability to work in harmony with both subordinates and superordinates.
    d. Warmth and friendliness in interpersonal relations.
    e. Sense of humor.
    f. Acceptable personal appearance and grooming.
    g. Loyalty and enthusiasm for the cause of education and dedication to student personnel work.

[14] C. H. Patterson. *Counseling the emotionally disturbed.* New York: Harper, 1958. Chapter 3, "The Personal Qualifications of the Counselor." See also Hill & Green, *op. cit.*

h. Self-respect and integrity.
7. One or more years of teaching experience "and/or other experience related to personnel services."
8. The total pattern should be used in selection.[15]

These requirements seem reasonable, and adequate evaluations should be possible using previous records of the applicant, references, ratings, interviews, and tests. Tests useful in evaluating intellectual qualities have already been mentioned. Tests which are of value in interest and personality screening include the Strong Vocational Interest Blank, the Edwards Personal Preference Schedule, the Minnesota Multiphasic Personality Inventory, and the Allport-Vernon-Lindzey Scale of Values.[16]

Work experience may be required for admission to graduate work. Teaching experience is the most frequent type mentioned, although experience in another field may be required, usually in conjunction with teaching experience, or as a related appropriate substitute for it. Experience is more often required for admission to doctoral work than to master's level work.[17]

Another factor in the selection of students for counselor training has seldom been mentioned. This is the nature of undergraduate preparation. Mathewson recommends a major in psychology and a minor in sociology.[18] The requirement may vary depending on the department or college in which counselor training is offered. Psychology departments may require or prefer an undergraduate psychology major. In a survey of 21 graduate training programs it was found that 9.5 percent required a psychology major, while 38.1 percent recommended it (19.1 percent did not respond to this question); 14.3 percent required

[15] American College Personnel Association, op. cit.

[16] (1) Dorothy M. Clendenen. Selection and training of counselors. In Vivian H. Hewer (Ed.) New perspectives in counseling. Minnesota Studies in Student Personnel Work No. 7. Minneapolis: University of Minnesota Press, 1955. (2) W. C. Cottle. Personal characteristics of counselors: I. A review of the literature. Personnel Guid. J., 1953, 31, 445–450. (3) P. H. Kriedt. Vocational interests of psychologists. J. appl. Psychol., 1949, 33, 482–488. (4) C. H. Patterson. Characteristics of rehabilitation counselor trainees. Urbana, Ill.: College of Education, University of Illinois, 1960 [mimeo]. (5) Wrenn, op. cit.

[17] MacMinn & Ross, op. cit., pp. 12–13.

[18] R. H. Mathewson. The general counselor. Personnel Guid. J., 1954, 32, 544–547.

a psychology minor, and 42.9 percent recommended it (28.6 percent did not respond). Only 4.8 percent required an education major, with 19.1 percent recommending it (38.1 percent did not respond); 19.1 percent required an education minor, and 23.8 percent recommended it (28.6 percent did not respond). Some schools required work in sociology, guidance, economics, and mathematics.[19]

An earlier survey by another committee of the American Psychological Association found that of 21 schools which had, up to 1953, trained the largest number of counselors, 60 percent required a psychology major or minor, and 40 percent, education.[20]

This emphasis upon a background in psychology raises a question, in view of the fact that counselors in the public schools come from teaching.

Should Counselors Be Teachers?

At the present time, as well as in the past, universal requirements for counselors in the public schools are (1) certification as a teacher, and (2) teaching experience. Hulslander and Scholl, in a survey of high-school and elementary-school principals, found that these administrators wanted counselors with teaching experience, often with experience in their own system.[21] That these requirements have become fixed is no doubt related to the method of entry into a career in counseling described above. While the requirements are still universal, there have been some questions raised recently about the necessity or desirability for retaining them. Teachers are the major source of supply of counselors, but this is because of the present requirements. Is teaching experience, however, essential to effective functioning as a professional guidance counselor?

[19] American Psychological Association, Division of Counseling Psychology, Committee on the Role of Psychology in the Preparation of School Counselors. *The role of psychology in the preparation of school counselors* [mimeo; no date].

[20] American Psychological Association, Division of Counseling Psychology, Counselor Training Committee, Sub-committee on Counselor Trainee Selection, *op. cit.*

[21] S. C. Hulslander & C. E. Scholl. U.S. school principals report their counselor needs. *Voc. Guid. Quart.*, 1957, 6, 3–4.

The qualities desired in a counselor, as discussed above, are not limited to teachers. Nor, as Keppers notes, does "the fact that good teachers have always done counseling mean that all teachers have done good counseling."[22]

While they would admit that teaching experience might not be necessary for all counselors, many educators insist that it is essential for counselors working in the schools. Weitz, in a survey of counselor employment policies which included forty-five states, asked whether trained people without a teaching certificate could be eligible to serve as counselors in the schools. None of the replies indicated that this would be possible, although six states suggested certain conditions under which they might be employed. Sixteen states thought they might qualify for provisional, temporary, or emergency certificates, or for special positions. In answer to a question regarding willingness to evaluate their certification requirements by employing such counselors on an experimental basis, five states gave an unqualified yes response, and eight more indicated a qualified willingness to try such an experiment. In spite of the fact that about two-thirds of the states reported a shortage of counselors, there was apparent reluctance to examine employment requirements with the possibility of modifying them to allow the employment of trained counselors who lacked a teaching certificate.[23]

It has been suggested that, with the amount of professional preparation needed to become a skilled counselor, it might be desirable to allow the counselor to master this knowledge and skill rather than spend time meeting requirements for certification as a teacher. It might be replied that the latter is done during undergraduate training, leaving graduate training to be devoted to learning counseling. Yet it has been suggested that undergraduate preparation in psychology and sociology would better prepare for graduate work in counseling, which now has to include much basic psychology.

Part of the insistence upon teaching as a background for counseling appears to be the result of a confusion of guidance with instruction, a failure to recognize differences in these func-

[22] Keppers, *op. cit.*

[23] H. Weitz. The role of the guidance worker in the schools. *Personnel Guid. J.*, 1958, **37**, 266–272.

tions. Guidance skills are considered as secondary to instructional skills. As a result, teachers are considered qualified to counsel on the basis of their teaching skills, without having to meet certification requirements for counselors. Persons are permitted to counsel without a counseling certificate, but not to teach without a teaching certificate.

Emphasis is put upon the value of knowledge of the school situation and of experience with the problems of the classroom teacher, rather than upon the value of professional training in counseling. Often, as has been suggested, it is felt that the counselor must have experience as a teacher in the same school system.

A recent report of a committee on the role of psychology in the training of school counselors stated that "Prospective school counselors should be and will continue to be drawn from a population of those with undergraduate preparation in teacher education." Four reasons were given for this statement: (1) need for an adequate orientation to education; (2) acceptance by school staffs, as well as the utilization of part-time counselors in teaching; (3) development of a better understanding of the problems of the classroom teacher; (4) no shortage of applicants for counseling training who have teaching certificates. The committee recognized that such students have deficiencies in basic psychological principles which would need to be provided in graduate preparation.[24] One member of the committee disagreed with the statement, feeling that a teaching certificate should not be *required*, even though the great majority of applicants would have one. He pointed out that some excellent counselors would be barred from preparing for and entering upon counseling positions in the schools if such a requirement were continued. Most counselor trainers have no doubt had the experience of turning down promising students with excellent undergraduate backgrounds for training in counseling because they lacked a teaching certificate.

That teaching experience can be useful to a counselor cannot

---

[24] American Psychological Association, Division of Counseling Psychology, Committee on the Role of Psychology in the Training of School Counselors, *op. cit.*

be questioned; but other kinds of experience can also be useful. The question is whether a teaching background is necessary. Such experience is not required of other personnel workers in the schools. In one sense everyone has some familiarity with the schools, having gone through the educational system as a student. It appears that many of the claims for the importance of teaching experience are not based upon any factual evidence, but upon emotional beliefs. While it is no doubt true that some counselors without such experience might encounter difficulties, they might have problems even with teaching experience. Some of the difficulty might result from lack of acceptance by teachers, rather than from inadequacies of the counselor. It seems that one of the main reasons for the insistence upon the teaching requirement is to promote acceptance by the teachers.

The shortage of trained counselors has led to consideration of the possibility of increasing the supply by recruitment from sources other than the teaching profession. A conference on the identification and guidance of able students reported that "ideally, the counselor will have had teaching experience and other educational background that will have made him familiar with pupil reactions and adjustments in the classroom. . . . In an era of drastic shortages in both teaching and counseling personnel, however, it may be impossible to meet the counselor shortage entirely by this means [by recruitment from teaching staffs]. Therefore, new sources of supply of counselors must be discovered. Potential counselors may well be found among those who have not had the familiar background of actual teaching and also job experiences outside the field of education."[25] The report goes on to suggest that field experience in the schools, presumably as part of the counselor's training, might be substituted for teaching experience. In spite of the shortage of counselors in the schools, however, the study by Weitz[26] indicated little inter-

---

[25] American Association for the Advancement of Science. *Identification and guidance of able students.* Report of Conferences on Testing and Counseling, University of Michigan, May 28–31, 1958. Washington, D.C.: The Association, 1958. P. 25. The recommendations of the 1960 White House Conference on Children and Youth also suggest that qualifications for certification "recognize and give credit to appropriate training and work experience in lieu of classroom teaching." See Appendix II.

[26] *Op. cit.*

est among school administrators in attempting to utilize adequately trained counselors without teaching certificates.

The belief that it is desirable for every counselor to carry some teaching has been strong. This has been justified on the basis that if a counselor has his counselees in his classes he will know them better, and that the better he knows them, or the more he knows about them, the better he will be able to counsel them. This justification represents a misunderstanding of counseling. If counseling were only a matter of giving information or advice, or solving another person's problems, the amount of information the counselor had about the client might be important. But counseling is a relationship in which the counselor must understand the client as the latter sees himself, and as he perceives the world; factual information is not necessary for this kind of understanding. Entirely too much time and effort has been devoted by teachers to obtaining such factual information about their students, and by textbook writers to encouraging this approach to helping students.

In addition, it has been recognized by experienced counselors and psychotherapists that relationships with a client outside the individual counseling relationship are undesirable, and hinder counseling. Parents cannot counsel their children, husbands cannot counsel their wives, employers cannot counsel their employees—nor can teachers counsel their students, if by counseling we mean a special relationship in which the client enters freely, easily, without reservation, without fear or threat of being judged or evaluated. No matter how hard he may try, even how successful he may be, in taking a nonjudgmental, counseling attitude, a parent, husband, employer, or teacher is likely to be unsuccessful in counseling. For even though he may distinguish between his role as a counselor and his other roles in relationships to the client, the client may not be able to do so. Students may find it difficult, if not impossible, to discuss personal problems with a teacher who is perceived as an authority, a judge or evaluator of his educational progress (the teacher must give grades). Of course the student may seek information, including information about possible vocational choices, and the teacher may be helpful in this area, but this is not counseling, at least not the professional counseling with which this book is concerned.

While many guidance functions may be adequately performed by persons who have other relationships with pupils, it is questionable whether this is true of the individual counseling relationship.

There is evidence that this difference between counseling and teaching is being recognized and accepted, not only by counselors, but by administrators and teachers. In one junior high school which has been reorganizing its counseling program, assignments are being made so that counselors, who also teach, *do not teach the students whom they serve as counselors.*

We shall return to the discussion of the relation between teaching and counseling from the point of view of the teacher's functions in a guidance program in Chapter 6. The fact that counseling in the public schools is one of the few professions (psychiatry might be another) which requires training in another profession prior to admission to practice at least raises a question regarding the desirability of continuing to adhere rigidly to this requirement.[27]

Summary

If we are to have adequate counseling and guidance services, it is essential that we have competent counselors. In this chapter we have discussed problems of recruitment and selection of individuals to be trained in counseling. The traditional method of recruitment by administrators from the teaching staff was questioned.

Selection is exercised by colleges and universities engaged in the training of counselors. Such selection is generally pretty much limited to the area of academic ability, however. But while it is recognized that other factors are important, particularly in the area of personality and personal qualifications, there is a

[27] The discussion of the relevance of teaching experience as a requirement for the school psychologist in Cutts is applicable to counselors. The Thayer Conference on the Functions, Qualifications, and Training of School Psychologists voted thirty-four to seven "that they thought there might be some other route to the profession of school psychologist other than that of classroom teaching." Norma E. Cutts, *op. cit.*, Chapter XIII, "The School in School Psychology." See also W. C. Trow. Diagnostician, Ed.S., and Ph.D. Programs for school psychologists in Michigan. *Amer. Psychologist*, 1961, **16**, 84–85.

problem in determining just what characteristics are important, and then measuring or evaluating these characteristics.

The problem of the requirement of a teaching certificate and teaching experience for counselors was considered, and it was suggested that while desirable, perhaps this background is not essential, and that consideration might be given to making this requirement more flexible.

SUGGESTED READINGS

American College Personnel Association, Professional Standards Committee. American College Personnel Association Professional Standards Committee studies graduate student selection. *Personnel Guid. J.*, 1954, **32**, 362–366. This is one of the few sets of recommendations of a professional group, based on a survey of counselor educators.

American Psychological Association, Division of Counseling Psychology, Counselor Training Committee, Sub-committee on Counselor Trainee Selection. An analysis of practices in counselor trainee selection. *J. counsel. Psychol.*, 1954, **1**, 174–179. A survey of counselor training institutions, emphasizing training in counseling psychology but of pertinence to the selection of guidance counselors.

Hill, G. E. & Green, D. A. The selection, preparation, and professionalization of guidance and personnel workers. *Rev. educ. Res.*, 1960, **30**, 115–130. A brief review of the recent literature in the area of selection and preparation of counselors.

CHAPTER 5

THE TRAINING AND
CERTIFICATION OF
SCHOOL COUNSELORS

No matter how well selected, how well adjusted or endowed with a "counseling personality," the individual must have training to be an effective counselor. There are some persons who seem to be natural counselors without training. But these people would be better counselors with training. To some extent, it is perhaps true that counselors are born, not made. Wrenn notes that "if certain attributes are not present at the beginning of the professional training, the individual will not become an effective counselor, no matter how excellent the training program. Training, after all, merely sharpens the effectiveness of a personality whose structure is fairly well determined before the onset of graduate work."[1] Nevertheless, training is essential. Effective counseling is not instinctive, and while a "counseling personality" is an asset, it is not sufficient. For effective counseling, a background of knowledge and information of various kinds is needed, as well as skills and techniques to implement the personal qualities and attitudes which are basic for counseling.

Before training can be discussed, it is necessary to determine what the training is for—what it is to be directed toward. Counseling is the major activity of the counselor, though it is not the only one. Hitchcock states that "education for most guidance positions is basically the education of the counselor and the counselor is the principal professional person in any guidance

[1] C. G. Wrenn. *Student personnel work in college.* New York: Ronald, 1951. P. 197.

program."[2] Accepting counseling as the essential professional activity of the guidance specialist, what are the knowledges and skills which are involved in effective counseling? In this chapter we shall consider the roles and functions of the guidance counselor, and then discuss the content of training for these roles and functions. The certification of counselors, which is closely tied to training, will also be considered.

Counselor Roles and Functions

There are numerous discussions of the duties and functions of counselors in the public schools. Surveys have been made of what various counselors do,[3] and opinions have been expressed by individuals and groups.[4]

[2] A. A. Hitchcock. By what means can the quality and quantity of guidance services, particularly in high schools, be increased? *Current issues in higher education*, 1958. Washington, D.C.: Association for Higher Education, National Education Association, 1958.

[3] For example, (1) D. L. Arnold. Time spent by counselors and deans in various activities. *Occup.*, 1949, **27**, 391–393. (2) *Counseling services in the secondary schools of Illinois.* Allerton House Conference on Education. Urbana, Ill.: College of Education, University of Illinois. (3) Rachael D. Cox. *Counselors and their work.* Harrisburg, Pa.: Archives Publishing Company of Pennsylvania, 1945. (4) C. W. Grant. The counselor's role. *Personnel Guid. J.*, 1954, **33**, 74–77. (5) W. L. Hitchcock. Counselors feel they should. *Personnel Guid. J.*, 1953, **32**, 72–74. (6) K. A. Martyn. We are wasting the counselor's time. *Calif. J. second. Educ.*, 1957, **32**, 439–441. (7) Florence E. Purcell. Counselor assignments and efficiency. *Voc. Guid. Quart.*, 1957, **5**, 111–113. (8) W. Tennyson. Time: the counselor's dilemma. *Personnel Guid. J.*, 1958, **37**, 129–135. (9) W. E. Truax, Jr. Critical requirements of small school counselors. *Personnel Guid. J.*, 1956, **35**, 103–106. Reprinted in G. F. Farwell & H. J. Peters (Eds.) *Guidance readings for counselors.* Chicago: Rand McNally, 1960. Pp. 499–506.

[4] For example, (1) American Association for the Advancement of Science. *Identification and guidance of able students.* Report of conferences on testing and counseling, University of Michigan, May 28–31, 1958. Washington, D.C.: The Association, 1958. (2) American Personnel and Guidance Association, Committee on Professional Training, Licensing and Certification. Professional training, licensing, and certification. *Personnel Guid. J.*, 1958, **37**, 162–166. (3) Institute for Human Adjustment. *Training psychological counselors.* Ann Arbor, Mich.: University of Michigan Press, 1950. (4) L. M. Miller (Ed.). *Counselor preparation.* Washington, D.C.: National Vocational Guidance Association, 1949. (5) National Association of Guidance Supervisors and Counselor Trainers, Committee on Duties, Standards, and Qualification. *Duties, standards, and qualifications of counselors.* Misc. 3314-1, 1949. Washington, D.C.: U.S. Office of Education, 1949. (6) E. D. Tooker. Counselor role: counselor training. *Personnel Guid. J.*, 1957, **36**, 263–267. Reprinted in Farwell & Peters (Eds.), *op. cit.*, pp. 93–100.

The duties and functions of counselors vary widely in different schools and different systems. Some counselors spend much of their time in nonprofessional activities, or activities which are not guidance. Many counselors are dissatisfied with the way they spend their time. There seems to be lack of understanding, or even a misunderstanding, of the counselor's functions, and misuse of his time, by some administrators, as well as by some counselors themselves. The statement of Cox, made in 1945, while now not as generally applicable, still seems to describe the counselor in many schools. She wrote: "A counselor needs to be an educational and vocational adviser, a social worker, a teacher, an organizer, a promoter, a public speaker, and even a public relations man. At the same time he needs some of the skills of a psychologist, some of the knowledge of a physician, some of the insights of a psychiatrist. Perhaps the hardest part of this amazingly complicated function is his need to know where and when his own work properly ends and that of some more specialized worker begins."[5]

Perhaps the most comprehensive and detailed outline of the counselor's function is that developed by the Committee on the Role of Psychology in the Preparation of School Counselors of the Division of Counseling Psychology, American Psychological Association. It is reproduced here because of its completeness.

ESSENTIAL FUNCTIONS OF THE SECONDARY
SCHOOL COUNSELOR

I. Intellectual Development of the Pupil
   A. Working With Pupils Directly
      1. Developmental activities
         a. Developing study skills
         b. Orientation to school
         c. Educational course planning
         d. Planning for post-high school education
         e. Encouraging optimal intellectual productivity
      2. Preventive-remedial activities
         a. Problems of course or program changes
         b. Problems of failing students
         c. Problems of lack of motivation in academic learning

[5] Cox, *op. cit.*, p. 36.

B. Working With Others Who Work With Pupils
   1. Developmental activities
      a. Helping teachers
         (1) Who are attempting to perform the same kinds of developmental activities as listed under I, A, 1
         (2) Identify individual differences in pupils
         (3) Discover and utilize school and community resources for assessment of intellectual capacity
      b. Helping administrators
         (1) Become aware of pupil characteristics as an aid in curricular development
      c. Helping parents
         (1) Develop realistic goals with respect to the educational potentialities of their children
         (2) Develop skills and understandings in procedures for working with children in educational planning
   2. Preventive-remedial activities
      a. Helping teachers search for causes of pupil academic failure
      b. Helping teachers discover and utilize school and community resources for pupils with special learning difficulties
      c. Working with other pupil personnel workers in the school; e.g., special education workers, remedial reading specialists, speech and hearing specialists, school psychologists, school social workers, in their attempts to aid youth in intellectual development

II. Vocational Development of the Pupil
   A. Working With Pupils Directly
      1. Developmental activities
         a. Helping pupils know and understand their vocational potentialities and interest
         b. Helping pupils know and understand their vocational opportunities
         c. Helping pupils make increasingly specific vocational decisions based on understanding of self and of vocational opportunities
         d. Helping pupils develop plans for putting vocational decisions into effect
      2. Preventive-remedial activities
         a. Helping pupils with unrealistic vocational goals to achieve a more realistic vocational orientation

B. Working With Others Who Work With Pupils
  1. Developmental activities
     a. Helping teachers
        (1) Collect, organize, and disseminate vocational information pertinent to their subject fields through classroom activities
        (2) To relate instructional activities to vocational goals of pupils
     b. Helping administrators relate curricular planning to changes in local or regional occupational structure
     c. Helping parents understand the process of vocational development in their children and the parent's role in this process
     d. Working with community agencies, institutions, and individuals interested in the vocational development of youth
  2. Preventive-remedial activities
     a. Working with community agencies, institutions, and individuals interested in helping vocationally handicapped youth

III. Personality Development of the Pupil
  A. Working With Pupils Directly
     1. Developmental activities
        a. Helping the pupil develop respect for himself as a member of society
        b. Helping the pupil develop competencies in interpersonal relationships
     2. Preventive-remedial activities
        a. Problems of teacher-pupil relationships
        b. Problems of peer relationships
        c. Problems of pupil-family conflicts
        d. Problems related to the development of self values
  B. Working With Others Who Work With Pupils
     1. Developmental activities
        a. Working with teachers in promoting positive mental hygiene concepts in the classroom
        b. Working with parents in developing understandings of normal behavior and the psychological needs of adolescents
     2. Preventive-remedial activities
        a. Working with teachers in the identification and referral of pupils with personality problems

b. Working with teachers in providing a classroom climate conducive to the psychological growth of pupils with personality problems

c. Working with parents of pupils with personality problems

d. Working with other pupil-personnel workers in developing and carrying out procedures designed to assist pupils with personality problems

e. Working with community agencies, institutions, and individuals in developing and carrying out procedures designed to assist pupils with personality problems

IV. Programming Responsibilities of the Counselor

A. Student Appraisal Procedures

1. Organizing, developing, collecting, studying and using pertinent appraisal data as a basis for stimulating the intellectual, vocational, and personality development of each pupil

2. Helping teachers develop competencies in student appraisal procedures

3. Working with school administrators responsible for conditions conducive to the operation of an effective program of student appraisal procedures

B. Informational Procedures

1. Organizing, collecting, studying, and using pertinent educational and occupational information in the development of the perspective which each pupil possesses of his environmental opportunities

C. Counseling

1. Developing suitable plans and procedures for individual counseling with each pupil

2. Developing suitable plans for enlisting the active participation of other school staff in the total counseling process

3. Developing suitable plans for referral of students with problems beyond the scope of competencies possessed by the counselor to appropriate agencies and individuals

4. Working with school administrators in developing physical facilities and time allowances essential for the work of the counselor[6]

[6] American Psychological Association, Division of Counseling Psychology, Committee on the Role of Psychology in the Preparation of School Counselors (K. B. Hoyt, Chmn.). *The role of psychology in the preparation of school counselors* [mimeo.; no date]. Pp. 4–8.

While individual counseling occupies a relatively small part of the outline of duties, in terms of time involved it accounts for about 50 percent of the counselor's time in those schools which provide adequate counselor services. It is therefore to be expected that this function would be emphasized in training programs.

Recommended Training for the School Counselor

With the variety of functions of the school counselor, due in part to the varying situations in which he works, but also related to differences of opinion, it would be expected that training programs would vary. This is, in fact, the case. Programs vary depending upon their location in departments of education or psychology, and upon the views of those operating the programs regarding the relative importance of various fields of knowledge and skills. Nevertheless, a survey of the literature concerning opinions and recommendations for training programs, as well as the nature of existing programs, indicates that there is considerable basic agreement and similarity in programs.

In 1949 two reports containing recommendations for the training of counselors were published, one by a committee of the U.S. Office of Education and one by the National Vocational Guidance Association, based upon the work of representatives of NVGA and seven other professional organizations: American College and Personnel Association, Division of Counseling and Guidance of the American Psychological Association (now the Division of Counseling Psychology), National Rehabilitation Association, U.S. Office of Education, National Association of Guidance Supervisors, U.S. Employment Service, and the Veterans Administration.[7]

The latter report has had considerable influence, and is still recognized as a valuable guide. A common core of training was proposed, consisting of the following areas: Philosophy and Principles; Growth and Development of the Individual; Study of the Individual; Collecting, Evaluating, and Using Occupational and Related Information; Administrative and Community Relationships; Techniques Used in Counseling; and Supervised Ex-

---

7 (1) Committee on Duties, Standards, and Qualifications, *op. cit.* (2) Miller, *op. cit.*

perience in Counseling. For counselors who are to engage in educational and vocational counseling, the following areas were suggested in addition: Group Methods in Guidance; Placement; Follow-up Techniques and Uses; and Methods of Research and Evaluation.

The most recent outline of recommended areas of preparation is that of the Committee on the Role of Psychology in the Training of School Counselors, whose outline of essential functions was reproduced above. This committee proposes two programs, a minimal program and a desirable program, as follows:

A Minimal Program of School Counselor Preparation

Academic Program Leading to an M.A. Degree or its Equivalent

A. Psychological Foundations—Basic Areas
   1. Child and Adolescent Psychology
   2. Psychology of Individual Differences
   3. Psychology of Learning
   4. Psychology of Personality
B. Educational Foundations—Basic Areas
   1. Curriculum
   2. Philosophy and History of Education
   3. Educational Administration
   4. Statistics and Measurement
C. Counseling and Guidance—Basic Areas
   1. Backgrounds and Principles of Guidance
   2. Student Appraisal Procedures
   3. Counseling
   4. Occupations and Vocational Development
   5. Group Procedures
   6. Supervised Practice in Counseling

A Desirable Program of School Counselor Preparation

Academic Program Leading to a Professional Certificate

A. Psychological Foundations
   1. Same as for minimum program
   2. Additional areas of preparation
      a. Social Psychology
      b. Psychology of Exceptional Children

    c. Abnormal Psychology
    d. Psychology of Reading
    e. Advanced Educational Psychology
B. Educational Foundations
  1. Same as for minimum program
  2. Additional areas of preparation
    a. Supervision
    b. Advanced Statistics and Advanced Measurement
    c. Comparative Education
C. Counseling and Guidance
  1. Same as for minimum program
  2. Additional areas of preparation
    a. Advanced Counseling
    b. Advanced Counseling Practicum
    c. Use of Referral Sources[8]

It is evident from both the NVGA report and the above recommendations, that psychology, or psychological foundations, is heavily represented in what is considered a desirable program of counselor training. The NVGA report notes that "Because the counselor deals with human beings his preparation must include extensive study in psychology."[9] With undergraduate preparation in education, this emphasis appears to be warranted. The recommendations of two other committees for the training of psychological counselors also contain this emphasis upon psychological content.[10]

As a summary of various recommendations, the areas of work and typical course titles in each area which might constitute an adequate training program for counselors are suggested as follows:

  I. Psychological Foundations
      Developmental Psychology, Child Psychology, Adolescent Psychology, Human Behavior, Abnormal Psychology, Behavior Disorders

    [8] American Psychological Association, Division of Counseling Psychology, Committee on the Role of Psychology in the Preparation of School Counselors, *op. cit.,* pp. 16–17.
    [9] Miller, *op. cit.,* p. 19.
    [10] (1) Institute for Human Adjustment, *op. cit.* (2) American Psychological Association, Committee on Subdoctoral Education of the Education and Training Board (a report of). The training of technical workers in psychology at the subdoctoral level. *Amer. Psychologist,* 1955, **10,** 279–282.

*Psychology of Learning
Social Psychology
Educational Psychology (Advanced)

II. Personality Organization and Development
   *Psychology of Personality, Personality Dynamics, Theories of Personality
   Psychology of Motivation
   *Psychology of Adjustment, Mental Hygiene

III. The Social Environment
   Culture and Personality
   *Social Foundations of Education
   *Occupational Information, Educational and Occupational Information
   Occupational Analysis and Classification
   Occupational Sociology, Industrial Sociology, Sociology of Work
   Occupational Trends, Labor Market Trends, Labor Economics, Labor Problems
   Industrial Psychology
   Community Organization, Sociology of the Community
   Social Organization and Disorganization
   Social Problems
   Vocational Education

IV. Appraisal, Assessment, or Evaluation of the Individual
   *Introduction to Tests and Measurements, Use of Tests
   Instruments or Techniques of Measurement
   Individual Testing
   Case Study Methods, Case Analysis
   Personality Testing, Personality Evaluation
   Individual Differences, Differential Psychology

V. Counseling Theory and Practice
   *Introduction to Guidance, Introduction to Counseling
   *Principles of Counseling, Counseling Theories and Techniques
   *Advanced Counseling, Interviewing Techniques
   *Counseling Practicum, Supervised Practice in Counseling
   Vocational Counseling, Occupational and Vocational Counseling
   *Group Counseling, Group Guidance

* The items preceded by an asterisk are a suggested minimum program for preparation for counseling.

It is apparent that this outline reflects the predominantly psychological nature of training in counseling. It will also be noted that there is no specific training in statistics. This is not because such training would not be desirable for all counselors, but because some line has to be drawn due to time limitations. For the nondoctoral counselor, the emphasis is upon preparation for practice rather than research. It is assumed, or perhaps only hoped, that courses in tests and measurements, as well as other courses, will include sufficient statistics for the practicing counselor.

It is also apparent that adequate training, which would include even the most essential courses in these areas, could not be completed in one academic year. This raises the question of the length of training for counseling.

It seems to be agreed that adequate training for psychological counselors, including school counselors, requires at least two academic years of work. The NVGA report referred to above notes that "two years of graduate work including at least three months of supervised experience or internship is basic to a professional status."[11] The two American Psychological Association reports also propose two years of training.[12] Mathewson,[13] as well as other authorities, recommends a two-year program including internship. The program of the Committee on the Role of Psychology in the Preparation of School Counselors, outlined above, includes a two-year program as a desired goal. While most current programs are one-year, perhaps because of the general practice of awarding a master's degree after a year of study, it is being increasingly recognized that this is a minimum, and even as a minimum is inadequate.

One reason for the inadequacy of a one-year program is the impossibility of including adequate or sufficient supervised field training or experience in such a short period. Field training is being increasingly recognized as a necessary part of counselor preparation. It was incorporated in the training of clinical and counseling psychologists at the doctoral level following World

[11] Miller, *op. cit.*, p. 20.

[12] (1) American Psychological Association, Committee on Subdoctoral Education of the Education and Training Board, *op. cit.* (2) Institute for Human Adjustment, *op. cit.*

[13] R. H. Mathewson. The general guidance counselor. *Personnel Guid. J.*, 1954, 32, 544–547.

War II, when these programs were supported by the Veterans Administration. More recently, field training has been incorporated in the two-year training programs for rehabilitation counselors supported by the Federal Office of Vocational Rehabilitation.[14] There is no reason why such a training experience could not be made available for school counselors. There is a sufficient number of schools with adequate staffs of trained and experienced counselors in which student-counselors could be placed for a quarter or a semester of supervised experience.

Current Preparation Programs

How do these recommendations compare with present programs for the training of school counselors?

The Committee on the Role of Psychology in the Preparation of School Counselors obtained information from eighty-one institutions training secondary school counselors in 1959. The Committee was interested in the proportion of the master's program of courses that were psychological in content. Over 50 per cent of the institutions reported that at least 50 percent of the courses were psychological in content, in the judgment of the staff members replying. Only five schools reported that less than 20 percent of the courses were psychological in nature. There were wide differences among the schools, ranging from less than 10 percent to 100 percent. Problems of definition and classification of courses make these results ambiguous, however.[15]

A more complete and detailed survey was conducted by the U.S. Office of Education in 1957. Of 223 institutions known to offer graduate work in guidance and student personnel work, 182 responded. Of these 182 schools, 128 offered training in elementary-school counseling, 174 in secondary-school counseling, and 95 in college personnel work. Courses required in the programs of 152 of the schools were classified by level of training (master's or doctor's), by type of program (elementary,

---

[14] L. M. Miller, J. F. Garrett & N. Stewart. Opportunity: rehabilitation counseling. *Personnel Guid. J.*, 1955, 33, 444–447.

[15] American Psychological Association, Division of Counseling Psychology, Committee on the Role of Psychology in the Preparation of School Counselors, *op. cit.*

secondary, college), and by areas of preparation. Table 1 summarizes the results of the survey.

TABLE 1. Requirement Data in Areas of Preparation by
Type of Program and Level of Degree

Areas of Preparation	Master's Level % of Institutions Requiring			Doctor's Level % of Institutions Requiring		
	Elem.	*Sec.*	*Coll.*	*Elem.*	*Sec.*	*Coll.*
Counseling	90	94	94	97	93	100
Analysis of the individual	90	92	92	92	83	100
Educational & occupational information	67	90	90	70	89	98
Philosophy and principles	77	82	87	90	81	80
Organization & administration	71	76	74	85	83	91
Methods of research	69	74	76	100	100	100
Psychological foundations	69	73	68	90	81	89
Practicum	60	59	65	87	81	96
Group procedures	32	32	32	54	44	40
Sociological foundations	16	16	19	33	30	31
Placement	8	7	10	5	7	7
Follow-up & evaluation	3	3	5	8	7	9
Economic foundations	1	1	1	5	4	4

SOURCE: Adapted from Table 9, P. MacMinn & R. G. Ross. *Status of preparation programs for guidance and student personnel workers.* Department of Health, Education, and Welfare, Office of Education, Bull. 1959, No. 7. Washington, D.C.: Government Printing Office, 1959.

The data in this table indicate that the majority of the schools provide training programs which include the areas recommended for such training programs. That the percentages are not higher for the master's level is no doubt due to limitations in what can be included in a one-year program. Some schools include certain areas, while others choose to include other areas.

The figures for practicum include not only field training, or internship, but campus courses with varying amounts of supervised experience. It is not possible to determine, therefore, what proportion of the programs includes intensive supervised practice or field-training courses. The probably relatively small proportion which do include this, and the small proportion of schools which require work in group procedures, represent the greatest departures from recommended training programs.

The intensive and extensive training programs in most counselor-training institutions raise a problem concerning the preparation of teachers, and of teachers and administrators working in guidance who desire to obtain training on a part-time basis. First of all, the obtaining of such training entirely through summer-school work requires a long period of time, during most of which the individual is not functioning adequately or in a highly effective manner as a counselor. Second, summer-school courses are often not the equivalent of courses offered during the regular academic year, usually being briefer or condensed. Third, most of the training programs involve sequences, or groups of courses which should be taken together. Programs are developed for full-time students, and are not always well adapted for students who can only attend summer sessions. Providing adequate supervised practice for the part-time student poses a particular problem. As a result of these factors, it would seem desirable that counselors be trained in regular academic-year programs rather than by taking part-time work over a long period of time.

Certification Requirements for Counselors

Certification is, or can be, an important factor in the education of counselors. It is a means of standardizing, and raising, professional standards among guidance personnel. Kremen, in a survey of supervisors of guidance, educators and counselor trainers, and state superintendents of education in twenty-three states, found the following reasons for certification put forward:

1. To raise professional standards, and improve the quality of counseling and guidance services.
2. To provide a means of selecting qualified persons as counselors.
3. To aid in establishing the professional status of counselors.
4. To provide some guides for counselor training institutions.
5. To develop uniformity in the philosophy and practice of counseling.
6. To encourage those interested in counseling to obtain adequate preparation.[16]

[16] B. G. Kremen. Counselor certification in the United States. *Occup.*, 1951, 29, 584–586.

It may be questioned whether certification has contributed greatly to any of these objectives. About the only standardization of requirements is the need for a teaching certificate and teaching experience for a counseling certificate. About half the states having certification laws also require some other paid work experience in addition to teaching. Other requirements vary tremendously among the states. In most instances the academic requirements are minimal, being as low as approximately half a semester of graduate work for some types of certification. They seldom include more than a year of graduate work. Such minimum standards do little to establish the professional status of counselors or to encourage a period of full-time training. While there is rather general agreement in regard to the areas of academic training, the requirements are limited. There is relatively little in the way of psychological foundations. The emphasis is upon techniques, methods, procedures, and tools. Moreover, it is possible for a candidate for certification to meet the requirements by presenting a mixture of graduate and undergraduate courses taken at various institutions, including extension and correspondence courses, with resulting great overlap in content and representing no integrated, progressive, or continuing sequence of training. Certification requirements thus fail to assure that the counselor will be adequately prepared to undertake professional counseling. They fall far short of meeting the recommendations and suggested programs discussed above. Various types of provisional or temporary certificates are designed to encourage further preparation—and no doubt achieve this—but the requirements for full or permanent certification are low.

Certification plans in some cases have no teeth in them, or are not enforced. A certificate is not necessarily required for employment as a counselor; the superintendent or principal may or may not require certification as a condition of employment. In one study, some administrators stated that they regarded teaching experience as sufficient, and professional training as unnecessary.[17] In many instances state policies read to the effect that those assigned counseling and guidance duties *should* (not must) meet the certification requirements. Accreditation may

[17] H. Weitz. The role of the guidance worker in the schools. *Personnel Guid. J.*, 1958, 37, 266–272.

not be affected by the fact that the school employs counselors who are not certified. In some instances, a period of time is provided before the employment of certificated counselors is required for accreditation. Counselors employed prior to this date are not required to be certificated, thus encouraging the appointment of noncertificated counselors prior to the deadline date. In some cases those devoting less than half-time to counseling may not be required to hold certificates.

The result of these conditions is that in many states, the great majority of counselors do not hold counseling certificates. In 1955 Wendorf found that only 14.3 percent of the counselors responding to his questionnaire (representing almost 50 percent of the schools in Ohio) were certified, and 57.7 percent of these had provisional certificates.[18] In 1956–1957 another study of certification of counselors in the 1138 secondary schools of Ohio was made, using the Annual Principal's Report submitted to the State Department of Education. Of the 469 counselors devoting half-time or more to counseling, and to whom the certification requirements therefore applied, a total of 95, or 20 percent, held certificates for some type of personnel service. About a third of these (31) were four-year provisional counselor certificates; another 28 held a "guidance certificate—no category given," and 20 held the 8-year provisional counselor certificate. The authors state that "The indications of these findings give support to the statement that administrators continue to give little consideration to the professional preparation and competencies of personnel when appointing them to positions that have counseling as a primary responsibility."[19] There is evidence that a similar situation exists in many other states.

Certification is desirable when it serves the purposes listed above. It must be accepted and applied to do this. If certification is not required for the performance of counseling duties, it is of little value. At present, rather than contributing to raising standards, certification, even at the minimal levels, apparently is of little value. It is sometimes argued that mandatory certification

[18] R. A. Wendorf. Qualification of guidance counselors in Ohio high schools. *Personnel Guid. J.*, 1956, **34**, 569–571.
[19] G. F. Farwell & A. M. Vekich. Status and certification of counselors in Ohio high schools, *Personnel Guid. J.*, 1959, **38**, 285–289.

at any adequate level would mean that there would be no eligible applicants. On the other hand, in the present situation there is no incentive for applicants to meet certification requirements. At some point it must be determined that it is better to get along for a time without counselors rather than with untrained counselors. As Arbuckle points out, "We do not improve the standards of a profession by having the certification requirements geared to the supply and demand."[20]

Certification has been growing since its beginning in Pennsylvania in 1924. In 1959, thirty-seven states and territories had mandatory certification requirements, four had optional requirements, and thirteen had no requirements.[21]

The National Defense Education Act and Counselor Training

A discussion of the training of school counselors must consider the impact of the National Defense Education Act of 1958 (Public Law 85–864). Title V (B) of this Act authorized counseling and guidance training institutes "to improve the qualifications of personnel engaged in counseling and guidance of students in secondary schools, or teachers in such schools preparing to engage in such counseling and guidance." (See Appendix I.)

While the National Defense Education Act did not incorporate some of the recommendations of educators and professional organizations in the counseling and guidance field, it has been hailed as almost the complete solution to the problem of supplying an adequate number of qualified counselors in our schools. It is not a panacea, however. Its intention was not to subsidize complete training for counselors, as desirable as such a program may be. There is no doubt the Act will have an impact on counselor training. There are some doubts, however, as to whether the effects are entirely favorable. The number of individuals affected will be large. The 50 institutes held during the summer of 1959 enrolled 2210 students. In 1960, 84 institutes were held, and 21 regular-session institutes were held during the 1960–

[20] D. S. Arbuckle. From the president: The counselor and his professional education. *Personnel Guid. J.*, 1959, 37, 694–695.

[21] R. Brewster. *Guidance workers certification requirements.* Department of Health, Education, and Welfare, Office of Education, Bull. 1960, No. 14, Washington, D.C.: Government Printing Office, 1960.

1961 school year. It is estimated that by the summer of 1961 over 6000 persons will have been in attendance at one of the summer or regular session institutes.

The Act is restrictive regarding the nature and conditions of the training provided for counselor trainees. The concern of Congress was not specifically to meet the shortage of trained counselors in our schools; its main concern was the identification and education of the talented. Title V is entitled "Guidance, Counseling, and Testing; Identification and Encouragement of Able Students." Moreover, the purpose of the Act was to stimulate education in certain areas, to "correct as rapidly as possible the existing imbalances in our educational programs which have led to an insufficient proportion of our population educated in science, mathematics, and modern foreign languages, and trained in technology."

Fears that this emphasis upon the identification of the able student and upon the encouragement of education and training in specific areas would unduly limit or restrict the training of counselors under the act have not materialized, however. As Tyler, in her evaluation of the first fifty institutes, notes, the NDEA "makes it possible to provide counseling service to a group that is likely to be slighted where counselors are scarce and problems are acute. It should broaden the scope of counseling activity in secondary schools, but should not change its basic purpose."[22]

The emphasis upon identification of talent would appear to be inconsistent with the limitation of training to secondary school counselors. It is generally agreed that early recognition and encouragement of talent is important and that it may be too late to utilize fully talent which has not been recognized and encouraged until high-school age. Yet, counselors at the elementary level are not eligible for training.

Tyler points out the possible danger of counselors, as well as the public, developing a distorted picture of the job of the counselor. The breadth of the training programs, however, seems

[22] Leona E. Tyler. *The national defense counseling and guidance institutes program: a report of the first 50 institutes.* Department of Health, Education, and Welfare, Office of Education, Bull. 1960, No. 31. Washington, D.C.: Government Printing Office, 1960.

to minimize this danger. The fact that the basic principles and methods of counseling the able or talented are the same as those employed in counseling other students keeps the training programs from becoming unduly narrowed. The restriction of the Act to identifying and encouraging the able student thus does not, or should not, result in a limited or narrow program of training.

Likewise, the concern that the emphasis upon tests and identification of able students would limit training to testing was unfounded. The Act allows training in counseling in a broad sense.

In fact, there appears to be real danger that the institutes have attempted too much, have developed in some instances training programs which have been so broad as to be necessarily shallow or superficial in some respects. Emphasis tends to be on techniques, with neglect of psychological fundamentals and theory. Some institutes have perhaps attempted to crowd too much into a session of a few weeks, have perhaps tried to provide a telescoped program of counselor training. This appears to be a result, to some extent at least, of the desire of the Office of Education to encourage institute programs which are concentrated and which combine or consolidate materials or subject matter usually dealt with in separate courses, and of the Office's insistence that institute students should constitute a separate group, isolated from regular students in the counselor-training programs of the institution. While there may be some advantages to such a policy, there are also some serious difficulties.

This leads to what is perhaps the greatest problem created by the NDEA program. The briefness of the training programs, whether of the short-term or regular-session type, means that it is not possible to provide a complete program of training in counseling for any student. While as indicated above, it was not the intent of the Act to do this, it may be questioned whether it is desirable to do anything less than this. Short-term training programs are inadequate for professional training. While the institutes have certainly served to upgrade the qualifications of counselors in the field, it has served only indirectly in increasing the number of fully trained counselors. Almost a third of the students enrolled in the institutes have been teachers with no previous training or experience in counseling. Such persons are eligible for training if they can demonstrate that they will be engaged in counseling following their institute experience. This circumstance leads to the encouragement of administrators to follow the procedure which has long been criticized—to appoint teachers with little or no training to counseling positions. Some of these persons will no doubt go on to obtain further training, but there is no evidence as to how many will do so. Many certainly will not. We thus have a situation where a condition which is generally regarded as undesirable is perpetuated—the assignment of inadequately trained persons to counseling duties.

The Act does to some extent raise the quality of counselors but its main effect is to increase the quantity of inadequately trained counselors. This effect is a serious matter for those who are concerned about the number of such counselors who are functioning in our schools. It seems to assure that for a long time to come our schools will be staffed mainly by such incompletely trained counselors. Tyler,[23] discussing the contribution of NDEA institutes to the untrained counselors, asks: "Is it really to the advantage of the counseling profession, from a long-range point of view, to give minimal training to relatively unmotivated people who are unlikely to supplement it on their own initiative? . . . Among professional workers there would be more general support, however, for a policy of trying gradually to replace such persons with well-trained professionals."

Dugan, in his evaluation of the effects of the Act, writes that "Quality, not quantity, is the important variable. The number of counselors has grown at a faster rate than the quality. Quality has increased in the individual case but has not kept pace with the demand for an increasing supply of professionally skillful school counselors to meet the needs of rapidly accelerating secondary school enrollments. . . . Emphasis extended by the national level program of counseling institutes might easily give the impression that counselor preparation requires only a short-term, 'crash type' training program. . . . Support . . . is needed at the national level by subsidizing agencies to help balance the demand for quantity of counselors with an equal concern about the *quality* of their preparation. Increasing support nationally is

[23] *Ibid.*, p. 76.

needed for a minimum of a two-year program of professional preparation."[24]

The insistence of the Office of Education upon the isolation of institute trainees from other counselor trainees appears to be questionable. The implication that the regular curriculum is inadequate may not be intended; the desire to provide an intense, condensed experience is no doubt the purpose. The close interaction and relationships developed in classes by those with similar backgrounds has also been advanced as a reason for this isolation. However, as Tyler shows,[25] the trainees in each institute were highly heterogeneous. Much may be gained by the interaction of institute students with regular counselor trainees, whose stronger backgrounds of recent or current academic work in basic areas could contribute greatly to the courses.

The NDEA program for training counselors introduces, then, some serious professional problems. It upgrades the qualifications of practicing counselors, and this, most would agree, is desirable. But this is not sufficient, and the support of short-term training programs is not an unmixed blessing. Few of those attending such programs are brought to an adequate level of professional functioning. For many it is and will be the only training they will have. Few will continue on their own to obtain adequate training. And for those who do, the varied and unstandardized content of the institutes will make their integration into regular training programs difficult.

School Counseling as a Profession

A few words should be said here about the professionalization of counseling. The criteria of a profession have been listed by Wrenn and Darley as follows: (1) the definitions of job titles and functions; (2) a body of knowledge and skills; (3) the application of standards of selection and training; (4) a self-imposition of standards of admission and performance; (5) the development of professional consciousness and professional groups; (6) the legal recognition of the vocation; (7) the development of a code of ethics; (8) the performance of a socially needed

---

[24] W. E. Dugan. The impact of NDEA upon counselor preparation. *Personnel Guid. J.*, 1960, **39**, 37–40.
[25] *Op. cit.*

function.[26] The discussion in this and the preceding chapter should help in determining whether school counseling meets these criteria. Perhaps the last is the only one which could be considered as being adequately met. Progress is being made in meeting some of the others, such as (1), (2), (3), (5), and (7).

The criterion of a body of knowledge and skills is inadequately met when one considers the diversity in this area, as discussed earlier in the chapter. Mueller notes that "any emerging profession must justify its claim to certain unique skills which other professions and the general public do not have access to."[27] There appears to have been progress, however, with a growing recognition that the central function and skill of the counseling and guidance worker is counseling. This is something which no other professional in education can claim as his function. Pierson and Grant urge that "personnel and guidance workers should build their profession around the concept 'counselor' rather than around the concept 'guidance worker.'"[28] It is hoped that in adopting such an approach, this book will contribute to the professionalization of counseling services in the school.

Summary

In this chapter we have considered the nature of the training of school counselors. Accepting the point of view that the unique professional function of the counselor is counseling, we have suggested that the basic training for this function is psychological in nature. Programs which have been recommended for counselor training were reviewed, and it seems apparent that they emphasize the psychological foundations of counseling.

While a minimum of one academic year of graduate training is necessary for counselors, it is generally recommended that two years is desirable. A review of current programs of counselor training indicated that the greatest deficiencies, imposed

[26] C. G. Wrenn & J. G. Darley. An appraisal of the professional status of personnel work. In E. G. Williamson (Ed.). *Trends in student personnel work.* Minneapolis: University of Minnesota Press, 1949. Pp. 264–287.

[27] Kate H. Mueller. Criteria for evaluating professional status. *Personnel Guid. J.,* 1959, **37**, 410–417.

[28] G. A. Pierson & C. W. Grant. The road ahead for the school counselor. *Personnel Guid. J.,* 1959, **38**, 207–210.

perhaps to some extent by the limitations of time, are in group counseling and supervised practice.

A review of certification requirements for counselors suggests that it is not achieving the goals which it should be achieving. Standards are minimal, and are not adequately enforced or adhered to in hiring practices. The great majority of those functioning as counselors are not certified, even though most of the states now have certification provisions.

Finally, the implications of the National Defense Education Act for supplying schools with adequately trained counselors were considered. While there is no doubt that programs of training under NDEA are providing training to more individuals, there is a question as to whether it is adding many fully trained counselors to the profession.

SUGGESTED READINGS

American Personnel and Guidance Association, Committee on Professional Training, Licensing, and Certification. Professional training, licensing, and certification. *Personnel Guid. J.*, 1958, **37**, 162–166. This report is concerned with minimum standards for counselor preparation, and includes a general statement of the areas to be covered in graduate training.

Arbuckle, D. S. The education of the school counselor. *J. counsel. Psychol.*, 1958, **5**, 58–62. Raises some questions about training counselors, including whether such training should be therapeutic for the student.

Brewster, R. E. *Guidance workers certification requirements*. Department of Health, Education, and Welfare, Office of Education, Bull. 1960, No. 14. Washington, D.C.: Government Printing Office, 1960. A state by state listing of certification requirements for guidance workers.

Feder, D. B. The emerging role of the professional personnel worker. In Henry, N. B. (Ed.) *Personnel services in education*. Fifty-eighth Yearbook, National Society for the Study of Education. Part II. Chicago: University of Chicago Press, 1959. Pp. 181–209. A discussion of the present professional status of personnel work.

MacMinn, P., & Ross, R. G. *Status of preparation programs for guidance and student personnel*. Department of Health, Education, and Welfare, Office of Education, Bull. 1959, No. 7. Washington, D.C.:

Government Printing Office, 1959. The most comprehensive survey of training programs yet accomplished.

Miller, L. M. (Ed.) *Counselor preparation.* Washington, D.C.: National Vocational Guidance Association, 1949. Still one of the most comprehensive recommendations for counselor training.

Wrenn, C. G. Status and role of the school counselor. *Personnel Guid. J.,* 1957, **36**, 175–183. Reprinted in Farwell, G. F., & Peters, H. J. (Eds.) *Guidance readings for counselors.* Chicago: Rand McNally, 1960. Pp. 660–675. A critical review of some of the journal literature on the counselor's role and functions, pointing up the psychological nature of the preparation required for performing these functions.

CHAPTER 6

THE TEACHER IN GUIDANCE

There appears to be considerable difference of opinion, if not confusion, concerning the teacher's role in guidance and personnel work. In this chapter we shall examine the issues involved and attempt to work out a resolution of the differences in terms of the concepts of counseling and guidance which underlie the approach presented in this book. We shall not, of course, be able to consider in detail the teacher's responsibilities, since, as in most of the other topics dealt with, adequate discussion requires a book in itself. As in other chapters, the suggested readings will provide the student with more detailed treatments of the field.

The Teacher as a Counselor

One point of view sees the teacher as the central or key person in guidance or personnel work. Guidance is equated with education and teaching. It is pointed out that the goals of education and of guidance are similar, if not identical. It is emphasized that the teacher is the closest person to the pupil in the school, and thus knows the pupil better than does anyone else. Therefore, the only person who can be continuously effective in guidance is the teacher. The guidance function cannot be assigned to a group of specialists who do not know the child.

This presumed intimate knowledge of the child in the teacher-pupil relationship is put forward as the basis for the slogan "every teacher a counselor." Arbuckle has presented the best statement of this view. He makes the important point that "the subject matter of every teacher is human adjustment; his concern is the development and the adjustment of the child."[1] It is, of course, almost trite now to say that the teacher teaches the child, not subject matter.

Arbuckle recognizes, however, that teachers are not trained for counseling, that the traditional teacher is unable to function as a counselor, and that to allow such teachers to perform counseling would have calamitous results.[2] He presents some of the typical approaches of such teachers to counseling.[3] But he feels that teachers can become passable counselors with some training, and that teachers should be trained in counseling: "The needs of children are great, and they are more likely to be met in the classroom by teachers who have a personal philosophy and a background of *professional* training in the area of guidance and counseling" [my italics].[4] The teacher trained as a counselor is an ideal, but it is a necessary goal, according to Arbuckle, since "the teacher *can* function as a counselor, in many modern schools he *is* functioning as a counselor, and if our children are to undergo the educational experiences that should be a part of their living in a democratic society, then he *must* function as a counselor" [italics in original].[5] It is further argued that counseling must be done by the teacher or it is not done at all in many cases.

There are numerous objections to the teacher functioning as a counselor. A major one is that teachers do not have the training or knowledge and skills to undertake counseling. Arbuckle proposes that this situation be remedied. Such a proposal is perhaps unrealistic, if not undesirable. It was questioned, in Chapter 4, whether counselors should be required to have training as teachers. It would appear to be even more unreasonable to insist that teachers be trained as counselors, which requires from one to two years of specialized graduate work. This is particu-

[1] D. S. Arbuckle. *Teacher counseling.* Cambridge, Mass.: Addison-Wesley, 1950. P. 9.

[2] *Ibid.*, p. 10.

[3] *Ibid.*, Chapters 3 and 4.

[4] D. S. Arbuckle. *Guidance and counseling in the classroom.* Boston: Allyn & Bacon, 1957. P. 14.

[5] *Ibid.*, p. 62.

larly the case when teachers are not devoting full time to counseling. If it is difficult to recruit and retain teachers at present,
this task would be tremendously increased if teachers were required to have graduate training in counseling.

There is a danger in insisting that all teachers should be counselors when many are untrained and unfitted to be. It leads to
teachers developing unrealistic expectations and demands of
themselves. Berlin notes that ". . . teachers are being made to
feel responsible for changing the personality of disturbed students . . . Those who would give teachers this responsibility
seem to be unaware that trained psychotherapists may work
with a family for years before they can detect any change in
attitudes."[6] Not only may the child be harmed by untrained
teachers acting as counselors, but the teachers themselves may
be harmed.

There are other reasons, which appear to make it impractical,
if not undesirable, for every teacher to be a counselor. One is the
fact that some teachers, at least, do not have the personal qualifications for counseling. Although there are similarities in teaching and counseling, they are different in many respects. Some
good teachers may not be able to become good counselors. In
addition, some teachers may not want to become counselors,
may have no interest in doing so, but may prefer to remain
good teachers.

There are practical limitations on the teacher functioning as a
counselor.[7] These are recognized by those who advocate teachers
being counselors, but are minimized unduly. In the first place,
the teacher is working full time as a teacher, and often in addition is performing many other duties, including clerical functions. It is hardly justifiable to require teachers to spend the
time necessary for individual counseling of students, without
released time. It is impractical, if not impossible, for the teacher

[6] I. Berlin. Teachers' self-expectations: how realistic are they? *School
Rev.*, 1958, **66**, 134–143.

[7] See (1) C. E. Vontress. Homeroom guidance: perennial patchwork. *Voc.
Guid. Quart.*, 1960, 8, 223–225. (2) C. W. Grant. The teacher-student
relationship is not counseling. *J. Counsel. Psychol.*, 1960, 7, 148–149. These
contain brief but pointed discussions of these limitations. (3) E. A. Wicas.
The teacher as a counselor. *J. Educ.*, 1957, **139** (4), 13–22.

to enter into a continuing counseling relationship with a pupil. As Gordon notes, "Counseling by the teacher is sandwiched in during the course of a busy day, almost on an impromptu basis created by some pressing situation. . . . It is almost always a haphazard process, on a catch-as-catch-can footing, of a short-time and short-term nature."[8] A very simple difficulty is the lack of private office space in which the teacher can counsel. While counseling can take place in very simple, crude surroundings, there must be freedom from interruption, and privacy from other people.

There is also the question, which was raised in Chapter 4, as to whether the teaching and counseling roles can be mixed, particularly with the same pupils. It is dubious that, as many claim, better counseling can be done with students one has in one's classes (or about whom one has information from other contacts or sources). It is not information or knowledge *about* the student that is important in counseling, but understanding *of* the student. Many teachers have a misconception of counseling. They think of it as being the giving of advice, making recommendations, or engaging in individual teaching or problem-solving of an intellectual or cognitive nature.

Whether the teacher-counselor desires it or not, the student perceives him mainly, if not entirely, as a teacher, and often will not, or cannot, change this perception sufficiently to enter into a true counseling relationship. The teacher may face a problem when "the school situation in general, with all its emphasis on evaluation and judgment of performance, increases the difficulty of the teacher in his efforts to accept and understand behavior in a nonevaluative fashion, as the counselor must."[9] Even the best or most student-centered teaching, though having the same goals as counseling, differs in techniques and methods, and this difference constitutes a problem both for the teacher and the pupil in shifting from one to the other.

Many of those who argue for the teacher's engaging in counseling recognize the lack of professional preparation and the

[8] I. J. Gordon. *The teacher as a guidance worker.* New York: Harper, 1956.
[9] *Ibid.,* p. 268.

obstacles listed above. It appears to be inconsistent to continue to insist on teachers functioning as counselors under such conditions. In one breath they admit it cannot be done, while in the next they encourage teachers to do it.

The point of view that every teacher is a counselor does not necessarily mean that there are no specialists in counseling in the schools. Where there are specialists, however, problems of the limits of the teachers, of when and what students to refer, arise. If teachers were trained in counseling, the proposal that the specialists serve as consultants to the teachers would be appropriate. But where, as is the case at present, teachers are not trained as counselors, they perhaps will, and probably should, refer most of their cases to the specialist. But the specialist then is unable to provide all the counseling services expected of him on the assumption that teachers are to do counseling.

The need for specialized counseling services is present at the elementary level also. There has been a strongly expressed opinion that the teacher should provide individual counseling services to children in the elementary school, and that the counselor should be a consultant to the teachers. But the arguments outlined above apply at this level also. The only reported study of the attitudes of teachers on this matter is that of Smith.[10] Of forty-two elementary school teachers who were asked: "Do you believe there is a need for specialized guidance workers in the elementary school?" 93 percent answered affirmatively. These teachers were also asked to list, in order of importance, the four or five jobs or functions which should be handled by a specialized guidance worker if one were available in her school. Heading the list of replies were those which indicated that the specialized guidance worker should engage in counseling, that is, working with the child who is socially or personally maladjusted. Seventy-nine percent of the teachers listed a function which could be classified under this category. It is thus possible that what teachers want in a guidance specialist at the elementary level and what many experts feel the specialist's function should be are divergent.

[10] L. M. Smith. An observation on elementary school guidance. *Personnel Guid. J.*, 1956, **35**, 179–180.

Counseling by Specialists

A second point of view recognizes that counseling is a professional function requiring extensive training which is not possessed by the teacher, and which the teacher should not be expected to possess. Counseling is not a part-time or overtime sideline of teaching, but a function which is important enough, and enough in demand, to warrant a full-time person or persons, even in schools of only two or three hundred pupils. While there may be the necessity for a part-time teacher-counselor in smaller schools, it is considered undesirable in larger schools to have a number of part-time teacher-counselors, rather than a smaller number of full-time counselors.

Counseling is a professional activity which is not the same as teaching, and which requires specialized training. It is not justifiable to combine the two professions into a single one with the same training. That approach, while apparently resolving some of the problems of viewing the child as a whole, is not practical, and runs counter to the increasing specialization which is necessary with the accumulation of knowledge. The problem of specialization is one which has been and is being faced in other fields also, with the same fears of losing sight of the whole person. But there appears to be no way of avoiding specialization, short of stemming the accumulation of knowledge, since there are limits to how much an individual can acquire within the time available for training.

The Teacher as a Guidance Worker

To say that the teacher is not, and should not be, a counselor is not to say that the teacher is not a guidance worker. Some of the confusion about the teacher's role in guidance is the result of terminology. Counseling means many things when we have not only psychological counselors but employment counselors, legal counselors, investment counselors, travel counselors, small-loan counselors, and beauty counselors, among others. Everyone who talks to people wants to be called a counselor. It is no wonder then that teachers, as well as many educators and some professional guidance people, are impressed by the "every teacher a counselor" slogan.

But if counseling is a professional activity, then it would appear, for the reasons outlined above, that it is not a function of the teacher. As with every staff member to some extent, the teacher does have certain personnel responsibilities or functions. Arbuckle writes that "there is increasing agreement among teachers and professional personnel workers that not only *can* teachers function as personnel works in the classroom, but that if they are to do an effective and positive job of teaching they *must* function as personnel workers.[11] This is different from saying that teachers must be counselors, however.

The identification of guidance with teaching has led to confusion. While there are similarities, particularly as to goals, there are also differences, particularly in techniques. Mathewson notes that "the failure to make a distinction between the guidance process and the instructional process has led to uncertainty and conflict among guidance specialists, teachers, and administrators."[12]

The teacher applies the guidance point of view to teaching. How is this accomplished? There seems to be general agreement that the teacher is responsible for the following personnel or guidance functions as a teacher in the classroom or general school setting (for more detailed discussion of these functions, see the Suggested Readings at the end of this chapter):

1. The classroom teacher is responsible for providing a situation which is optimal for learning. This means that the teacher must be aware of the noncognitive factors in learning. The fact that the child's personality and emotions affect his learning means that teachers are concerned with the child as an individual, as a person. Teachers must therefore have an understanding of child and adolescent psychology, and apply this understanding in their teaching. The implementation of such a point of view is exemplified in pupil-centered teaching. An atmosphere which is conducive to learning must recognize and take into

[11] Arbuckle, *Guidance and counseling in the classroom, op. cit.*, p. 55.
[12] R. H. Mathewson. *Guidance policy and practice.* (rev. ed.) New York: Harper, 1955.

consideration the pupil's needs and motivations, and differences among pupils. An important element is the absence of threat, since it is recognized that learning is inhibited or restricted when the individual feels threatened.[13]

2. The teacher may perform important guidance functions in the vocational and occupational area. This includes a recognition of, and attention to, the occupational significance of the courses which he teaches, and often the inclusion of a unit on occupational information. The teacher is also a source of occupational information to the individual student, and may be used as a resource by the counselor in the course of vocational counseling.

3. The teacher is a source of assistance to the professional counselor in ways other than by providing occupational information. The counselor depends upon the teacher to recognize and make referrals of those students needing specialized counseling help. The teacher can contribute information concerning the child's needs to the counselor, either directly upon referral, in the case conference, or by supplying material for the pupil inventory or cumulative record. And the teacher also assists in the counseling service by administering group tests in the classroom, the results of which are used in the counseling process.

4. The teacher is a source of information, and often a model, for social habits and skills. This is an important area in social development which is often slighted, and for which no one in the school has a designated responsibility.

5. The teacher is responsible for providing a classroom atmosphere which is conducive to good personal-social adjustment and development in pupils. To a considerable extent, the same conditions which promote learning in the classroom are those which promote good personal-social adjustment. These include the recognition of individual differences, in personality as well as in learning ability; an acceptance of and respect for pupils as individuals or persons; and the absence of threat with the resulting freedom of the child to express himself.

This last responsibility of the teacher is often referred to as the mental-hygiene function. Because this function is important, and because so much has been written about it—some of it mislead-

[13] A. W. Combs & D. Snygg. *Individual behavior: a perceptual approach to behavior* (rev. ed.) New York: Harper, 1959.

ing and confusing—we shall deal with this aspect of teaching in more detail.

The Teacher and Mental Hygiene[14]

As the demand that teachers be counselors creates in teachers unrealistic expectations of themselves, frequently so does the emphasis of the importance of the teacher in mental hygiene. Teachers who are impressed with the complexity of counseling and psychotherapy, and with the possibly serious and tragic consequences of poor mental hygiene, are sometimes hesitant, even afraid, to take on any responsibility in the mental health area. Rather than meddle in something about which they realize they know little, and for which they are unprepared, they do nothing, for fear they will do or say the wrong thing.

Now this attitude is a healthy one when dealing with a seriously disturbed child. The teacher should not attempt to be an amateur psychotherapist. So often there is a total misconception, fostered to some extent by the popular press, of the approach and techniques of the psychotherapist.

On the other hand, teachers deal mainly with normal children. They must relate to these children on an individual basis, and in this relationship they exercise an influence upon the personality development of the child. It is therefore important that the teacher have an understanding of the basic principles of good human relationships. It is these principles, rather than a knowledge of abnormal psychology and psychiatric disorders, which are important in teaching.

Unfortunately, it is usually the latter which is emphasized in the training of teachers in mental hygiene. The teacher is trained in the recognition, or diagnosis, of emotional problems. Emphasis is placed upon the collection and compiling of extensive, detailed, and voluminous case histories or case studies of children. Many teachers have become quite skilled in recognizing emotional disturbances in children who should be referred for special treatment. This is well and good, since early treatment

[14] This section is based in part upon the following reference: C. H. Patterson. Counseling as a relationship. *J. Rehab.*, 1959, **25** (6), 13–15. Reprinted in C. H. Patterson (Ed.). *Readings in rehabilitation counseling.* Champaign, Ill.: Stipes Publishing Co., 1960. Pp. 122–125.

is desirable. But emotional disturbance is a matter of degree, and there are many less serious problems, or beginning problems, which cannot be treated by the limited number of counselors, psychologists, and psychiatrists available. And there are the more or less normal or temporary emotional disturbances of the "average" or "normal" child. The teacher has a responsibility in these cases also, so that emotional development will continue on a normal course. The teacher should maintain a healthy environment for the emotional development of all pupils.

Little has been done to help the teacher meet this responsibility and opportunity. But the teacher must acquire and be able to put into practice the attitudes and techniques of good mental hygiene. What, then, are these principles?

Basically, they are the principles of good human relationships. While these principles are in general known, they are not usually emphasized in the training of teachers or even of counselors. Nor are they widely practiced outside of counseling and psychotherapy. While it might appear that, since we are all engaged daily in human relationships, everyone should be an expert in this area, this is unfortunately not the case. The principles, while simple, are not obvious to the average person, nor are they necessarily easily or automatically put into practice.

Good human relationships are those which are productive of, or conducive to, good mental and social-psychological health. The goal of counseling or psychotherapy is of course the attainment of good mental health. It is thus apparent that the basic principles of good human relations and counseling are the same. Both relate to the mental and emotional health of people. I suppose you could say that the providing of good human relationships *keeps* people healthy, while in counseling and psychotherapy we are concerned with *restoring* people to good mental health or improving it. What is helpful toward the latter goal should be useful toward the former; conversely, what is good in keeping people healthy should be useful in helping to restore or improve mental health.

What are the requirements of good mental health which can be met by other people as they interact with an individual, whether in general human relationships, or in specific situations such as teacher-student, employer-employee, or counselor-client relationships?

The first and basic requirement of every individual if he is to be mentally healthy is that he have at least a modicum of self-esteem, that he accept himself, that he feel that at least in some respects he is a person of worth, and that he can respect himself. The achievement and maintenance of this self-esteem is the basic drive and motivation of every person. To have it is to be, to the extent that it is present, mentally healthy. An environment which facilitates the development and maintenance of self-esteem is a healthy environment. Since the major and most significant aspect of our environment is the social environment, then it follows that a healthy social environment is one that is conducive to the development of such self-esteem. Good human relationships, then, are relationships which are characterized by their ability to foster self-esteem in their participants.

How does one go about providing such an environment? What can one do to promote self-esteem in other people? We have some evidence, both from research and experience, regarding the conditions which promote or foster self-esteem or mental health.

It is difficult, if not impossible, to accept or respect oneself if one is not accepted or respected by others. One of the first principles of human relations, therefore, is the acceptance of others. Acceptance involves recognition of another as an individual, a unique person, who is respected as a person and treated as worthy of respect. Acceptance includes the recognition of the right of another to be himself, and not to conform to what you might want him to be. One accepts others by being interested in them as individuals, in showing interest in and respect for their opinions or contributions or expressions of feeling. It is shown by taking time to listen to what others have to say.

It is not always easy to accept others as they are, particularly when they differ greatly from ourselves. We tend either to ignore or reject those who are unusual, or attempt to change them. It is easy to be critical, derogatory in our remarks, belittling and condemning. Our own needs for self-esteem may interfere with our accepting and respecting others. We may want to feel superior to others to bolster ourselves. Our own unsatisfied need for self-esteem thus prevents us from esteeming others. And so a vicious circle develops. To be able to respect others one must respect oneself. But to respect oneself one must have the respect of others. So we have a situation where the mutual respect which is necessary for good human relationships and good mental health is lacking. The circle must be broken by those who have some security, some degree of self-esteem, and who are able to show respect for others, and so on.

Acceptance and respect for another as a unique individual is the foundation for the second basic principle of good human relations. Acceptance leads to understanding. People want and need to be understood. They need to feel that others know and appreciate what they are, who they are, and why they are like they are and behave and think as they do. Understanding is more than what is referred to by the phrase, "Knowing what makes people tick," however. It is more than being able to use psychological terminology glibly in talking about a person. Understanding of another is not obtained by standing on the outside and looking at him. It comes only from getting on the inside and looking out, putting oneself in the place of the other and looking at things as he does. Only when one is able to see things as another does is one really able to understand another. It is this feeling of being understood that people want, so that they do not feel that they are alone, isolated, so different that no one else sees things as they do.

A third factor in good human relationships is confidence and trust in another person. There is confidence that others are competent to make their own decisions. There is recognition of the *right* of others to make their own decisions, and of their freedom of action. One may not agree with another's decisions or acts, but one respects the other's right to them, within, of course, the limits of the rights of other people. The recognition of freedom of thought and action means that the manipulation of others, either by subtle or overt methods, for one's own goals, or even for the presumed good of those manipulated, is not consistent with good human relations.

Finally, good human relations are characterized by openness, sincerity, integrity, and honesty. There is no place for deceit, trickery, or subterfuge. Such activity is inconsistent with respect, understanding, and recognition of the freedom of choice of others.

The existence of these conditions in human relationships appears to make possible the optimal development of the individual. They lead to the development of self-esteem, self-confidence, independence, and responsible decisions and behavior. These are the characteristics of good mental health. Taken together, these conditions provide an optimum environment for the development of the individual. An important characteristic of this environment is the absence of threat. We are beginning to realize that only where strong threat is not present can the individual develop to his fullest potential. A threatened individual is anxious, tense, afraid, inhibited, withdrawn. Threat leads to a narrowing or restricting of perception, of thinking, of activity. Learning, or modification of behavior, does not occur. A person under threat is emotionally disturbed. An accepting, understanding, trustworthy, dependable, and consistent environment is not threatening. Only in a nonthreatening environment can the individual be free to learn, to solve problems, to make adequate decisions and choices, to act intelligently, to express himself—in short, to be mentally healthy.

What Can the Teacher Do?[15]

As a background for dealing with emotional maladjustment, it is essential that the teacher understand what the emotionally disturbed child is like. There are several points which must be kept in mind.

1. *The emotionally maladjusted child is not a malingerer.* He is not faking; he is not pretending or feigning in order to gain something, inventing complaints for his own ends. He is not deliberately manufacturing excuses and alibis.

2. *Emotional maladjustment is not a willful or consciously de-*

---

[15] This section is based upon the following reference: C. H. Patterson. The classroom teacher and the emotional problems of children. *Understanding the child*, 1952, **21**, 67–72. Condensed in *Education Digest*, 1952, **18**, 15–17, and in J. M. Seidman (Ed.). *Readings in educational psychology.* Boston: Houghton-Mifflin, 1955. Reprinted in W. A. Fullager, H. G. Lewis & C. F. Cumbee (Eds.). *Readings in educational psychology.* New York: Crowell, 1956.

veloped condition. It is not brought on by conscious design, but develops against the will of the child. It is not an indication of wickedness, stubbornness, laziness, or perverseness. It is not true, as is sometimes thought, that an emotionally maladjusted child can cure himself if he only wants to, if he will only "buckle down," try to control himself, or "snap out of it." Of course, maladjusted behavior serves a purpose, but it is not consciously developed as a clever trick to avoid something unpleasant.

3. *The physical complaints so common in emotional maladjustment are not imaginary.* Another mistaken notion is that the aches and pains of the emotionally maladjusted individual are not real. But the fact that a symptom or pain is of functional or psychological origin rather than of physical origin does not make it any the less painful or annoying. The nervous child actually suffers from his physical symptoms. A functional pain or symptom is just as real and painful and disabling as one due to organic disease.

4. *An emotional disturbance is not a sign of weakness.* It is trite to say that everyone has his breaking point, but it is true. The stresses and strains of military life were severe enough to cause many individuals to become emotionally maladjusted who might never have become so if they had continued in civilian life. There are many emotionally disturbed—or neurotic—individuals who are very successful in business, the professions, and the arts. Many are hard-working, ambitious, conscientious individuals, who perhaps take things too seriously at times. Emotional maladjustment is not something to be ashamed of; it is a misfortune, not a disgrace. The emotionally disturbed child is therefore not to be considered inferior, worthless, or untrustworthy. He is not of tainted heredity. He is not a slacker or coward. During the war the proportion of medals was as great among those who broke down in combat as among those who did not.

5. *Emotional maladjustment takes many forms.* It has been called the great imitator. It may manifest itself in tremors, headaches, backaches, other pains, shortness of breath, palpitation of the heart, rapid pulse, high blood pressure, excessive perspira-

tion, anorexia, vomiting, indigestion, stomach upset, constipation, diarrhea, irritability, fatigue, restlessness, inability to concentrate, fears and phobias, functional blindness, deafness or muteness, stuttering, functional paralyses, as well as hostility, overaggressiveness, etc. Because of the physical symptoms, it is important that a physical examination be given to check for any organic disease. However, if after thorough examination no physical basis for the complaint is found, an emotional disturbance is probably present. It has been estimated that from one-half to two-thirds of those individuals seen by the average doctor have a psychological, or emotional, basis for part or all of their complaints.

Many of these symptoms are present at times in all of us, without any physical basis. We are all familiar with the headache which develops—on a purely unconscious level—when we face an unpleasant engagement. A temporary emotional disturbance may be responsible for a variety of physical and psychological symptoms, without, however, warranting the classification of the individual as a neurotic.

With the general understanding of emotional disturbances just discussed, what can the teacher do for the emotional needs of the child? Without being a psychologist or a psychiatrist, how can she handle emotionally disturbed children, or the temporary emotional upsets of the average child? We shall discuss briefly some of the attitudes and techniques which are important in such situations. First, there are several "don'ts" which follow from the characteristics of the emotionally disturbed individual just presented.

1. Since the emotionally disturbed child is not a malingerer, or pretender, he should not be treated as such. He shouldn't be accused of faking, of making up or exaggerating his complaints. He is honest and sincere in his claims, and should be respected as such, with belief, not suspicion.

2. Since emotional maladjustment is not willful, but is beyond conscious control, no one should be blamed for it. Don't condemn the maladjusted child. It does no good to tell him to use his will power, to "snap out of it"—he would if he could. Lectures, sermons, exhortations are usually useless. Avoid such comments

as "you should know better"; "you're old enough not to do that"; "what if your mother knew about this?"; "you should be ashamed of yourself."

3. Since the pains and physical complaints are real, not imaginary, don't deny them, or tell him to forget them, or try to argue him out of them. Accept his aches and pains; recognize them as unpleasant and disabling. Don't deny him medical attention—if he doesn't need it, the doctor will tell him so.

4. Since the emotionally disturbed child is not a weakling or coward, he should not be condemned as one, or blamed or censored as if he had committed a crime. Anger, reproval, "telling him off," are harmful to his attempts to adjust. His feelings of self-condemnation, guilt, and failure are so strong that reproach or condemnation by others may drive him deeper into despair and hopelessness.

5. Don't diagnose or label or classify the emotionally maladjusted child as abnormal, neurotic, or "a mental case." It is not necessary to be familiar with psychiatric terminology; applying a psychiatric label to the child doesn't help him, but will probably hurt him. The psychiatrist is the only one qualified to make a psychiatric diagnosis.

6. Don't talk about the child in his presence to his parents or to anyone else. Frequently teachers have been overheard talking about a child, in very uncomplimentary terms, while he is present but ignored, as if he weren't present, or didn't count—almost as if he weren't a person at all, but an inanimate object. Such treatment is damaging to the child and to his self-respect. He should be treated as a human being who has feelings.

The teacher should be able to do more than to avoid these mistaken attitudes, however. She should be able to do something positive to foster the adjustment of the child. Teachers frequently complain that they don't have training in mental hygiene, or that they don't have time to study each child as an individual. But it is not necessary to have extensive training in mental hygiene to be helpful. Nor is it necessary to have a detailed, complete case history, to know all the facts about the background, development, and home life of each child. There are certain basic, fundamental attitudes and techniques that are applicable in all situations involving emotional expression, which teachers can cultivate with no more background in mental hygiene than has been just discussed.

1. The most essential element in handling emotional disturbances is that there be a real understanding and acceptance of the child as he is, with his negative attitudes, hostility and aggression, destructiveness, etc. These emotional reactions are just as natural as the more positive ones—they are not bizarre, "crazy," or shameful, but natural expressions under the circumstances. Realizing this, the teacher must avoid condemnation, criticism, and moralizing. It is not necessary that the exact cause of the behavior be known; it is enough to know that it is natural under certain conditions. These conditions almost always involve situations in which the child has been hurt, frightened, or threatened. It is only natural that resentment, aggressiveness, anger, and other negative emotional behavior result. The test of the ability of a teacher to handle emotional disturbances constructively is whether or not she can accept such negative, hostile emotions and resulting behavior as natural responses.

The most important need of the child is to be understood and accepted—to be able to share his thoughts, without fear, suspicion, or defensiveness. The maladjusted child feels aggressive because he feels threatened. He actually is threatened by others, usually the adults in his environment, when they criticize, condemn, exhort, or shame him. He needs to feel understood, to feel that someone accepts him as he is for what he is, with all his faults, and that someone knows how he feels.

2. If one really understands the emotionally disturbed child, and accepts his negative, hostile behavior as natural under the circumstances, the next step is to realize that emotions, once stirred up, need to be expressed or released. This may seem to be contrary to the attitude of many teachers, who feel that negative behavior and emotions must be controlled. They believe that the child cannot be allowed to express hostility, anger, or hatred of others, including his parents and teacher. If he cannot control these emotions, the teacher attempts to suppress them. But such attempts to exert control result only in suppression, or perhaps gradually in repression by the child himself —the emotions continue to exist, and to cause emotional maladjustment in the child. Contrary to general opinion, the free-

dom to express the emotions of hostility and hatred does not result in an increase of such negative emotions and behavior, after the initial period following such freedom. It rather allows the negative emotions to drain themselves off, so that the more positive, constructive emotions and behavior have a chance to show themselves. Discipline and punishment are thus not the answers to negative emotions and behavior. Expression rather than suppression or repression is necessary if the child is to reach a stage of better adjustment.

This does not mean that the child is allowed to be physically assaultive or destructive. There must be limits set to prevent injury to other children and adults, and damage to property. But while destructive behavior is prohibited when it injures others, there is no limit to the expression of destructive and aggressive thoughts and feelings, and if possible the expression of such behavior on substitute objects, such as rubber toys—for example, dolls representing the individuals toward whom the child feels aggressive or resentful. Verbalization of feelings and emotions is to be encouraged, and accepted without surprise or shock. It is important that the teacher really be able to accept such feelings, without actually condemning or judging the child in her thoughts. Children are acutely aware of our feelings and sense if they are really being understood and accepted, or if we are only pretending to do so. If it is the latter, the child will know it and be suspicious, afraid of being tricked into saying or doing something for which he will be punished. We must really prove to him that we are accepting and understanding. Being able to express in words those feelings which the child himself is unable to verbalize is often helpful in showing him that we do understand.

The activities of the teacher discussed above differ considerably from the concepts of many teachers about how to be helpful. Moreover, they differ from much of the training given teachers in the area of mental hygiene and adjustment. There is no effort to discover "causes" for the child's behavior in terms of his past history. There is no requirement that the child's history and environment be probed into, and a complete case history compiled. There is no concern with the so-called objective facts.

Understanding, and being able to help, a child does not depend on knowledge of the details of the child's life. The "facts" provide information *about* the child, from an external point of view. This approach might be called the Sergeant Friday, or detective, approach to human behavior. But the objective facts have little or no meaning in themselves. It is the way the child sees or perceives himself and his environment which is important. It is how he experiences things, how he feels about them, which are the important facts for understanding him. As Moustakas points out, "Selecting material reported as fact in the child's past record may set up expectations and prejudices in the mind of the teacher."[16] Understanding is achieved by being able to put oneself in the place of the child, to see things as he does. From this point of view, objectivity is "the completely unbiased attitude of seeing what an experience means to the child, not how it fits into or relates to other experiences, not what causes it, why it exists, or for what purpose."[17] Combs and Snygg comment upon this difference in approach to understanding as follows:

Teachers who understand that behavior is caused by present perceptions behave quite differently from those who believe that the causes of behavior lie primarily in the student's past. Teachers who see people's behavior as solely the product of history, for example, will need to acquire vast quantities of information and records about their students' lives. . . . Too strong a belief in such a concept of causation may even result in disillusion and discouragement, for if the causes of behavior all lie in the past, the teacher's present role becomes unimportant and of little consequence. . . . On the other hand, teachers who see behavior as the product of present perceptions will behave quite differently. They will need less detailed and extensive information about their students' pasts, and will be much more concerned with understanding their students as they are. For many teachers it will come as a great relief that they do not *have* to be amateur psychiatrists to carry on their jobs successfully.[18]

[16] C. E. Moustakas. *The teacher and the child.* New York: McGraw-Hill, 1956. P. 4. See also W. P. Angers. The Adlerian approach to the dangers of evaluative labeling. *Voc. Guid. Quart.,* 1958, **7,** 26–30.

[17] Moustakas, *op. cit.,* p. 3.

[18] *Op. cit.,* pp. 400–401.

Summary

The place of the teacher in guidance has been ambiguous. Some have accorded the teacher a central position. The point of view taken here is that counseling is the essence of a counseling and guidance program. Since counseling is a professional activity requiring specialized training, then the teacher, as a teacher, is not a counselor and should not be expected to perform the counseling function.

The teacher has an important place in the guidance program, however, and consideration is given to the functions of the teacher in a guidance program. An important responsibility is that of maintaining and fostering an atmosphere conducive to good mental health in students. Detailed consideration was given as to how the teacher can meet this responsibility.

We may conclude that although the teacher is not a counselor, he must understand and apply the basic principles of good human relationships in his contacts with pupils. Although these principles are basic to counseling and psychotherapy, they are implemented somewhat differently in the counseling relationship. The teacher is not a therapist, but can and should maintain a therapeutic environment. Such an environment makes it possible for the pupils to relate therapeutically with the teacher (as described above). But it also respects the privacy of the individual, and his decision not to reveal himself. The teacher should not question or probe into the personal affairs and feelings of the pupil, make interpretations, or give advice. These are not therapeutic; they may only make matters worse.

The contribution of the teacher to guidance lies not so much in providing any specific or special services, but in functioning as a teacher with a particular approach or attitude.

The teacher is, then, a teacher. But the teacher is, as are all professional people, responsible for contributing to the optimum environment for mental health. The teacher who is being a good teacher in this respect is doing enough, without trying to be a counselor or a psychotherapist. The purpose of training in mental hygiene is "to help teachers deal with emotional problems from the standpoint of sound instructional techniques. . . . Mental hygiene's contribution is to help teachers become effective teachers, not part-time therapists."[19]

The teacher should have enough sensitivity to emotional elements in children to be able to sense and empathize with the child who is going through an emotional crisis, and to understand that he needs acceptance and understanding rather than reprimand or scolding. The following poem is a poignant illustration of such a situation:

ONE SULLEN BOY

His father, unmet and unknown,
The mother overworked and overwhelmed.
Six siblings, assorted ages and sizes,
Three dreary rooms, heat sporadic.

The baby brother but two years old,
Caught cold suddenly,
And more suddenly died!
For the teacher next morning, his story—
"I couldn't do my spelling last night."

Samuel C. Gilburt[20]

SUGGESTED READINGS

American Personnel and Guidance Association. *Basic approaches to mental health in the schools.* Washington, D.C.: The Association, 1959. This is a reprint of a series of significant articles from the *Personnel and Guidance Journal,* describing six programs for training teachers in mental-hygiene concepts and practices. The teacher will find some useful ideas here.

Arbuckle, D. S. *Teacher counseling.* Cambridge, Mass.: Addison-Wesley, 1950. One of the exponents of teachers as counselors presents the nondirective or client-centered approach for teachers as counselors and in the classroom. Examples of interviews by teachers of various degrees of training and skill are included.

Arbuckle, D. S. *Guidance and counseling in the classroom.* Boston:

[19] M. L. Falik, Mildred Peters, M. Levitt & B. O. Rubenstein. Observations on the psychological education of teachers in a school-based mental-hygiene program. *Ment. Hyg.,* N.Y., 1954, 38, 374–386.

[20] From the *Graduate School Record,* Long Island University, Spring, 1960; reprinted in the *Personnel Guid. J.,* 1960, 39, 217.

Allyn & Bacon, 1957. In this book Arbuckle expands his argument for teachers as counselors. His discussion of counseling includes examples of teacher-counselors in action and a case study, as well as consideration of testing and group activities. The discussion is more appropriate for teachers who are part-time counselors, rather than for the average teacher.

Brown, R. W. The teacher as a guidance worker. *J. Educ.*, 1957, **139** (4), 3–12. A brief but comprehensive statement of teacher activities in guidance.

Combs, A. W. & Snygg, D. *Individual behavior: a perceptual approach to behavior.* (rev. ed.) New York: Harper, 1959. Chapters 17 and 18. This is a unique discussion of learning as change in perceptions, and of the ways in which such changes can be facilitated in teaching.

Gordon, I. J. *The teacher as a guidance worker.* New York: Harper, 1956. While the major part of this book discusses concepts of human development important for the teacher, it has chapters on the teacher as a group worker, as a counselor, and as an action researcher.

Moustakas, C. E. *The teacher and the child.* New York: McGraw-Hill, 1956. This book reports the experiences of teachers in a human-relations seminar conducted to assist teachers in developing understanding of their pupils and the application of the principles of human relationships to school procedures.

Moustakas, C. E. *The alive and growing teacher.* New York: Philosophical Library, 1959. This is a report of a group of classroom teachers and principals working together on problems of human relations, learning to work and live together.

Rogers, C. R. *Client-centered therapy.* Boston: Houghton-Mifflin, 1951. Chapter 9. The principles of student-centered teaching.

Strang, Ruth. *The role of the teacher in personnel work.* (4th ed.) New York: Bureau of Publications, Teachers College, Columbia University, 1953. This is a comprehensive book, with extended discussion of techniques in personnel work as well as chapters on guidance in the classroom, in the home room, and in extraclass activities. It emphasizes and illustrates the teacher's guidance role as a person interested in children and providing good human relationships with them.

PART III

BASIC COUNSELING
SERVICES

CHAPTER 7

THE NATURE OF

COUNSELING

We have suggested several times that counseling is only a part of student personnel work, or of the guidance services of the school. But we have also indicated that it is, or should be, the major service. Counseling is the core of the personnel services provided by the school. Moreover, it is the most highly skilled activity of the professional personnel worker. It is for these reasons that we use the word counselor to refer to the professional worker in guidance. Hatch and Stefflre state it clearly when they say that "the primary responsibility of the counselor is counseling. Additional duties serve as diluting agents and may result in a teacher or an administrator with the title of counselor. A situation of this kind is a prostitution of the counselor's abilities and results in a guidance program that is based on an inadequate or imaginary foundation."[1]

As in the case of the other aspects of counseling and guidance services in schools, the counseling services cannot be covered in detail here. The purpose of the discussion in this and the following chapters is not to make a counselor of the reader, but to provide an orientation to counseling for the nonspecialist and for the beginning student in counseling.[2] The student should be reminded that the discussion presents a particular point of view of the counseling process.

[1] R. N. Hatch & B. Stefflre. *Administration of guidance services.* Englewood Cliffs, N.J.: Prentice-Hall, 1958. P. 163.

[2] The reader who is interested in a more detailed presentation of the point of view summarized here may consult the author's *Counseling and psychotherapy: theory and practice.* New York: Harper, 1959.

What Is Counseling?

In these days when it is not only claimed that teachers are counselors, but that the clergy, lawyers, and doctors are counselors, it is difficult to know what counseling is. In addition to these professional people who counsel, we have all types of commercial counselors. It seems that everyone who talks with a customer or client is a counselor. Or perhaps more specifically, anyone who as part of his work or services provides information or advice or makes recommendations of any kind wants to be called a counselor.

But counseling does not consist, as the layman thinks, of giving advice and making recommendations. Nor is it the giving of answers to questions, or solutions to problems; it is not simply information-giving. This is one of the first things a student of counseling must learn. And it is sometimes the most difficult thing which a teacher who wants to become a counselor has to learn. The teacher—or at least the traditional teacher who is concerned with imparting subject matter, or even inculcating problem-solving skills—must overcome certain habits of teaching before he can become a counselor. This is necessary even if the teacher is to function as a guidance worker (as discussed in the last chapter), rather than as a counselor.

As a matter of fact, the basis of counseling lies in the same principles of good human relationships which were summarized as essential for the teacher's functioning as a guidance worker. Fiedler, in a study of the ideal therapeutic relationship, found that therapists of different views agreed in their descriptions of this relationship. Moreover, nontherapists described the ideal therapeutic relationship in the same manner as therapists, leading Fiedler to conclude that "the therapeutic relationship may therefore be but a variation of good interpersonal relationships in general."[3]

Counseling is a *relationship;* it is not a bundle of techniques or a bag of tricks. One may well ask, if counseling is nothing more than the practicing of good human relationships, why it is so difficult to become a counselor—why shouldn't everyone, including

[3] F. E. Fiedler. The concept of an ideal therapeutic relationship. *J. consult. Psychol.,* 1950, 14, 239–245.

the teacher, be a counselor? To some extent, everyone who practices good human relationships is a counselor, at times, with some people. But there are certain characteristics of counseling which set it aside as a specific kind of relationship.

In the first place, the principles of good human relationships, though some of them are known, are not obvious, nor necessarily natural, nor easily practiced. If they were, we should be much more advanced as a society, much happier, with less mental disorder or disturbance, than is the case at present. The understanding of the nature of good human relationships is something that must be learned.

Second, the practice of these principles requires training and experience. The ability to apply the principles is related to the psychological characteristics, or mental health, of the individual applying them. It is not a matter of information or knowledge; it is a matter of attitudes.

Third, the implementation of these principles in a counseling relationship differs somewhat from their practice in everyday relationships. This is because the counseling relationship is a special kind of relationship. It is a formal relationship between two persons who may, and perhaps preferably, have no other relationship. The counseling relationship is for the sole purpose of improving, or restoring, the mental health, adjustment, or functioning of one of the participants. The counselor consciously and purposefully practices, or applies, the principles of good human relations for the benefit of the counselee.

Fourth, the relationship is usually established between a trained individual and another individual who is in need of help or assistance by reason of being disturbed, unhappy, or in conflict because of an unresolved problem or another condition resulting in dissatisfaction with himself, or lack of self-respect or self-esteem. Whereas the application of the principles of good human relationships in general is for the purpose of *maintaining* good mental health among normal, or average, individuals, their application in counseling is to *restore or improve* the mental health of disturbed persons.

Fifth, the relationship is established at the request or desire of the disturbed individual, is continued at his wish, and is characterized by certain conditions: privacy, confidentiality, set time limits, and regularity, on an appointment basis.

Sixth, the counseling relationship, even though it is a formal relationship, and may be very limited in terms of time relative to the life of the individual (seldom more than an hour a day, more often an hour a week), is a closer, more intense, and deeper relationship than any ordinary social relationship. This is due to its purpose, and to the application of the principles of good human relations in their purest form, divested of the formalities of the usual social relationships.

While it is difficult to give a succinct definition of counseling, an approximation may be attempted. Counseling is a professional relationship, established voluntarily by an individual who feels the need of psychological help, with a person trained to provide that help. This definition makes it clear that it is not the techniques which are basic, that it is not the information or knowledge possessed by the counselor which is most useful in helping the client; nor is it what the counselor does to, or for, the client in terms of services that is important. The significant factor is the kind of relationship which is provided.

The Counseling Relationship

It should be apparent that the description of good human relationships in the last chapter almost constitutes a description of the counseling relationship. As indicated above, however, the application of the principles differs in the professional counseling relationship. In this section we are concerned with the description of the specific nature of the counseling relationship, in terms of its assumptions and principles. In the following section we shall consider the implementation of these principles in the relationship itself.

The basic approach to the counseling relationship which is taken in this book is the client-centered approach. It is felt that this point of view toward the counseling relationship best fits the philosophy of education and of personnel services outlined in Chapters 1 and 2. Indeed, it appears to be the logical, necessary expression of this philosophy in the counseling relationship. The philosophy of client-centered counseling is simple, and may be summarized in three beliefs, assumptions, or attitudes:

1. Each individual is a person of worth in himself and is therefore to be respected and valued as such.
2. Each individual is capable of assuming responsibility for himself. He can, and will, under appropriate conditions, make the best, or right, decisions or choices for himself. Jersild suggests that ". . . human beings, from an early age, have more capacity for learning to face and to understand and to deal with the realities of life than we hitherto assumed in our psychological theories and in our educational practices."[4]
3. Furthermore, each individual has the *right* to self-direction, to choose or select his own values and goals, to make his own decisions.

The counselor thus recognizes and respects the client as a unique, autonomous individual, worthy of acceptance as a human being, a person. His right to freedom of choice, to self-determination of his behavior, to live his own life, is recognized and respected.

Moreover, it is recognized that coercion and pressure are detrimental to the client's taking responsibility for himself and reaching adequate decisions. Such conditions inhibit, rather than facilitate, the inherent growth force, the self-actualizing tendency, which is assumed to exist in all persons.

What are the conditions under which the individual grows, develops, takes responsibility for himself, reaches adequate decisions? Again, they are very simple. They are the conditions for good mental health which have been touched upon in the last chapter. The counseling relationship is one in which an atmosphere is created in which the individual is able to take responsibility for himself, to begin developing, or restoring, the self-esteem which is necessary for his functioning as a healthy, responsible, independent human being, able to make adequate decisions and resolve problems.

In the first place, the atmosphere in which this can take place

[4] A. T. Jersild. Self-understanding in childhood and adolescence. *Amer. Psychologist*, 1951, 6, 122–126.

is more dependent on the attitudes and feelings of the counselor toward the client than upon the techniques which he uses. These attitudes are expressions of the basic philosophy of the counselor toward other people. They consist of a genuine respect for the client, so that he is treated as a worthy person. Being respected by another is often the first step in achieving self-respect. There is an attitude of acceptance on the part of the counselor. He accepts the client as he is, without judgment or condemnation, criticism, or ridicule. This is not a perfunctory, verbal acceptance. It is a genuine feeling of acceptance, of interest in and liking for the client as a person. This combination of respect and acceptance appears to be what is expressed by Rogers as an "unconditional positive regard for the client."[5]

A second major characteristic of the atmosphere or conditions for client progress is understanding on the part of the counselor, and the communication of this understanding to the client. It is important to recognize just what is meant by understanding. The kind of understanding which appears to be most effective in counseling is not knowledge of or about the client. It does not consist of the results of a battery of tests, nor of the data in the cumulative record, nor of extensive case studies, no matter how voluminous or complete. The understanding which appears to be most effective is an empathic understanding. It is an understanding which has no trace of evaluation or judging, nor of categorizing or labeling in terms of some problem area or complex or presumed etiological conditions. An empathic understanding is a "feeling with" another, the entering into his frame of reference—the internal rather than the external frame of reference—so that one sees the world and the other person, insofar as possible, through the eyes of the other. The counselor places himself, or attempts to place himself, in the client's place. He realizes that in order really to understand another's feelings, attitudes, and behavior, he must see things as the other sees them. For one does not behave in response to the world as it exists—

---

[5] C. R. Rogers. The necessary and sufficient conditions of therapeutic personality change. *J. consult. Psychol.*, 1957, **21**, 95–103. Reprinted in H. B. McDaniel, *et al.* (Eds.). *Readings in guidance.* New York: Holt, 1959. Pp. 185–195.

or is assumed to exist—in "reality," but in response to the world as one perceives it.[6]

A central characteristic of the counseling relationship as viewed here is the absence of threat. Although it may appear to be a negative way of looking at counseling and mental health, the concept of threat appears to be extremely important. Threat to the self and the self-concept seems to be the basis for personality disturbances, or poor mental health. The basic need of the individual is the preservation and enhancement of the self; all other needs or drives may be subsumed under this. Frustration of, or threat to, the satisfaction of this basic need results in a lowered evaluation of the self, a loss of self-esteem, a reduced self-regard. It seems to be becoming clear that the loss of self-esteem is the core of personality disturbance.

The influence of threat upon behavior has been demonstrated in many areas. Perception is narrowed, so that the individual literally does not see many aspects of the situation. Under threat the individual may withdraw, even to the point of freezing under extreme threat, being literally paralyzed with fear. On the other hand, under less extreme threat, the individual may become defensive, or aggressive. It may be that what has often been considered instinctive or natural aggressiveness is always a reaction to threat, a reaction which is universal, because threat, in some form or other, is universal. That is, while threat, or frustration, may lead to other reactions besides aggressiveness, aggressiveness is always a result of threat or frustration.[7] Another method of defense against threat which may occur, in addition to not recognizing or seeing it, and withdrawal and aggression, is self-

[6] For consideration of the significance and implications of this statement, consult (1) the writer's book referred to above. (2) E. C. Kelley. *Education for what is real*. New York: Harper, 1947. (3) A. W. Combs and D. Snygg. *Individual Behavior: a perceptual approach to behavior*. (rev. ed.) New York: Harper, 1959.

[7] Bibring, a psychoanalyst, suggests this possibility, raising the question "whether there are any phenomena of aggression at all outside the field of the ego-preservative function," and notes "the empirical fact that aggressiveness appears only or almost only when the life instincts or the ego instinct are exposed to harm." E. Bibring. The development and problems of the theory of instincts. In C. L. Stacy & M. F. De Martino (Eds.) *Understanding human motivation*. Cleveland: Howard Allen, 1958.

deception, which serves as a method of avoiding loss of self-esteem, or of restoring it.

In everyday life we are aware of the results of pressure or threat. The individual is unable to perform effectively or efficiently. He is unable to learn easily; he persists in ineffective attempts at problem-solving rather than in fruitful exploration. We know that we create resistance when we attempt to change people by pressure or threat, from the child who becomes more insistent on doing what he wants to do, to the girl who insists on marrying the clearly unsuitable boy to whom her parents object.

Change in attitudes and behavior, self-actualization, the development of independence and responsibility—in short, mental health or adequate personality development—occur only under conditions of absence of serious threat to the self and the self-concept. Since the goal of counseling is the preservation, or restoration, of good mental health, or of self-esteem, then it follows that the counseling situation must be characterized by an absence of threat. Respect for the client, interest in and acceptance of him as a person, absence of evaluative attitudes, and understanding of him by seeing his point of view—all contribute to an atmosphere devoid of threat. It then becomes possible for the client to examine and explore himself and his situation, to see or recognize aspects which he could not see before, and to change his attitudes, concepts, or perceptions, which can then lead to changed behavior.

What Does the Counselor Do?

Our emphasis has been upon the attitudes of the counselor, as forming an atmosphere in which the client can achieve a feeling of security and self-esteem. But what does the counselor do; how does he act; what does he say? How does he express these attitudes; how does he understand the client and convey this understanding to him? While the attitudes of the counselor are of first importance, their implementation must also be considered. Their expression in a therapeutic manner is not usually natural or automatic. And while it is true that their expression must become natural, so that the counselor may be himself, genuine and not playing a role, it is also true that he must be his counseling or therapeutic self, not his social, or even teaching, self.[8]

The objectives of the counselor are to show his genuine interest in the client, to show that he accepts the client as someone worthy of respect and esteem, and to understand the client and communicate this understanding to him. How can the counselor do this, while at the same time allowing the client to be responsible for himself, for his behavior and decisions, including his communications to the counselor, from the beginning of the counseling process?

The methods, or techniques, by which this can be accomplished, appear to be simple, and yet they are often difficult to practice. The first, and basic, activity of the counselor is *listening*. To listen is often a difficult thing for a counselor to learn. It is difficult to listen to another because one is thinking about what one wants to say. This kind of listening in order to have one's say in turn is not what is meant by listening in counseling. Listening is not, on the other hand, a passive thing, but an active following of what the client is saying, or trying to say. It is listening without interference by one's own personal reactions and associations. The counselor's attention and interest are concentrated upon the client's communication. The listening is complete, in that the client is given freedom to express himself as he desires, to tell his story in his own way, without interruption, without questioning, without probing, without judgments. Remember that the counselor is not a Sergeant Friday trying to get "the facts," but is trying to see things as the client sees them. He is not concerned with obtaining an ordered, complete, life history, to be recorded and filed away, but in helping the client express his attitudes, feelings, concerns, and perceptions of himself and the world.

Listening in this manner to what another has to say is a simple but basic manifestation of interest and respect; the client is worth listening to, and what he has to say is important. It is the first step in the client's taking responsibility for himself. The client who begins by asking the counselor what the latter wants

[8] C. H. Patterson. A note on counselor personality and therapeutic techniques. *J. counsel. Psychol.*, 1961, 8, 89–90.

to know, what the counselor wants him to talk about, or who suggests that the counselor ask him some questions, is expressing his dependency, his lack of responsibility and self-esteem. The counselor responds by pointing out that the client may decide what he wants to talk about, that the counselor is interested in whatever he has to say, and that the counseling time is his to use to discuss his concerns.

Listening of this kind is the basis for the empathic understanding described above. It is the way by which the counselor is able to learn how the client sees things, and thus he is able to perceive from the point of view of the client. Listening and understanding are the basis of, or perhaps constitute, empathy. Empathy is the ability to place oneself in the place of another, to take his role as it were, and to think and feel as he does. Rogers defines empathy as the ability "to perceive the internal frame of another with accuracy, and with the emotional components and meanings which pertain thereto, as if he were the other person, but without ever losing the 'as if' condition."[9]

While listening is perhaps the most important way of showing interest in and respect for the client, there are other ways of expressing interest and respect. Simple *acceptance* responses, such as "Yes," "I see," "Uh huh," or "Mm . . . hmm," are useful. These responses also may represent the second major class of techniques or responses used by the counselor. They indicate to the client that he is understood by the counselor. Simple acceptance responses, of which the above are illustrations, indicate that the counselor is following the client. The simple statement, "I understand," may be all that is necessary at times. To some extent simple restatement of the client's statements, usually called reflection of content, indicates to the client that the counselor understands.

But perhaps the most appropriate way of communicating understanding is by what is known as *reflection and clarification of the client's feelings and attitudes.* Rogers defines reflection as the attempt "to understand from the client's point of view and to communicate that understanding."[10] The ability to reflect and

---

[9] C. R. Rogers. *Client-centered therapy.* Boston: Houghton-Mifflin, 1951. P. 38.
[10] *Ibid.,* p. 452.

clarify the feelings and attitudes of the client requires genuine understanding, based upon empathy. It requires skill in focusing upon attitudes and feelings expressed by the client, rather than attention to the content or the objective facts being expressed by the client. In counseling, the significant facts are the attitudes and feelings. This skill must be acquired through training and experience, including supervised practice in counseling.

It is important that the counselor not pretend that he understands when in fact he does not. If the counselor is not able to follow the client, which may happen when the client is confused himself, then he should say so. He may say, "I don't follow you," "I don't understand," or "I'm not sure I know what you're saying." Or if the counselor has some idea, but is not sure, of what the client is expressing, he may say, "Is this what you are saying . . . ?" or "Let me see if I follow you. Are you saying . . . ?" etc. It is not necessary, indeed it is impossible, for the counselor to understand completely all that the client says or feels. He may misunderstand, and show this in his reflections. But the client will correct him, if a nonthreatening atmosphere is maintained. As long as the client feels that the counselor is trying to understand him, and shows some evidence of doing so, it appears that progress can occur.

What Does the Counselor Avoid?

The application of the simple methods described above, at least by a skilled and understanding counselor, appears to be effective in helping clients. These seem to constitute the necessary and sufficient conditions for therapeutic personality change.[11]

It does not appear to be necessary for the counselor to question, probe, interpret, give advice, etc. From the point of view of counseling adopted in this book, such techniques are inconsistent with the assumptions and goals of counseling. Interpretation, questioning, and probing may be threatening to the client. Support, persuasion, and advice may prevent the client from assuming responsibility for himself and for the solution of his problems.

[11] C. R. Rogers. The necessary and sufficient conditions of therapeutic personality change, *op. cit.*, pp. 95–103.

It will be noted by the reader that no techniques for achieving rapport have been prescribed, because such techniques are neither necessary nor desirable. They are usually the result of insecurity on the part of the counselor rather than the need of the client. Counseling is not a social relationship, nor a social conversation, and should not be begun as such. If the client has come to the counselor voluntarily, he has not come to discuss the weather or the pending football or basketball game. And if he is referred and comes involuntarily, he knows he was not sent to discuss such topics. The counseling interview should be started simply and directly, recognizing what the client comes for. "What's on your mind?" "What would you like to talk about?" or "Where would you like to start?" are usually all that is necessary to begin the counseling session.

Rapport is not something to be achieved by artificial techniques or social devices. It is something that develops and exists where the counselor is genuinely interested in the client and his problems. The expression of the attitudes described in this chapter are sufficient for the establishment of rapport.

It must be emphasized again that counseling is not a matter of techniques, even the techniques suggested above. Counseling is a relationship in which the attitudes of the counselor are expressed. This expression must be genuine and spontaneous, not labored, forced, or self-conscious. It would perhaps be better if we abandoned the word *technique,* since it has connotations of being a deliberate, conscious, artful device for achieving a goal, even of manipulating a situation. The expression of the attitudes of the counselor in the counseling situation is not a matter of techniques in this sense. It is a matter of making known to the client his respect, his interest, his understanding, in simple, genuine, spontaneous, natural ways.

This chapter is of course not sufficient for the practice of counseling. The student will require considerably more background and training before he attempts a counseling relationship with a disturbed client. We have attempted only to summarize the basic and essential elements in the counseling relationship, from the point of view of the philosophy of human relationships adopted in this book.

While the particular methods and techniques discussed here

are most specifically applicable to counseling clients with personal-social-emotional problems, the philosophy and attitudes are basically applicable to other areas, such as educational-vocational problems. Their expression may be supplemented by other methods, but the basic philosophy and attitudes are appropriate to all counseling situations. In the following chapters we shall discuss their application to educational-vocational counseling.

Summary

While counseling is only one aspect of counseling and guidance services, it is the most professionally oriented, the most time-consuming, and thus the major activity of the counselor. This chapter has attempted a definition of counseling: counseling is a professional relationship, established voluntarily by an individual who feels the need of psychological help, with a person trained to provide that help. The emphasis is upon counseling as a relationship rather than upon techniques. The nature of this relationship is considered, and the basic assumptions of the client-centered point of view are stated: (1) each individual is respected and valued as a person of worth; (2) each individual is capable of assuming responsibility for himself; and (3) each individual has the right to self-direction and freedom of choice.

Accepting as the goal of counseling the ability of the individual to assume responsibility for himself and his decisions, the conditions under which counseling operates to foster this outcome are outlined. This atmosphere is one of acceptance of and respect for the client, an understanding of him as a unique individual, and the avoidance of the introduction of threat into the counseling relationship.

A brief discussion of the implementation of these conditions by the counselor in terms of techniques followed. The major techniques of the client-centered counselor are listening, acceptance, and the communication of understanding through reflection and clarification of feelings. Techniques to be avoided, because they are threatening, were mentioned.

This chapter is merely an introduction to the principles of counseling, and is provided to give the counselor an understanding of the nature of counseling, and not to prepare him for the practice of counseling.

SUGGESTED READINGS

Combs, A. W., & Snygg, D. *Individual behavior: a perceptual approach to behavior.* (rev. ed.) New York: Harper, 1959. This is the most complete and detailed discussion of the basic psychological theory or point of view underlying client-centered counseling.

Patterson, C. H. *Counseling and psychotherapy: theory and practice.* New York: Harper, 1959. This book develops the discussion in the present chapter, and includes discussions of the implications of client-centered counseling for various problems in the field.

Porter, E. H., Jr. *An introduction to therapeutic counseling.* Boston: Houghton-Mifflin, 1950. An excellent book for the beginning counselor, since it discusses the practical problems involved as he begins actual work with clients.

Rogers, C. R. *Client-centered therapy.* Boston: Houghton-Mifflin, 1951. The basic reference for the counseling point of view adopted in the present text. It is the systematic development of the client-centered approach to counseling by its originator.

Snyder, W. U. (Ed.) *Casebook of nondirective counseling.* Boston: Houghton-Mifflin, 1947. A series of cases, transcribed from recordings or detailed notes, illustrating the application of client-centered counseling as it was practiced fifteen years ago. Some changes have occurred since then.

CHAPTER 8

EDUCATIONAL-

VOCATIONAL COUNSELING

Educational and vocational counseling are considered together, since they are closely related. One function of education is preparation for a vocation. Educational choices are thus prevocational choices, being vocationally oriented. We shall use the term *vocational* rather than *educational-vocational* for simplicity, and because our concern is with the vocational implications of educational counseling.

Importance of Vocational Counseling

Our society is a work-oriented society. It is likely that it will continue to be so for some time to come, although with increased leisure brought about by greater productiveness (resulting in part from automation) other aspects of life will receive more attention. However, work now occupies the major part of the adult's waking hours, or about one-third of his activities. Work is universal, being present in all societies, even the most primitive, because of the necessity of wresting subsistence from the environment. It is, or has been, often regarded as a curse, a penance for sin. In Genesis we read that God said to Adam after he had eaten the apple, "Cursed be the ground because of you; in toil shall you eat of it all the days of your life; in the sweat of your brow you shall eat bread."

Yet, on the other hand, work is not always unpleasant or distasteful. Man does not as Freud suggested always have to be forced into work. We not only work to live, but we live to work. Work is the natural exercise of the body and mind. It satisfies the need for physical and mental activity. Anne Roe points out that "in our society there is no single situation which is potentially so capable of giving satisfaction at all levels of basic needs as is the occupation."[1]

Work also serves other needs in our society. Work offers the individual the opportunity to contribute to society, to give something in return for the goods which society makes available for his life and living. There is a psychological satisfaction in working to support oneself and one's family. Work provides security to the individual; to be unemployed, or to be fearful of unemployment, is psychologically devastating. It reduces or destroys one's self-esteem or self-respect.

Work is more than a means of subsistence, then. In our complex society it has an immense influence on our whole lives. Perhaps more than any other single thing, a man's occupation molds his life. It determines his social class, his place of living, his style and manner of living, his dress, his hours of work—and thus his hours at home and his avocations. Indirectly it affects his attitudes and opinions; his goals and values, including the way he feels about education; his outlook on life; and his politics. These influences are not directly related to amount of income, either, since groups with similar income levels differ greatly in these respects. Health is related to occupation, both in terms of occupational hazards and diseases, and in terms of nutrition and medical care. Length of life is related to one's occupation, with educators, lawyers, and business executives being among those with long life spans, doctors falling in the middle, and poets being among the lowest. Mental disorders also appear to bear some relationship to occupational class and level.

Work thus involves the whole person, influencing his total personality. Anne Roe states that "if one wishes to understand the total psychology of any person, it is at least as important to understand his occupational behavior as it is to understand his sexual behavior."[2] In view of this importance of work to the individual, it is surprising that it is only recently that attention has been focused on the psychology and sociology of work. The choice of an occupation is an important factor in an individual's

[1] Anne Roe. *The psychology of occupations.* New York: Wiley, 1956. P. 31.
[2] *Ibid.*, p. vi.

life—almost as important as the choice of a marriage partner—and should be approached with as much preparation as possible.

Work is of great importance to society also. The necessity for the most effective utilization of the nation's manpower needs no emphasis. The wise use of the abilities of our people goes beyond the meeting of current needs in science and technology; it includes the cultivation of those abilities and aptitudes which can lead to contributions in the arts, the humanities, and human relations, including politics and the social sciences.

In a democratic society it is essential that there be freedom of choice in one's occupation. Individuals are not assigned to occupations, even on the basis of adequate testing of aptitudes and abilities. The individual's preferences and interests are factors in occupational choice. There need be no conflict between the needs of society and the needs of the individual, however. Indeed, in a democracy, it is assumed that what is good for the individual is good for society. Of course, society may influence the choices of an individual. The rewards of prestige and income may be used to attract people to perform needed work. These are factors which society introduces into the occupational market place to be considered by the individual in his choice of an occupation.

But while there is and should be freedom of choice, the complexity of our present-day society makes this choice a difficult one for many, if not most, of our young people. In this complex and changing society, the young person frequently needs some assistance in making an intelligent and appropriate choice and in planning and preparing for a career in the field of his choice. Such assistance is provided by educational and vocational counseling.

Development of Vocational Counseling[3]

Vocational counseling is usually considered to have begun with the work of Frank Parsons in Boston in the early years of this century. Others, of course, before this were concerned about the

[3] For detailed histories of the vocational counseling movement, see: (1) J. M. Brewer. *History of vocational guidance.* New York: Harper, 1942. (2) Anna Y. Reed. *Guidance and personnel services in education.* Ithaca, N.Y.: Cornell University Press, 1947.

vocational and occupational problems of youth, but he developed an approach to assisting youth which, in its essence, characterizes vocational counseling today. His point of view was developed in a book which was published just after his death in 1908. In it he defined vocational guidance as "the choice of a vocation, adequate preparation for it, and the attainment of efficiency and success." He told youth that "in the wise choice of a vocation there are three broad factors: (1) a clear understanding of yourself, your aptitudes, abilities, interests, ambitions, resources, limitations, and their causes; (2) a knowledge of the requirements and conditions of success, advantages, compensations, opportunities, and prospects in different lines of work; (3) true reasoning on the relations of these two groups of facts."[4] The responsibility for a choice rested with the client. This pattern of vocational counseling has continued to appeal to vocational counselors and is perhaps the most widely accepted approach at the present time.

Parsons began his work not in the schools, but in an independent agency called the Breadwinner's Institute. In 1908 a Vocation Bureau was established which provided services to school-leavers and out-of-school youth. Counseling services were offered in some schools as early as 1895, notably by George Merrill in California, Jesse B. Davis in Michigan, and Eli Weaver in New York City. The first formal public-school department was apparently the Vocational Information Department established in Boston in 1913. The first National Conference on Vocational Guidance met in Boston in 1910, leading to the organization of the National Vocational Guidance Association in 1913 in Grand Rapids, Michigan. A publication, the *Vocational Bulletin*, was established in 1915, becoming eventually the *Personnel and Guidance Journal* of today.

World War I stimulated the vocational guidance movement by spurring the development of tests and testing. Donald G. Paterson of the University of Minnesota was one of the pioneers and important contributors, beginning with his article on the vocational testing movement,[5] and continuing through the 1920s

---

[4] F. Parsons. *Choosing a vocation.* Boston: Houghton Mifflin, 1909. P. 5.

[5] D. G. Paterson. The vocational testing movement. *J. Personnel Res.*, 1922, **1**, 295–305.

and 1930s with the development of the Minnesota Mechanical Ability Tests and the Minnesota Employment Stabilization Institute. Paterson has summarized these developments in a paper read at a conference held in recognition of his contributions.[6] Another pioneer in vocational counseling, Harry D. Kitson, also recently summarized his association with vocational counseling.[7]

Although neither Parsons, Paterson, nor Kitson viewed vocational counseling as a routine matching of the aptitudes of individuals to the requirements of jobs, this concept has been widely accepted and practiced. There has been an implied, if not expressed, hope that eventually measurements of aptitudes would become precise enough, and the requirements of jobs could be specified objectively enough, that the matching could be handled by machines.

But vocational counseling is more difficult and complex than fitting square pegs into square holes and round pegs into round ones, even if we admitted different sizes and degrees of roundness and squareness. There is, as has been repeatedly pointed out, no one occupation which is the "best" for any individual. Nor are all the factors entering into the choice of an occupation objective or rational. And finally, an occupational choice is not something which is to be faced on a particular fine day, or even in a particular period of time.

The recognition of the psychological complexity as well as the importance of choosing an occupation has led to consideration of the problems in a broader perspective. Not everyone has accepted this point of view. Very recently the point of view of vocational choice as a problem for concern by skilled counselors, or one with which they can be helpful, has been questioned. Eli Ginzberg, an economist, questions the assumption that vocational counseling must deal with the total person.[8] He asks: "How does this assumption hold up in the face of the fact that to help bring

[6] D. G. Paterson. Developments in vocational counseling technique. In Williamson, E. G. (Ed.) *Trends in student personnel work.* Minneapolis: University of Minnesota Press, 1949. Pp. 80–96.

[7] H. D. Kitson. Psychology in vocational adjustment. *Personnel Guid. J.,* 1958, **36,** 314–319.

[8] E. Ginzberg. Guidance—limited or unlimited. *Personnel Guid. J.,* 1960, **38,** 707–712.

about significant changes in the individual's basic personality usually requires three years of psychoanalytic treatment at a cost of $10,000 or more?" It might be pointed out in reply that first, it is not a "fact" that personality does not change without a lengthy psychoanalysis, and second, that basic personality changes are not necessary for vocational adjustment in most people. Ginzberg then questions the assumption that the counselor has a responsibility for helping the individual to understand himself better, stating that "it has always been a mystery to me why a reasonably intelligent, young person should not know what he is interested in or what his capacities are." Strange as it may seem to some, those who are closely in contact with young people, as well as young people themselves, recognize their need for assistance in understanding themselves in many cases. Ginzberg sees the function of the counselor as being limited to providing information about the world of work. He feels that counseling can be of little help to the individual in the light of the influences of heredity, socioeconomic class, the home and the family, the school, the church, the community and the culture at large. Yet he points out that many young people waste their potentialities by failing to aim high enough, failing to develop a flexible strategy of decision-making, and failing to take advantage of their opportunities. These are certainly not problems which will be solved merely by providing occupational information.

In the same issue of the journal in which Ginzberg's article appeared, Bell presents some cases illustrating the influence of ego-involvement in vocational decisions.[9] In one case a high school student chose nuclear physics as his vocational goal. His grades were good, and the choice seemed reasonable. But when he entered college, he was unable to master the required mathematics, lost his self-assurance, and had to give up his objective. When he changed to psychology, which was consistent with the results of tests of interests and aptitudes, he was able to obtain his Ph.D. Here obviously was an individual who did not know

[9] H. Bell. Ego-involvement in vocational decisions. *Personnel Guid. J.*, 1960, **38**, 732–735. See also Anneliese F. Korner. Origins of impractical or unrealistic vocational goals. *J. consult. Psychol.*, 1946, **10**, 328–334.

his own interests and aptitudes, and who was perhaps prevented from realizing them because of emotional attitudes which developed around an early vocational choice which became part of his self-concept.

Most authorities, however, recognize the importance of personality factors in vocational choice and success. That vocational choice is not entirely a rational, logical process, entered upon at a particular time, has led to the development of some significant concepts for counselors. Although we can only touch upon them here, they warrant our attention even in the limited space available in this introduction to vocational counseling.

Theories of Vocational Development and Choice

We have indicated that a multitude of factors affect the vocational choices of individuals. It might be argued that, when it comes down to it, the individual actually has little choice, as Ginzberg suggests. Parental occupations and parental pressure, socioeconomic factors, and limited opportunities in the local community are sometimes major factors in determining one's occupation. But more and more the individual is being given a freedom of choice, and even with the limitations imposed on everyone, some freedom remains. That some freedom has existed in the past is indicated by the tendency of those in certain occupations to be similar in some respects. Occupational stereotypes—the typical businessman, salesman, scientist, farmer, teacher—suggest that occupations are selective. It is doubtful that the occupations mold their members into similar characteristics, though there is no doubt some such influence. The development of some of our instruments for vocational counseling, such as the Strong Vocational Interest Blank, is dependent upon the fact that those in an occupation have selected it as appropriate to their needs and interests.

If there is freedom of choice, and if persons seem to gravitate to particular occupations, what are the factors influencing occupational choices? That these factors include characteristics of the individual's personality is the core of recent theories of vocational development and choice. Psychoanalysis provided perhaps the earliest modern theory of vocational choice. This theory related personality characteristics determined by the person's psychosexual development to the occupation which he entered. Thus the compulsive (anal) character would be attracted to routine, exact work such as tabulating and statistics. While this theory has many defects,[10] it does bring out the importance of personality in occupational choice and satisfaction.

One of the most extensive studies of vocational choice is that of Ginzberg and his associates.[11] Although the study was inadequate, being based on a small number of cases mainly at one socioeconomic level, and the results were not particularly new,[12] it did bring a number of theoretical ideas together and stimulated interest in concepts of vocational choice. The theory included four aspects: (1) Occupational choice is a developmental process, occurring over a period of about ten years. (2) The process is essentially irreversible, since certain choices cannot be changed. (3) The process culminates in a compromise between interests, capacities, values, and opportunities. (4) The process can be divided into three stages: a stage of fantasy choice; a stage of tentative choices (beginning at about age 11) influenced first by interests, then by capacities and finally by values; and the stage of realistic choices, involving exploration, crystallization, and specification phases, and beginning at about age 17.

This theory is inadequate because of its limitations rather than because of its being erroneous. Super points out that it does not utilize existing knowledge of interests, that choice means preference at one stage and action at another, and that the theory does not describe or analyze the compromise process. Super then goes on to list twelve main elements of an adequate theory, and presents a summary statement of a comprehensive theory in a series of ten propositions:

[10] See Chapter 11, Selecting a vocational objective, of my book, *Counseling the emotionally disturbed*. New York: Harper, 1958.

[11] E. Ginzberg, J. W. Ginsburg, S. Axelrod, & J. L. Herma. *Occupational choice*. New York: Columbia University Press, 1951.

[12] D. E. Super. A theory of vocational development. *Amer. Psychologist*, 1953, 8, 185–190. Reprinted in G. F. Farwell & H. J. Peters (Eds.). *Guidance readings for counselors*. Chicago: Rand McNally, 1960. Pp. 271–282.

1. People differ in their abilities, interests, and personalities.
2. They are qualified, by virtue of these characteristics, each for a number of occupations.
3. Each of these occupations requires a characteristic pattern of abilities, interests, and personality traits, with tolerances wide enough, however, to allow both some variety of occupations for each individual and some variety of individuals in each occupation.
4. Vocational preferences and competencies, the situations in which people live and work, and hence their self-concepts, change with time and experience (although self-concepts are generally fairly stable from late adolescence until late maturity), making choice and adjustment a continuous process.
5. This process may be summed up in a series of life stages characterized as those of growth, exploration, establishment, maintenance, and decline, and these stages may in turn be subdivided into (a) the fantasy, tentative, and realistic phases of the exploratory stage, and (b) the trial and stable phases of the establishment stage.
6. The nature of the career pattern (that is, the occupational level attained and the sequence, frequency, and duration of trial and stable jobs) is determined by the individual's parental socioeconomic level, mental ability, and personality characteristics, and by the opportunities to which he is exposed.
7. Development through the life stages can be guided, partly by facilitating the process of maturation of abilities and interests and partly by aiding in reality testing and in the development of the self-concept.
8. The process of vocational development is essentially that of developing and implementing a self-concept: it is a compromise process in which the self-concept is a product of the interaction of inherited aptitudes, neural and endocrine make-up, opportunity to play various roles, and evaluations of the extent to which the results of role playing meet with the approval of superiors and fellows.
9. The process of compromise between individual and social factors, between self-concept and reality, is one of role playing, whether the role is played in fantasy, in the counseling interview, or in real life activities such as school classes, clubs, part-time work, and entry jobs.
10. Work satisfactions and life satisfactions depend upon the extent to which the individual finds adequate outlets for his abilities, inter-

ests, personality traits, and values; they depend upon his establishment in a type of work, a work situation, and a way of life in which he can play the kind of role which his growth and exploratory experiences have led him to consider congenial and appropriate.[13]

There are three main concepts in this formulation. The first is that of *vocational adjustment as a developmental process.* Although this has long been recognized, emphasis has continued to be placed upon the choice of an occupation as occurring at some particular time. It is true, of course, that choices are and must be made, but these are events in a process; the process includes a series of choices, each of which influences the life work of the individual. In the process of vocational development, numerous factors operate, or interact, including the characteristics and potentialities of the individual and the environment. It is apparent that this process is similar to other developmental processes, so that vocational development is one aspect of the individual's total development, as Beilin and Super point out.[14]

The process of interaction is a compromise or synthesis.[15] Super prefers the term *synthesis* for the normal developmental process, feeling that the term *compromise* is more appropriate when development is delayed or retarded and the reality-testing process begins later than it should. However, it is probable that in many, if not in most, cases, compromises must be made between the needs and desires of the individual and the requirements and opportunities of the environment. Synthesis, or compromise, involves the personal needs and resources of the individual on the one hand, and the economic and social resources and demands of society on the other. The synthesizing process is a learning process which often takes place in role-playing and role-taking. It operates through the attempt of the individual to satisfy his various needs. The individual tries himself out, some-

[13] *Ibid.*

[14] (1) H. Beilin. The application of general developmental principles to the vocational area. *J. counsel. Psychol.*, 1955, **2**, 53–57.   (2) D. E. Super. *The psychology of careers.* New York: Harper, 1957. Pp. 185 ff.

[15] (1) D. E. Super. Vocational development: the process of compromise or synthesis. *J. counsel. Psychol.* 1956, **3**, 249–253.   (2) D. E. Super. *The psychology of careers, op. cit.*, Chap. 21.

times in fantasy, sometimes in exploratory activities, in various
roles, with or without clear awareness of what he is doing—
"trying on" various roles.

The second major conception in this formulation is that of
career patterns.[16] This concept hypothesizes that the occupational histories of individuals follow patterns. The pattern is the
result of influences within and outside the individual. The determinants of career patterns are not clearly known, though there
is some information available about some of the individual and
sociological or economic factors which operate. But we need
more data to answer the following questions posed by Super:
(1) What are the typical entry, intermediate, and regular adult
occupations of persons from different socioeconomic groups?
(2) To what extent do "regular adult occupations" exist, and what
is the relationship between parental socioeconomic level and
having a regular adult occupation? (3) What are the lines and
rates of movement from entry toward regular adult occupation?
(4) What factors are related to the direction and rate of movement from one job or occupation to another? (5) What is the relationship between occupational field and factors such as accessi-
bility of the occupation or industry, and the possession of various
aptitudes, interests, values, and personality characteristics? (6)
What is the relationship of differences between actual and parental occupational levels to possible causal factors, such as acces-
sibility of the occupation or industry, and the possession of
attitudes, interests, values, and personality characteristics?

The third major element in the process is the *self-concept.*
Super sees vocational development as the implementation of the
self-concept.[17] The importance of one's occupation to one's self-
concept is indicated by the fact that in response to the question
"Who are you?" many people reply by stating their occupation.

The importance of the self-concept in personality and behavior is being increasingly recognized. It has become the central element in several theories of personality, including the

[16] (1) D. E. Super. Career patterns as a basis for vocational counseling.
J. counsel. Psychol., 1954, **1**, 12–19.   (2) D. S. Super. *The psychology of
careers, op. cit.,* pp. 70–79.

[17] (1) D. E. Super. Vocational adjustment: implementing a self-concept.
Occup., 1951, **30**, 88–92.   (2) D. E. Super. *The psychology of careers, op.
cit.,* Chapter 13.

client-centered theory.[18] It is only natural, therefore, to expect it to be an important factor in vocational development. Vocational development is thus an aspect of personal development. A person's occupation is, as has been emphasized earlier, an important part of his life. It must be consistent with other aspects of his life if he is to be happy and satisfied. This means that the individual must view his work, or his occupation, in terms of his self-concept. Is his occupational role compatible with his concept of himself?

Implications for Vocational Counseling

It thus becomes apparent that vocational counseling is more than the matching of aptitudes, abilities, and interests with job demands and job requirements. A definition of counseling as assisting the person to develop an understanding of himself and of his environment, and to integrate the two to enable him to resolve problems, make choices, and develop and carry out plans, is perhaps still adequate. However, this requires more than the use and interpretation of tests and the providing of occupational information. Super prefers a revised definition: "Vocational guidance is the process of helping a person to develop and accept an integrated and adequate picture of himself and of his role in the world of work, to test this concept against reality, and to convert it into reality, with satisfaction to himself and benefit to society."[19]

Super presents an excellent comparison of the traditional approach to vocational counseling and that of vocational counseling as aiding in the development and implementation of a self-concept which is drawn upon here.[20] The traditional method is described essentially as information-giving. In it the counselor, by questioning and by the administration of tests, obtains and synthesizes information about the client. This is commonly referred

[18] (1) C. R. Rogers. A theory of therapy, personality, and interpersonal relationships, as developed in the client-centered framework. In S. Koch (Ed.) *Psychology: a study of science. Study I. Conceptual and systematic. Vol. 3. Formulations of the person and the social context.* New York: McGraw-Hill, 1959. (2) C. H. Patterson. The self in recent Rogerian theory. *J. Indiv. Psychol.,* 1961, **17,** 5–11.

[19] Super. *The psychology of careers, op. cit.,* p. 197.

[20] *Ibid.,* pp. 191–197.

to as the individual inventory. The individual's assets are then matched with job requirements, and the client is assisted in examining appropriate occupations. The questions to which answers are sought are: What are the client's aptitudes and interests? In what jobs are they likely to be useful? What is the demand for such services? How can the client prepare for, enter upon, and advance in such work? As Super notes, "Implicit in the use of such methods of vocational guidance has been the assumption that vocational maladjustment is generally the result of lack of information about oneself or about the world of work. And it goes on to assume that the best way to promote vocational adjustment is to give people information about themselves and about occupations."[21]

Another approach considers vocational counseling as personal counseling. This approach, the client-centered method, is seen by Super as conflicting with the traditional approach. Its emphasis is upon attitudes and feelings rather than so-called objective *facts*. The client-centered counselor, according to Super, does not discuss these facts or provide information, but helps the client explore his attitudes and feelings. The client develops self-understanding and self-acceptance, which enables him to make choices, to select goals, and to carry out plans for their attainment. All of this, Super implies, occurs with no specific consideration of the usual content of traditional vocational counseling.

The two approaches appear to be antithetical or in conflict, as Super notes. This apparent conflict has been a source of difficulty for the counselor engaged in vocational counseling in the schools. On the one hand, he recognizes the importance of non-rational, or emotional, factors in vocational development and choice. On the other, he feels the need for tests and for occupational information in vocational counseling. His concept of client-centered counseling is one in which the counselor does not ask questions, give tests, or provide any information. Although he often feels guilty about it, he usually ends up using tests and providing information. He usually concludes that the client-centered approach is not useful in vocational counseling.

This situation, in the opinion of the writer, is the result of a misconception of the client-centered approach. It is based on a

21 *Ibid.*, p. 193.

conception of client-centered counseling as consisting of a group of techniques. But the client-centered approach is essentially an *attitude* rather than a series of techniques. The attitude may be implemented in different ways in different situations. In counseling on problems of personal adjustment, the techniques of simple acceptance and reflection of feeling are sufficient. In counseling dealing with problems of vocational choice, tests may be used and occupational information provided. It is, or should be, done in ways which are consistent with the basic attitudes or assumptions of client-centered counseling as referred to in the preceding chapter. Later chapters will indicate how this is accomplished.

From this point of view, there is no conflict between client-centered counseling and educational-vocational counseling. Tests and occupational information are appropriate where they are needed, and where they are useful to the client in the solution of his problems.[22] The techniques as used in personal-adjustment counseling are appropriate when dealing with attitudes and feelings of the client in vocational counseling.[23]

Super's approach to vocational counseling is consistent with this interpretation of client-centered counseling and is actually not a synthesis of two approaches, or an eclectic approach, but essentially client-centered vocational counseling. The questions considered are listed by Super as follows: "What sort of person do *I think* I am? How do I feel about myself as I think I am? What sort of person would *I like* to be? What are my aptitudes and interests? What can I do to reconcile my self-ideal with my real self? What outlets are there for me with my needs, values, interests, and aptitudes? How can I make use of these outlets?"[24]

As Super notes, the distinction between vocational and per-

[22] C. R. Rogers. Psychometric tests and client-centered counseling. *Educ. psychol. Measmt.*, 1946, **6**, 139–144.

[23] For a more detailed discussion of client-centered vocational counseling, see Part IV (Chapters 7–12) of the author's *Counseling the emotionally disturbed.* New York: Harper, 1958. See also (1) R. H. Bixler & Virginia H. Bixler. Clinical counseling in vocational guidance. *J. clin. Psychol.*, 1945, **1**, 186–192.   (2) A. W. Combs. Nondirective techniques and vocational counseling. *Occup.*, 1947, **25**, 261–267.   (3) B. J. Covner. Nondirective interviewing techniques in vocational counseling. *J. consult. Psychol.*, 1947, **11**, 70–73.

[24] D. E. Super. *The psychology of careers, op. cit.*, p. 196.

sonal counseling seems artificial. "In order to do an effective job for vocational guidance the counselor must have a good understanding of the personal adjustment which he is trying to further. And in order to help with many commonly encountered problems of personal adjustment the counselor must have a good understanding of the tools, techniques, and resources of vocational guidance."[25] Problems of vocational choice are to some extent emotional because, like parent-child, marital, or any other type of problem, they involve the self. In this context, it is misleading to try to distinguish between vocational problems which are symptoms of personal maladjustment, or personal maladjustment which is the result of vocational problems. Super presents a case in which vocational counseling enabled a rather severely disturbed person to function adequately in his total life, and suggests that "emotionally maladjusted persons who have genuine problems of vocational adjustment, which can be worked on directly, will find that improvement in the latter will bring about improvement in the former."[26]

Nevertheless, there appears to be some practical value in distinguishing extreme cases. In most instances vocational counseling may be considered as concerned with relatively normal individuals facing the usual problems of occupational choice, with emotional factors being present, but not of primary concern. On the other hand, there are individuals with severe emotional problems which affect their entire adjustment, including the vocational. Such individuals usually need therapeutic counseling or psychotherapy rather than, or preceding, vocational counseling. Other clients may be in need of counseling regarding personal problems which are not related to vocational development. It therefore seems desirable to retain such terms as *vocational counseling* and *personal counseling*, to indicate the focus of the concern, without implying that there are any sharp lines involved.[27]

A second implication of this approach to vocational counseling is related to the concept of vocational development. If voca-

---

[25] *Ibid.*, p. 192.

[26] D. E. Super. Personality integration through vocational counseling. *J. counsel. Psychol.*, 1955, 2, 217–226.

[27] A. S. Thompson. Personality dynamics and vocational counseling. *Personnel Guid. J.*, 1960, 38, 350–357.

tional choice is a process, then there is no one point at which *the* vocational choice is made. Various choices are made at different points in the process. Moreover, the process begins very early in life. Anne Roe discusses some of the early determinants of vocational choice in the individual. While hereditary factors are present, they are limiting rather than specifically determining factors. The development of special abilities, within these limits, is influenced by early experiences of satisfactions and frustrations of needs. Early experiences of the child in the family thus have strong influence on the basic attitudes, interests, and capacities which the individual develops, and which are expressed later in broad vocational choices.[28]

The child, then, is developing the basis for his occupation from birth, and is shaping his vocational life by the many choices he makes in expending his energies, developing his abilities, and expressing his interests. Vocational counseling, entering rather late into the picture, is only one factor in helping to crystallize the direction of vocational development. The specific choice of a beginning job or occupation is only one choice, although it may be the most important. But in view of the total process of vocational development, it should be obvious that the choice cannot, or should not, be forced at any particular time. There is no age at which a specific vocational choice should or must be made, in terms of the process of vocational development. As in other types of development, the process is an individual one, proceeding at different rates in different individuals. Vocational counseling may be helpful at various points, or stages of the process, and is not necessarily directed to the goal of having the client make a specific choice. The fact that a large percentage of high-school students have not reached a decision regarding their life occupation has been alarming to some people, who have used this as evidence of inadequate vocational counseling services. But there is no reason why a specific vocational choice must be made in high school, particularly in the case of those students who will continue their education. The fact that the socioeconomic situation sometimes requires a specific decision does enter in, of course, and often the counselor's job is to help a student reach

[28] Anne Roe. Early determinants of vocational choice. *J. counsel. Psychol.,* 1957, 4, 212–217.

the best decision in the light of circumstances, even though the latter may not be prepared to make an adequate choice.

This leads to consideration of the implication of the career-pattern concept for counseling. The career pattern is the continuation of vocational development in the individual's adult occupational life. It might not appear to be particularly useful to school counselors. However, it brings in some considerations of which the counselor should be aware. First, the career pattern emphasizes the importance of the nonpersonal, or external factors, in vocational development and choice. It thus should direct the counselor's attention to the importance of the socioeconomic factors in occupational choice. The importance of other family-background factors is also emphasized. The career-pattern concept states in effect that the future of an individual is closely related to his past. While a pattern can be broken, it requires effort to do so. Thus, a very superior student, from a family, a neighborhood, a socioeconomic or other group in which education and professional activities are not valued, *can* become a successful college student and professional person, but the influence of his background must be considered.

The career-pattern concept provides another important point of view to the counselor. A pattern, while having certain elements of constancy, also suggests change. It does not imply that once a clerk, always a clerk, or once a carpenter, always a carpenter. There is an element of change and progression, even though it may be within a general context or pattern. Therefore, an entry occupation is just that—an entry into a field of work, or career, in which the individual may progress. Again, the concept of pattern must not be interpreted too rigidly. Change is characteristic of the occupational lives of many people. Going from job to job is not necessarily indicative of lack of success. It may indicate successful progression. The occupational histories of some of our leading figures show some major changes in occupation. While in some cases they may indicate the breaking of a pattern, the development of rather different careers, in other cases a pattern of development may be discerned. The counselor, therefore, must take the long view, and think in terms of broad career patterns, rather than in terms of narrowly defined occupations.

There is a third important implication of this concept of vocational counseling. The recognition of vocational development as a process points up the importance for the school to be concerned with vocational development in the curriculum as well as in providing counseling services. While it is recognized that counseling is a continuing process, which should begin in early childhood, it is also true that because of lack of counselors, counseling services are inadequate. Moreover, even where services are available, students may not utilize them sufficiently. They tend to seek out a counselor only when faced with an immediate choice or decision. In addition, continued, intensive counseling is not necessary in most cases. There are other more efficient and perhaps more effective ways of assisting the student in his vocational development. We have already mentioned teachers as a source of information about occupations. Information about the world of work should be incorporated in the curriculum from primary grades onward (see Chapter 10). The student can be helped to develop increased understanding of himself through curricular activities which incorporate such materials as those developed by the Educational Testing Service and Science Research Associates.[29] These and other approaches will be considered in the chapter on group-guidance activities.

The importance of these noncounseling activities is emphasized by the concept of vocational development. They are vehicles for providing materials which are helpful in the developmental process, and which are preparatory for more specific vocational counseling.

Individual vocational counseling is usually not considered as necessary or desirable below the ninth grade. This attitude appears to be related to the concept of vocational counseling as the making of a vocational choice, rather than as a means of assisting the student in his vocational development. It is true that even at the ninth-grade level, students are unprepared for vocational counseling which requires the making of occupational decisions. Super, reporting on an extensive study of vocational maturity of

[29] (1) M. R. Katz. *You: today and tomorrow.* Princeton, N.J.: Educational Testing Service, 1958. (2) S. A. Stouffer. *Your educational plans.* Chicago: Science Research Associates, 1959.

ninth-grade boys,[30] concludes that "typical ninth grade boys, in a typical small city high school, with a typical guidance program, were at a stage of vocational development which is characterized by readiness to consider problems of prevocational and vocational choice but also by a general lack of readiness to make vocational choices. Ninth graders are clearly in an exploratory stage, not a decision-making stage, of vocational development . . . ninth graders are ready to look into things, to try themselves out, but have not yet developed to a point at which it is reasonable or desirable to expect them to commit themselves to a vocation."[31]

Concern with vocational development, rather than vocational choice, is thus the focus of guidance and related services in the junior high and elementary school. While much of this concern can be expressed in curricular and extracurricular activities, it does not follow that there is no place for the counselor trained in vocational counseling in elementary and junior high schools. The counselor is the expert on materials for inclusion in the curriculum, and is a consultant to teachers and the administration, as well as being available for some special instruction and assisting in developing special programs.

Nor is individual vocational counseling out-of-place in the upper elementary and junior high school. While vocational choices are not necessary, educational choices which have vocational implications are. Curriculum choices are made in the sixth, seventh, eighth, and ninth grades which in many cases should be made only with individual counseling, whether we call it vocational or prevocational.[32] And of course vocational counseling should be provided for drop-outs at this level.

The concept of vocational development, then, points up the need for concern with preparation for vocational choice from the beginning of the school years. The identification and development of abilities, aptitudes, and interests of vocational sig-

[30] D. E. Super & Phoebe L. Overstreet. *The vocational maturity of ninth grade boys.* New York: Teachers College, Bureau of Publications, 1960.

[31] D. E. Super. The critical ninth grade: vocational choice or vocational exploration. *Personnel Guid. J.,* 1960, 39, 106–109.

[32] M. Newman. Pre-high school vocational counseling. *Voc. Guid. Quart.,* 1957, 6, 6–8.

nificance are therefore a concern of guidance and counseling services in elementary and junior high as well as in the high school. It is because of this fact that the National Defense Education Act, which limits training programs to secondary-school counselors, is inadequate.

Unrealistic Vocational Aspirations

Counselors have long been concerned about the fact that many students express unrealistic vocational preferences, both in terms of the opportunities available and of their aptitudes and abilities.[33] The discussion of the relation of occupational choice to personality, or the self-concept, makes it clear why this occurs.

Vocational preferences of high-school students tend to fall in the upper and middle occupations of the occupational scale, including those with higher salaries and greater prestige.[34] It seems clear that these factors are important to many students because of the need for status.

It should be apparent that where unrealistic vocational choices or preferences are determined by such personal needs, simple information-giving will be of little help. Statistics on the distribution of the population among the occupations will be unheeded, and information on the student's aptitudes will be ignored or not accepted. Counseling must consider the emotional or attitudinal factors behind the preference, and deal with them therapeutically.

It might be well here to include a brief discussion of the realism of vocational preferences. It has been widely assumed, on the basis of early group studies that, since the majority of high school students express preference for upper-level occupations, these preferences are unrealistic. In terms of existing opportunities, this may be so, at least to a great extent. But the occupational picture is changing, with increasing demands for professional manpower.

In addition, studies of the realism of vocational preferences have usually not analyzed the preferences in terms of individual aptitudes and abilities. A recent study in which this was done

[33] For a review of studies in this area see Anne Roe. *The psychology of occupations.*

[34] R. M. Stephenson. Realism of vocational choice: a critique and an example. *Personnel Guid. J.,* 1957, **35**, 482–488.

found that 95 percent of a sample of 508 high-school graduates had vocational preferences that were judged to be realistic by judges utilizing information on the student and on the preferred job. In fact, 37 percent of the students were judged to have chosen a vocation *below* their ability levels.[35] It has been pointed out that *aspirations,* or *preferences,* may be unrealistic in terms of opportunity, although they represent the success orientation of our culture. *Plans* or *choices* on the other hand may be more realistic.[36]

Summary

One of the major areas of counseling in the school is educational and vocational counseling. Work is an important aspect of our society. One's occupation exerts a significant influence on one's whole life. The choice of an occupation is thus a serious decision. It is becoming increasingly recognized that occupational choice is more than fitting one's aptitudes and abilities to a job. The individual's personality is an important factor, and a central aspect of personality is the self-concept. Vocational choice may thus be seen as the implementation of the self-concept. The implications of this for the vocational counseling process were pointed out.

This chapter has presented a developing point of view in vocational counseling. It is representative of the trend toward working with students as well as with other individuals in terms of recognizing the person as an integrated whole which cannot be broken up or compartmentalized. Vocational development is a part of general development, vocational problems are involved with the personality, the self-concept is important in occupational choice and adjustment as in other areas of life. If he is to do a good job of vocational counseling, the vocational counselor must be more than what he has been narrowly defined as being in the past. He must be broadly trained and qualified in counseling, in order to be able to acquire an understanding of vocational development as a part of the total development of the individual over his life span.

[35] W. V. Lockwood. Realism of vocational preference. *Personnel Guid. J.,* 1958, **37**, 98–106.
[36] Stephenson, *op. cit.*

SUGGESTED READINGS

Blum, M. L., & Balinsky, B. *Counseling and psychology.* New York: Prentice-Hall, 1951. A text on vocational counseling, for nonpsychologists, yet presenting the psychological foundations of vocational counseling.

Roe, Anne. *The psychology of occupations.* New York: Wiley, 1956. This book is a survey of some of the literature on the psychological aspects of occupations. It also presents an occupational classification which takes into consideration the psychosocial characteristics of occupations.

Sanderson, H. *Basic concepts in vocational guidance.* New York: McGraw-Hill, 1954. While not directly related to the concept of vocational counseling adopted in this chapter, Sanderson's book does attempt to place vocational guidance in a larger context than the traditional approach.

Super, D. E. *The psychology of careers.* New York: Harper, 1957. This book is the most detailed and definitive statement of the point of view taken in this chapter. Anyone engaging in or preparing for vocational counseling should be familiar with it.

White, R. W. *Lives in progress.* New York: Dryden, 1954. There is a dearth, indeed almost a complete lack, of case histories of vocational development. The cases in this book include the vocational aspects, and as such are of value to the vocational counselor as illustrations of the concepts developed in this chapter.

CHAPTER 9

TESTING IN THE
GUIDANCE PROGRAM

The use of tests has been increasing by leaps and bounds, not only in our schools, but in other areas of our life, including industry, the government, and the armed services. Pitirim Sorokin, the Harvard sociologist, has written as follows about the ubiquitous use of tests:

At the present time in the Western countries almost every individual is tested from the cradle to the grave, and before and after every important event in his life. He is given a battery of tests after his birth, in his nursery school and kindergarten, in his elementary, high school, and college, before and after his draft into the armed forces, before and during his marriage, before and after his gainful employment, and so on, up to the tests preceding and following death. His life career is largely determined by these tests. Beginning with intelligence tests and ending with the tests of loyalty and subversity, various testers have replaced the old-fashioned angel-guardians that supposedly guided the life-course of each person. We are living in an *age of testocracy*. By their tests of our intelligence, emotional stability, character, aptitude, unconscious drives, and other characteristics of our personality, the testocrats largely decide our vocation and occupation. They play an important role in our promotions or demotions, successes and failures, in our social position, reputation, and influence. They determine our normality or abnormality, our superior intelligence or hopeless stupidity, our loyalty or subversity. By all this they are largely responsible for our happiness or despair and, finally, for our long life or premature death.[1]

[1] P. A. Sorokin. Testomania. *Harvard educ. Rev.*, 1955, 25, 199–213.

While the writer knows of no psychological test which can be administered after death, and while it is an exaggeration to say that tests determine our lives or careers, it is undeniable that they are an influence. It is incorrect to say that tests *determine* normality or abnormality, or intelligence, since these actually determine test results, but the results of the measurement of these characteristics by tests are important factors in the careers of many people.

The comments of some responsible educators are similar. Kelley and Rasey write as follows: "We have been too fond of standardized tests. . . . We have seen IQ tests given to whole groups of students together, without regard for their condition at the particular time. Scores have been computed and have been used to categorize people from that time hence. In some schools these scores have been posted on the bulletin board. There have even been reports that teachers have seated their students according to the scores! Because of the weaknesses of the tests and because of their misuse and misinterpretation, we believe that as of today the testing movement has done more harm than good."[2] Tests are not perfect. Test scores are not completely accurate or infallible. Tests must therefore be used with caution and only by those trained in their use and interpretation.

The emphasis placed upon tests and testing by the National Defense Education Act of 1958 (Public Law 85–864) has led to expansion of testing programs in the schools, and has given rise to concern about overtesting. In some instances, it almost appears that a school is judged by the number and frequency of tests administered, or the weight of test information per student in the files. Criticisms concerning the use of tests by untrained personnel, the dangers in the acceptance of tests as completely accurate, and their uncritical use in making important decisions about students have increased.

It is important to consider the use to which test results are to be put in developing any testing program. Testing per se is not necessarily desirable. There must be a purpose behind the testing program, and the tests must be useful to the school and the students in the achievement of some goal or end.

[2] E. C. Kelley & Marie I. Rasey. *Education and the nature of man.* New York: Harper, 1952.

Uses of Tests

Tests may be and are used in schools for a variety of purposes. The most common uses may be grouped under three headings: for administrative purposes, for classroom purposes, and for counseling and guidance purposes. These can be outlined as follows:

Administrative Purposes:
Determining emphasis to be given different areas of instruction.
Measuring the progress (or changes) in the school from year to year.
Identifying the changing character of the student body.
Determining the appropriateness of the school curricula for students of differing characteristics or ability levels.
Determining how well students are attaining educational goals.
Evaluating curricular experimentation.
Evaluating the school as a unit.
Providing evidence for improvement of public relations.
Providing information for outside agencies.
Providing basis for student placement and the formation of classroom groups or curriculum tracks.
Providing basis for pupil promotion or retardation.

Classroom Purposes:
Grouping pupils for instruction within a class.
Guiding activities for specific pupils, including individualizing of instruction.
Determining reasonable level of classroom achievement for each pupil.
Identifying pupils who need special diagnostic study and remedial instruction.
Measuring class progress over a period of time.
Appraising relative achievement within a class.
Assigning course grades.

Counseling and Guidance Purposes:
Building realistic self-pictures on the part of pupils.
Helping pupils to set educational and vocational goals.
Helping pupils choose an occupation or plan for further education.
Discovering interests of which the pupil may not be aware.
Improving counselor, teacher, and parent understanding of problem cases.
Helping pupils select suitable courses of study.

Predicting success in future educational work.

Identifying superior or gifted students for scholarship purposes.[3]

It is apparent that there is some overlap in the major purposes listed above. For example, teachers as well as counselors may use tests to help identify gifted students, or this may be considered in some instances to be an administrative use of tests. Research may be the purpose of testing in any one or all of the three areas.

In this book we are concerned with the use of tests in counseling, and the remainder of this chapter will be limited to a discussion of this use. Specifically, we shall attempt to answer the question of how tests are used in counseling as it has been described in the preceding two chapters. The discussion will not be concerned with the use and interpretation of specific tests, nor with the kinds of tests which are appropriate in certain situations. Rather, it will be a consideration of the integration of tests in the counseling process from the counseling point of view adopted in this book. Again, the reader must remember that there are other points of view regarding the use of tests in counseling.

Are Tests Consistent with Client-Centered Counseling?

It was indicated in the last chapter that some counselors, and some writers, have felt that the use of tests in counseling is not consistent with the client-centered approach. This feeling appears to be based upon a misconception of client-centered counseling. It is true that testing has been minimized in client-centered counseling, due mainly to this approach being applied in the past almost exclusively in cases involving problems of personal adjustment, where the problem is not one in which tests are ordinarily useful, even where there are vocational aspects to the problem. Essentially, the objections to tests in client-centered counseling are concerned with the way in which they are used rather than with their use as such. Rogers wrote that "psychometric tests which are initiated by the counselor are a hindrance to the counseling

[3] Adapted from H. H. Remmers, N. L. Gage, & J. F. Rummel. *A practical introduction to measurement and evaluation.* New York: Harper, 1960. Pp. 80–81.

process whose purpose is to release growth forces. They tend to increase defensiveness on the part of the client, to lessen his acceptance of self, to decrease his sense of responsibility, to create an attitude of dependence upon the expert."[4] This may be true when tests are introduced routinely by the counselor.

But Rogers goes on to say that "tests are not necessarily completely excluded from the counseling process, however. The client may, in exploring his situation, reach the point where, facing his situation squarely and realistically, he wishes to compare his aptitudes or abilities with those of others for a specific purpose. . . . Consequently, when the request for appraisal comes as a real desire of the client, then tests may enter into the situation. It should be recognized, however, that this is not likely to occur frequently in practice."[5]

This last statement is usually true in counseling in the area of personal adjustment. It does not usually apply in vocational counseling, however. Here, the client usually expects tests, if indeed he does not feel that counseling consists entirely of taking tests and having them interpreted. It must be recognized that tests may not be appropriate or useful with every client with a vocational problem. In most cases they are of some help.

The Purpose of Tests in Counseling

Probably one of the reasons that the use of tests has been felt to be inconsistent with client-centered counseling is the identification of tests with evaluation. If tests are not all of evaluation, they constitute the principal tool or technique of evaluation. They measure, appraise, or assess aptitudes, abilities, and other characteristics of the individual.

Counseling, on the other hand—at least client-centered counseling—is nonevaluative. The nonjudgmental nature of client-centered counseling is one of its central and distinctive characteristics. This being the case, testing would appear to violate the nonevaluative requirement of client-centered counseling. How

[4] C. R. Rogers. Psychometric tests and client-centered counseling. *Educ. psychol. Measmt.*, 1946, **6**, 139–144.
[5] *Ibid.*

can the counselor be client-centered and at the same time introduce evaluation into the counseling process?

The apparent dilemma arises from a misconception of testing and the use of tests. Tests *are* instruments of evaluation, but the use of tests does not necessarily make the counselor an evaluator. While counselors often use tests to evaluate a client, there is no reason why tests must be used in this way. In other words, a counselor may use tests without making evaluations of the client.

What then is the purpose of tests in client-centered counseling? The answer should be clear. *Tests are used to assist the client in evaluating himself.* It is the client who evaluates, not the counselor. The ultimate purpose of the tests—indeed the purpose of counseling—is not to help the counselor understand the client (though they may do this, and understanding of the client by the counselor is necessary) but to help the client understand himself. This confusion about the ultimate goal of counseling, the failure to recognize that this goal is not knowledge about or understanding of the client by the counselor for its own sake, has led to a misunderstanding of the place of data and information about the client in counseling. The result has been an overemphasis upon the collection of data, including test data, by the counselor. It is not what the counselor knows about the client, but what the client knows about himself, which is important. The client must make his own decisions; therefore he must make the evaluations.

Although it is rather generally accepted that the client must make his own decisions, this does not appear to be acted upon in many instances. Counselors often seem to act as if *they* are to make the decisions, and they appear to obtain and collect data as if they must do so. The client has and is aware of much of the data and information which counselors spend time obtaining and recording, and it is not necessary that the counselor have and record all the details. In the case of the characteristics which tests measure, however, the client may not have information, or accurate information, about himself. Tests are useful because they provide more objective information than the client can obtain elsewhere, even from the counselor's estimates.

Even if the counselor could make good estimates of the characteristics which are measured by tests, it would not be desirable that he do so, and then provide these estimates to the client rather than use tests. To do so would be setting himself up as an evaluator, which would be inconsistent with a client-centered approach. Hence, the use of tests, where they are appropriate, may *preserve* the client-centeredness of the counseling relationship. Objective test results, while they may be threatening to a client, are less likely to disrupt the counseling relationship than the judgments or estimates of the counselor.

This use of tests is the essential difference between counseling and selection. In selection, the client—or applicant—is being evaluated by the tester or the interviewer (the employer or his representative). In counseling, the client is evaluating himself by means of tests. The same tests may be used, but they are used differently.

When and How Are Tests Introduced?

If tests are not necessarily or routinely used in counseling, and if they are not prescribed by the counselor, even on the basis of a knowledge of the individual client and his problem, when and how are they used?

It seems clear that tests would not be administered prior to the counseling interview. The procedure used in many counseling centers, where the client takes a series of tests before he sees the counselor for the first time, does not appear to be consistent with the counseling approach presented here. It may be argued that there are certain tests which all clients should take, and that it is more efficient if they are taken prior to counseling. But the essence of our approach is that there are no standard batteries of tests which every client should have. It is true that in practice a counselor may find that for the clients with whom he works he tends to find certain tests used with almost all of them. Nevertheless, even in this situation, the tests should not be administered prior to counseling.

The prohibition of the administration of a standard battery of tests to all clients before counseling begins does not mean that mass or group testing of students in schools is not approved. It will be remembered that there are other uses of tests besides counseling, and it is efficient to administer tests on a group basis for these purposes. In addition, where it is felt that particular tests would be useful in the counseling of many students, it is economical and justifiable to administer them to all students so that the results will be available for counseling use later.

The essential basis for the use of tests in counseling is that *they provide information which the client needs and wants.* They should provide information concerning questions which the client raises in counseling. Thus the information is relevant to the client and his questions, not to what the counselor would like to know or thinks the client should know. Since answers to questions are useful only after the questions have been asked, tests are not used until the need for the information arises in counseling. The information is relevant and significant only when the client recognizes its pertinence and his need for it.

The recognition by the client of the usefulness of tests may be expressed in different ways. It is not necessary, as is sometimes thought, that in order for the client-centered counselor to use tests, the client must ask for specific ones. If the client brings up problems to which test results would be relevant, the counselor may indicate that tests might be helpful to the client, who then decides whether he would like to take them. The process of test selection in client-centered counseling has been discussed by Bordin and Bixler and by Seeman.[6]

Since the client may raise questions at different times during counseling, rather than all at once, it follows that testing may be distributed throughout the counseling process. Thus a test or tests may be used at different times or different points in counseling or spread throughout the counseling process as the need for the particular information which they may provide arises. Early questions may be general. The questions which develop

---

[6] (1) E. S. Bordin & R. H. Bixler. Test selection: a process of counseling. *Educ. psychol. Measmt.*, 1946, **6**, 361–373. Reprinted in A. H. Brayfield (Ed.) *Readings in modern methods of counseling.* New York: Appleton-Century-Crofts, 1950. Pp. 173–183. (2) J. Seeman. A study of client self-selection of tests in vocational counseling. *Educ. psychol. Measmt.* 1948, **8**, 327–346.

as counseling proceeds may become more specific, and testing thus becomes more specific. This method of testing has been referred to by Super as "precision testing," as distinguished from "saturation testing," where a complete battery of tests is given at one time.[7]

Since the tests are used to provide information for the client, and since the client's questions are individual in nature, the use of tests is on an individual basis. However, since there are many questions which are raised by many, if not most, clients, the same tests will frequently be used with different clients. This, however, should not be an excuse for routine testing prior to the counseling interview.

Tests, then, are introduced in counseling when the client, either overtly or covertly, indicates a desire or need for the kind of information which tests can help to provide. The counselor indicates the kinds of information which the tests may provide, describing the appropriate tests in nontechnical terms. The client indicates whether or not he would like this information. If he does, the counselor arranges for the administration of the appropriate test or tests. This is all done in a simple, matter-of-fact way without disturbing the attitude of respect for the client or infringing upon his responsibility for making decisions. There is no implication that the tests, or the counselor's use of tests, will solve the client's problems. Tests are presented as one source of information, and the decision as to whether to use this information is left up to the client.

This method of introducing and selecting tests preserves the client's autonomy and yet does not make the process overcomplicated or artificial, as some descriptions of client-selection of tests would seem to make it. The counselor, in some of these illustrations, seems to be leaning over backward in a hands-off attitude toward test selection, perhaps creating an unpleasant or frustrating experience for the client. This may be the source of some of the dissatisfaction which has been expressed by some clients with whom such attempts at client-centered methods of test selection have been made.

[7] D. E. Super. Testing and using test results in counseling. *Occup.,* 1950, **29**, 95–97.

Using Test Results in Counseling

Once tests have been administered and scored, how are the results used in counseling?

Before discussing the problem of test interpretation in counseling, it might be well to mention an obligation of anyone who administers tests. It is the opinion of the author that anyone who takes a test has a right to some information concerning the results of the test. This should apply even outside of the counseling situation. The administration of a series of tests to large groups such as an entire class raises some problems in this regard. While it may be desirable to offer to discuss the tests with any student who wishes to do so, it may be impossible to issue such an invitation because of lack of counseling staff. This situation is an unfortunate one, since, in addition to denying the student something to which he should be entitled, it also fails to utilize a method of contact with students who need counseling services. The offering of an opportunity to discuss the results of tests taken in a group testing program is one method of offering counseling services and encouraging their use by students who may need them.

In the counseling situation, there is no excuse for not informing the client about the results of tests he has taken. Tests are of no use to the client unless he knows the results. How then are tests interpreted in client-centered counseling?

If the client is to use the results of tests, he must (1) understand them, and (2) be able to accept them. There are several implications for test interpretation in these requirements.

First, the emphasis is upon the understanding of the client, not of the counselor. For this reason, the word *interpretation* may not be the best one to indicate the use of test results in counseling. It tends to emphasize the activity of the counselor. We should be more concerned about the activity of the client. It is suggested that perhaps the *communication of test results* might be a better phrase than the interpretation of test results. For communication to be successful there must be understanding on the part of the client.

We shall not discuss here the detailed methods and procedures for communicating test results to clients, since this is a matter for courses on the use of tests in counseling. The Bixlers and Bordin have discussed test interpretation in the counseling interview.[8] But the matter of technique involves a general principle which is a second implication of the conditions under which the client is able to use test results. This is that the results must be communicated objectively, that is, without the introduction of judgments or evaluations by the counselor. The results of the tests must be allowed to speak for themselves, after adequate explanation of the meaning of the scores by the counselor. An illustration of what is meant by objective presentation of the results is the interpretation of a score on a college aptitude test. The statement, "Three out of four persons with scores like yours do not complete the first year of college," is objective. The statement, "Your score indicates that the chances are three out of four that you will not complete the first year of college," while apparently objective, is somewhat loaded. But the statement, "With a score such as yours you should not attempt college," is definitely evaluative and judgmental, and goes beyond the presentation of information to the client.

A third implication of the requirements for adequate use of test results by the client involves the conditions under which the results will be accepted by the client. Test results may not be received by the client as information on a logical, rational level. Any information about the self has emotional implications to an individual. Unfavorable information particularly may be threatening. Test results, then, may be reacted to emotionally. They may not be accepted as accurate, they may be rejected, they may be disbelieved, or they may be rationalized.

In presenting test results to the client, "the significant elements with which the counselor deals are the emotional attitudes of satisfaction, doubt, or fear which the test creates. It is not the

8 (1) R. H. Bixler & Virginia H. Bixler. Clinical counseling in vocational guidance. *J. clin. Psychol.*, 1945, 1, 186–196. (2) R. H. Bixler & Virginia H. Bixler. Test interpretation in vocational counseling. *Educ. psychol. Measmt.*, 1946, 6, 144–155. Reprinted in A. H. Brayfield (Ed.) *Readings in modern methods of counseling.* New York: Appleton-Century-Crofts, 1950. Pp. 184–192. (3) E. S. Bordin. *Psychological counseling.* New York: Appleton-Century-Crofts, 1955. Pp. 272–279.

factual test results but the attitudes of the client toward the test results which are important in the counseling process."[9]

The counselor, then, must be prepared to deal with emotional attitudes toward test results. If in addition to the emotional reactions to the objective results, the counselor also arouses emotional reactions toward himself by introducing his own judgments and evaluations, the situation becomes more difficult to handle and may lead to the failure of counseling or the breaking off of it by the client. The objective presentation of the results is thus important. However, more than this is necessary: The counselor must handle emotional reactions to the test results in a therapeutic manner.

The fact that the client is emotionally involved in his test results, and may react against them, leads to several suggestions for therapeutic handling of test results in counseling: (1) The client should not be abruptly faced with the test results, nor should these be presented all at once or too rapidly. There should be time for the client to absorb their meanings and implications. (2) The client should be given opportunity to express and discuss his reactions and feelings. The counselor should be alert to the client's reactions. It might be well to begin by obtaining his reaction to the test or tests in general before presenting any results. Some such question as "Well, what did you think of the tests?" might elicit some feelings and attitudes and serve to prepare the counselor for specific emotional reactions. (3) When feelings are expressed, the counselor should recognize them and handle them therapeutically. They should not be ignored or passed over. Nor should resistance to acceptance of test scores be handled by defense of the tests or of their reliability and validity, by arguments, "reasoning," persuasion, or attempts to "sell" the client on the tests. Resistance or objections must be allowed expression—accepted by the counselor as feelings and not reasoned with. Only by such therapeutic handling is the client likely to come to accept the results and integrate them into his self-concept.

[9] C. R. Rogers, *op. cit.*

This approach to test interpretation involves the active participation of the client in the process. It is not a one-sided presentation of results. There is some evidence that client participation in test interpretation is effective in counseling. Dressel and Mattson found that client participation was positively related to improved self-understanding and to greater feeling of security in choices made, although there was no relation to client satisfaction with counseling.[10] Rogers found that a self-evaluative interview was more effective than a test-centered interview with less-intelligent college students (bottom four deciles on the ACE Psychological Examination). Active participators in the self-evaluative interview increased in self-understanding more than less-active participators and more than the students in the test-centered group.[11]

However, Gustad and Tuma found no differences among different methods of test interpretation.[12] Further analysis of the data of this study indicated that methods cannot be studied apart from the personalities of the counselors.[13] The interpersonal relationships in the counseling interview are probably more important than techniques, so that the attitude of the counselor rather than specific techniques of test interpretation must be given attention.

Kamm and Wrenn found that client acceptance of test information was best when the following conditions were present: (1) the counselor and the client were completely at ease; (2) the client took a positive attitude throughout counseling; (3) the client was ready to respond on the basis of new information; (4) the information presented was related directly to the client's problem; and (5) the information presented was not in conflict with

[10] P. L. Dressel & R. W. Mattson. The effect of client participation in test interpretation. *Educ. psychol. Measmt*, 1950, **10**, 693–706.

[11] L. B. Rogers. A comparison of two kinds of test interpretation interview. *J. counsel. Psychol.*, 1954, **1**, 224–231.

[12] J. W. Gustad & A. H. Tuma. The effects of different methods of test introduction and interpretation on client learning in counseling. *J. counsel. Psychol.*, 1957, **4**, 313–317.

[13] A. H. Tuma & J. W. Gustad. The effects of client and counselor personality characteristics on client learning in counseling. *J. counsel. Psychol.*, 1957, **4**, 136–141.

the client's self-concept.[14] These conditions represent a situation where the client is not defensive or does not feel threatened. However, the client may be threatened even when the counselor attempts to create and maintain a nonthreatening situation, since the test information itself may constitute a threat. It is in these instances where it is important that the counselor be able to enter into a therapeutic relationship.

Parents and Test Results

The question arises whether test results should be communicated to parents as well as students. Test results are confidential information. They certainly should not become common knowledge by posting them on bulletin boards or listing them in the community newspaper. James H. Ricks of the Psychological Corporation provides an excellent discussion of the problem of parents and test results.[15]

In answer to the question, "should parents be told about their children's test results?" Ricks states: "Parents have the right to know whatever the school knows about the abilities, the performance, and the problems of their children. . . . Few educators will dispute [this] principle. It is in parents that the final responsibility for the upbringing and education of all children must lie. This responsibility requires access to all available information bearing on educational and vocational decisions to be made for and by the child."

This seems to be an acceptable principle. Parents make certain decisions about the child, particularly about younger children, and they should have all the information available. Wolfle suggests that "when a counselor finds a very bright child from a home that is not likely to stimulate educational ambition, it is desirable to call the family into consultation so that the situation

[14] R. B. Kamm & C. G. Wrenn. Client acceptance of self-information in counseling. *Educ. psychol. Measmt,* 1950,**10**, 32–42.

[15] J. H. Ricks. On telling parents about test results. *Test Service Bulletin,* No. 54 (December, 1959). New York: The Psychological Corporation, 1959. This discussion contains excellent material on how to interpret test scores to parents, material which applies also to presenting test results to the student himself.

can be explained and an effort made to enlist its interest and support."[16]

But what about the desires and the rights of students in this? School grades are routinely provided to parents, and teachers have conferences with parents routinely, without consulting the child. Is this same procedure appropriate for counselors in respect to test scores? Some justification might be made for this practice in regard to scores on tests administered as part of a school group testing program. But what about tests administered as part of the counseling process with an individual student? What responsibility does the counselor have to the student in this situation?

It is suggested that since the counseling relationship, including the results of tests incorporated in it, is a confidential relationship, its contents should not be discussed with others, even the student's parents, without the knowledge and permission of the student. Such a policy is necessary if adequate counseling services are to be maintained and accepted and used by the student. The securing of the student's permission to discuss test results with parents preserves the confidentiality of the relationship and manifests respect for the student. It should therefore become the accepted practice in all schools.

The Teacher and Tests

A related question is whether test results should be accessible to teachers. It is common practice to record all test results in individual folders or cumulative records which, in most cases, are accessible to any member of the school staff. Is this a desirable situation?

A study of twenty-eight Illinois schools (the schools represented in the 1959 National Defense Education Act summer institute at the University of Illinois)[17] obtained the following data (Table 2) from teachers in response to the question: What meth-

[16] D. Wolfle. Guidance and educational strategy. *Personnel Guid. J.*, 1958, **37**, 17–25.

[17] J. T. Hastings, P. J. Runkel & Dora E. Damrin. *Effects on use of tests by teachers trained in a summer institute.* Cooperative Research Project No. 702, U.S. Office of Education. Urbana, Ill.: Bureau of Educational Research, 1961 (mimeo). Appendix J, Vol. II.

ods does your school use in informing teachers of scores on standardized tests?

TABLE 2.   Practices Employed by Schools to Provide Teachers
with Information About Test Results

| Practice | Number of Schools in Which the Majority of Teachers Say That the Practice: | |
	Is Done[a]	Is Not Done
Scores are kept in the administration office, and any may look them up who wish	22	6
Scores are kept in a particular office, and the appointed person will discuss the test results with any teacher who asks	16	12
Reports of results in some form are given to the teacher *to give to the students,* and the teacher can look them over before handing them out	0	28
Copies of actual scores are given to the teacher to keep	3	25
Copies of test results in descriptive form (not actual scores) are given to the teacher to keep	0	28
Group meetings are held at which test results are explained and discussed with the teachers	2	26
Conferences are scheduled with individual teachers to discuss test results	0	28

a In the few instances where teachers were equally divided on the matter, the school was tallied in the "*is* done" column.

SOURCE: J. T. Hastings, P. J. Runkel & Dora E. Damrin. *Effects on use of tests by teachers trained in a summer institute.* Cooperative Research Project No. 702, U.S. Office of Education. Urbana, Ill.: Bureau of Educational Research, 1961 (mimeo). Appendix J, Vol. II.

The most common practice is to place some or all of the test data in the files in the central office and to make these available to any teacher who wishes to use them. The next most common practice is the more controlled method of having the data filed in a particular office and having the teacher go to an appointed person for information. Some schools employ both methods, perhaps for different types of tests.

The teachers were also asked: Do you think these methods are desirable? The results will be found in Table 3.

TABLE 3. Practices Which Teachers Believe Ought to be Employed to Provide Teachers with Information About Test Results

Practice	Number of Schools in Which the Majority of Teachers Say That the Practice:	
	Is Desirable[a]	Is Not Desirable
Scores are kept in the administration office, and any may look them up who wish	16	12
Scores are kept in a particular office, and the appointed person will discuss the test results with any teacher who asks	22	6
Reports of results in some form are given to the teacher *to give to the students,* and the teacher can look them over before handing them out	0	28
Copies of actual scores are given to the teacher to keep	5	23
Copies of test results in descriptive form (not actual scores) are given to the teacher to keep	0	28
Group meetings are held at which test results are explained and discussed with the teachers	19	9
Conferences are scheduled with individual teachers to discuss test results	5	23

a In the few instances where teachers were equally divided on the matter, the school was tallied in the "*is* desirable" column.
SOURCE: J. T. Hastings, P. J. Runkel & Dora E. Damrin. *Effects on use of tests by teachers trained in a summer institute.* Cooperative Research Project No. 702, U.S. Office of Education. Urbana, Ill.: Bureau of Educational Research, 1961 (mimeo). Appendix J, Vol. II.

It is apparent that teachers desire more explanation and discussion of test data than the schools presently provide. They also want *actual* test scores and *direct* information, not descriptive materials or access to reports given to students. It thus appears that while teachers are interested in specific scores, they also recognize the need for assistance in interpreting or understanding them.

Most teachers do not have an adequate background to interpret test scores without assistance. Tests are technical tools, and the use of test results requires training. Cook discusses what teachers should know about measurement. The following are a few of the items listed:

1. Be able to analyze a standard test in the subject and at the grade level he teaches with reference to skills, subject matter and mental processes tested, ease of administration and scoring, and the nature and adequacy of the norms provided.
2. Know the proper procedures and ethics of administering, reporting, and using teacher-made and standardized tests.
3. Know how to compute percentile ranks, percentile scores, and standard scores and interpret them with reference to equal units on the base line of the normal frequency curve, and how to convert raw scores to standard scores by either the linear or the area method. (This will involve ability to use the following statistics: median, mean, standard deviation and normal probability curve.)
4. Know how to compute and interpret coefficients of reliability and validity with an understanding of the factors inherent in the test (speed factors, length, homogeneity, difficulty, order of items, etc.), of the factors inherent in the students (fatigue, emotional state, etc.), and of the factors inherent in the situation (distraction, timing, etc.) which influence each.
5. Know how to interpret a test score with reference to the standard error of measurement.
6. Know what to anticipate regarding the extent and nature of individual and trait differences when a battery of tests is administered to a class.[18]

If teachers had the background represented by the knowledge contained in this list, then there would be no problem about making test scores available to teachers. Until they do, however —and it is doubtful that most teachers do—then it would appear to be best that actual scores on tests not be available to teachers except through someone who is qualified to assist them in understanding the scores and interpreting them correctly. In the case

[18] W. W. Cook. What teachers should know about measurement. In Edith M. Huddleston (Ed.) *The Fifteenth Yearbook of the National Council on Measurements Used in Education.* New York: The Council, 1958.

of tests administered as part of the counseling process, the stu
dent's permission should be obtained before discussing the test
with a teacher. In situations where test scores are available to
teachers directly, scores of tests used in counseling should no
be recorded in the files or cumulative records.

Summary

This chapter began with a consideration of the place of tests
in the school. The main concern, however, was with the use of
tests in the individual counseling process. Although it has often
been felt that the client-centered approach to counseling had no
place for tests, this seems to be a misconception of that approach.
The fact that tests are instruments of evaluation, while counseling
should be nonevaluative, seems to pose a dilemma. But tests
need not be used by the counselor to evaluate the client. They
may be used to assist the client in understanding and evaluating
himself. Principles involved in the selection and interpretation of
tests in a client-centered approach to counseling are stated.

Since the results of tests, even when not used by the counselor
to evaluate the client and even when presented objectively to
the client may be threatening to the client's self-concept, it is important that the counselor recognize and deal with emotional reactions of the client.

Consideration was also given to the problem of discussing test
results with parents. The problem of the access of teachers to test
scores was dealt with. It was concluded that since teachers do
not have the training or background necessary for an adequate
understanding and use of test scores, it is best to make the test
scores of their students available to them through a counselor
or other staff member who is trained in testing, and who can
help teachers understand and utilize the scores effectively.

SUGGESTED READINGS

Anderson, S. B., Katz, M. R., & Shimberg, B. *Meeting the test.* New
York: Scholastic Magazines, Inc., 1959. This is a series of fifteen
articles reprinted from *Senior Scholastic, World Week,* and *Practical English,* 1958–1959. While directed to students as test-takers,
the articles are well worth reading by teachers and counselors.

Cronbach, L. J. *Essentials of psychological testing.* (2nd ed.) New York: Harper, 1960. A comprehensive treatment of tests and testing, from individual intelligence tests to projective tests.

Goldman, L. *Using tests in counseling.* New York: Appleton-Century-Crofts, 1961. This is the only text devoted to the problems of using tests in counseling.

McLaughlin, K. F. (Ed.) *Understanding testing: purposes and interpretations for pupil development.* Washington: Government Printing Office, 1960. Originally published in *School Life* (September, 1959), these eight articles plus a glossary of terms are available in pamphlet form. They are written at an elementary level for parents and interested citizens as well as for teachers.

Remmers, H. H., Gage, N. L., & Rummel, J. F. *A practical introduction to measurement and evaluation.* New York: Harper, 1960. An elementary, brief, and concise but comprehensive treatment directed to teachers. While the emphasis is upon evaluation of classroom instruction rather than of interests or aptitudes, a teacher who has mastered the contents of this book is fairly well qualified to handle such test scores.

Rothney, J. W. M., Danielson, P. J., & Heiman, R. A. *Measurement for guidance.* New York: Harper, 1959. A highly critical introduction to testing.

Sorokin, P. A. Testomania. *Harvard educ. Rev.,* 1955, 25, 199–213. An attack on tests and testing which, although inaccurate and unfair, makes some valid points and gives cause for questioning the extent to which tests have become a part of our lives.

Super, D. E. *Appraising vocational fitness by means of tests.* New York: Harper, 1949. Deals with the problems, methods, and results of vocational testing, reviewing the values and limitations of the most widely used tests.

CHAPTER 10

OCCUPATIONAL
INFORMATION IN
COUNSELING

It is a basic tenet of American democracy that each individual has the right and should have the opportunity to choose his own occupation. There are, of course, limitations to such a choice, such as the aptitudes and abilities of the individual and the opportunities available at particular times and places. These are not necessarily undemocratic. There are other limitations which are undemocratic, including discrimination on the basis of race, creed, color, sex, or disability. These are of concern to all of us as citizens, though as counselors we must accept them, within limits, at a particular time.

There is another limitation which it is the function of the counselor to remove, insofar as possible. This is the matter of information about occupations and occupational opportunities. Freedom of choice of an occupation, within the limitations mentioned above, is not possible without knowledge of the opportunities which exist. The function of occupational information is to provide this knowledge.

Counseling includes the development in the client of an understanding of his environment as well as of himself. In many counseling situations or problems, lack of knowledge of the environment is not a factor, or at least not an important factor. This may perhaps be taken as evidence of the effectiveness of our educational process, since one of the main functions of education is the cultivation of knowledge and understanding of the environment. This is a part of the curriculum of the school, of the teaching and instructional program rather than the pupil personnel or guidance program.

In some areas, however, the standard instructional program needs supplementation. One of these places is in the area of knowledge and understanding of the world of work, or occupational information as it is usually called. The world of work is so complex that it requires special attention if young people today are to make an intelligent choice among the many occupations and jobs available.

The standard curriculum may be supplemented in two ways. One of these is the addition of courses or units of courses on occupations to the regular curriculum, or the scheduling of special classes or sessions dealing with occupational information. This method will be discussed in the chapter on group approaches. The second way in which such information is provided is in the counseling process. This chapter is concerned with the utilization of such information in the approach to vocational counseling which is developed in this book.

Before we can consider this specific topic, however, we must indicate briefly what is included in occupational information.

What Is Occupational Information?

The field of occupational information is impossible to define in a simple or succinct manner. Hoppock defines occupational information as "any and all kinds of information regarding any position, job, or occupation, providing only that the information is potentially useful to a person who is choosing an occupation."[1] It is more than knowledge of local job openings and more than knowledge of the national and local labor-market situation and trends, although it includes these. It includes knowledge of the educational and training requirements of jobs, and how and where the education and training may be obtained. It includes knowledge of the physical and temperament requirements of jobs, the nature of the work, working conditions, economic returns, and lines and opportunities of advancement.

[1] R. Hoppock. *Occupational information.* New York: McGraw-Hill, 1957. P. 6.

Hoppock has prepared a check list of facts about jobs for use in vocational counseling which in effect gives a description of the content of occupational information. It is reproduced here:

Employment Prospects

Are workers in demand today? Is employment in this occupation expected to increase or decrease?

Nature of the Work

What is the work of a typical day, week, month, year? What are all the things a worker may have to do in this occupation, the pleasant things, the unpleasant things, the big and little tasks, the important responsibilities and the less glamorous details?

Qualifications

Age. What are the upper and lower age limits for entrance and retirement?

Sex. Is this predominantly a male or female occupation? Are there reasonable opportunities for both? Is there any more active demand for one than for the other?

Height and weight. Are there any minimum or maximum requirements? What are they?

Other physical requirements. Are there any other measurable physical requirements, e.g., 20/20 vision, freedom from color-blindness, average or superior hearing, physical strength, etc.?

Aptitudes. Has there been any research on aptitudes required, e.g., minimum or maximum intelligence quotient, percentile rank on specific tests of mechanical aptitude, clerical aptitude, finger dexterity, pitch discrimination, reaction time, etc.?

Interests. Have any vocational interest tests been validated against workers in this occupation?

Tools and equipment. Must these be supplied to the worker at his own expense? What is the average cost?

Legal requirements. Is a license or certificate required? What are the requirements for getting it?

Unions

Is the closed shop common or predominant? If so, what are the requirements for entrance to the union? Initiation fees? Dues? Does the union limit the number admitted?

Discrimination

Do employers, unions, or training institutions discriminate against Negroes, Jews, others?

Preparation

Distinguish clearly between what is desirable and what is indispensable.

How much and what kind of preparation is required to meet legal requirements and employers' standards?

How long does it take? What does it cost? What does it include?

Where can one get a list of approved schools?

What kind of high school or college program should precede entrance into the professional school? What subjects must or should be chosen?

What provisions, if any, are made for apprenticeship or other training on the job?

Is experience of some kind prerequisite to entrance?

Entrance

How does one get his first job? By taking an examination? By applying to employers? By joining a union? By registering with employment agencies? By saving to acquire capital and opening his own business? How much capital is required?

Advancement

What proportion of workers advance? To what? After how long and after what additional preparation or experience?

What are the related occupations to which this may lead, if any?

Earnings

What are the most dependable average figures on earnings by week, month, or year?

What is the range of the middle 50%?

Are earnings higher or lower in certain parts of the U.S. or in certain branches of the occupation?

Number and Distribution of Workers

Are the workers evenly distributed over the U.S. in proportion to population, or concentrated in certain areas? Where? Why?

Can a person practice this occupation anywhere that he may wish to live?

Do conditions in small towns and rural areas differ materially from those in urban centers? How?

Advantages and Disadvantages

What do workers say they like best and dislike most about their jobs?

Are hours regular or irregular, long or short? Is there frequent overtime or night work? Sunday and holiday work?

What about vacations?

Is employment steady, seasonal, or irregular? Does one earn more or less with advancing age?

Is the working lifetime shorter than average, e.g., professional athletes?

Are the skills acquired transferable to other occupations?

Is the work hazardous? What about accidents, occupational diseases?

In comparison with other occupations requiring about the same level of ability and training, in what ways is this one more or less attractive?[2]

Fine attempts to integrate occupational information by viewing a job as "a job-worker situation, a dynamic relationship between what workers do and the methods and techniques of industry and technology, both operating on materials, products, and/or subject matter to produce a given end."[3] This view led him to organize occupational information as follows:

I. The Structure of the World of Work
   A. Economic: The contribution of various work processes to survival, resulting in a classification based on the flow of goods from the natural state to the consumer.
   B. Sociological: The world of work from the standpoint of social status, leading to a hierarchical classification of occupations.
   C. Methods Groups: A classification reflecting the specific knowledge and experience of workers.

II. How Workers Function
   A. Relation to Things: Physical capacities and performance aptitudes are important.
   B. Relation to Data: Mental aptitudes and special interests are significant.
   C. Relations to People: Personality and temperament are significant.

III. Job-Worker Situations as Behavior
   Human relations and human engineering factors. Job satisfactions derived from the work and the work environment.

This approach to occupations has led to the development of a new occupational classification structure by the United States

[2] (1) R. Hoppock. A check list of facts about jobs for use in vocational guidance. *Amer. Psychologist,* 1948, 3, 417–418.   (2) R. Hoppock. *Occupational information, op. cit.,* pp. 18–21.

[3] S. A. Fine. What is occupational information? *Personnel Guid. J.,* 1955, 33, 504–509.

Employment Service.[4] This functional classification is related to a new approach to and method of estimating worker requirements.[5]

Essentially, this development represents a recognition of the psychological and sociological aspects of work, referred to in the chapter on educational-vocational counseling. We still know relatively little about these aspects of work, however. But it should be apparent that if we accept the importance of the self-concept in occupational development these factors are important. The counselor must be concerned with more than the matching of aptitudes and physical capacities to the physical demands of the job. He must recognize the potentialities, or lack of potentialities, of the job to satisfy the individual's psychological needs, particularly the need for status and its importance for self-esteem. Occupational information, then, includes the psychology and sociology of work as well as the economic aspects.

Obtaining and Filing Occupational Information

It is apparent that the field of occupational information is vast in terms of the facts and items of information it includes. No counselor can have it all at his finger tips; if he did he would be a walking encyclopedia. It is not necessary that a counselor be a mine of such information. It is necessary, however, (1) that he have easily available the most commonly needed or used kinds of information, and (2) that he be familiar with the sources of occupational information, so that he can obtain data which he does not have on hand.

[4] (1) W. S. Studdiford. A functional system of occupational classification. *Occup.*, 1951, 30, 37–42. (2) W. S. Studdiford. New occupational classification structure. *Employment Secur. Rev.*, 1953, 20 (9), 36–39. (3) S. A. Fine & C. A. Heinz. The functional occupational classification structure. *Personnel Guid. J.*, 1958, 37, 180–192.

[5] (1) S. A. Fine & C. A. Heinz. The estimates of worker trait requirements for 4,000 jobs. *Personnel Guid. J.*, 1957, 36, 168–173. (2) S. A. Fine. USES occupational classifications and Minnesota Occupational Rating Scales. *J. counsel. Psychol.*, 1957, 4, 218–223. (3) Department of Labor, Bureau of Employment Security, U.S. Employment Service, *Estimates of worker trait requirements of 4,000 jobs as defined by the Dictionary of Occupational Titles.* Washington, D.C.: Government Printing Office, 1957.

To have adequate occupational information available requires that the counselor have, or build and maintain, an occupational library. An occupational library includes both books and unbound occupational materials. The books may be a part of the school library. In this case the counselor will want to maintain a card file of pertinent books. They may be maintained as a separate section of the library, or such books and references may constitute a collection which is maintained in the counseling offices.

In addition to books and permanent materials, the occupational information library should include a collection of materials containing detailed information on specific occupations. The amount of such material is voluminous. This means that what is collected and retained must be evaluated. Since much of the information is time-bound, effort is required to keep materials current. The Guidance Information Review Service Committee of the National Vocational Guidance Association conducts a continuous review of occupational literature, publishing its results under "Current Occupational Literature" in each issue of the *Vocational Guidance Quarterly,* and periodically assembling them in book form.[6]

The tremendous amount of information available requires some method of classification and filing. Several classification and filing systems have been developed, and the counselor must adopt or adapt a system to make his information accessible and usable.

In addition to books and materials which are filed, there are available current materials of a display nature, including charts and graphs. These materials are useful for posting in the library, in the waiting room, or in a reading room. Since occupational information in many instances should be used directly by clients, provision must be made for such use, whether in the library, a waiting room, or a special reading room.[7]

Detailed treatment of the sources of occupational information

[6] For example: National Vocational Guidance Association. *NVGA bibliography of current occupational literature.* (1959 ed.) Washington, D.C.: The Association, 1959.

[7] Recent discussions of filing and displaying occupational information include the following: (1) E. Diamond. Bring the occupational file out into the open. *Voc. Guid. Quart.,* 1959, **7,** 219–221. (2) Dolores Kable. Guidance bulletin boards: a new look. *Voc. Guid. Quart.,* 1958, **7,** 9–10. (3) L. Utter. Filing career information. *Voc. Guid. Quart.,* 1957, **6,** 76–77.

and its classification and filing will be found in the standard texts listed at the end of this chapter. The establishing and maintaining of an adequate library of occupational information is an important, though time-consuming, task for the counselor.

Perceptions of Students About Occupations

Psychologists are recognizing more and more the influence of an individual's perceptions on behavior. The vocational counselor must take into consideration the perceptions of students about occupations and the world of work. One of the aspects of the perception of occupations which has been studied rather extensively is the prestige values or social status rankings of various occupations.

Perhaps the earliest study was done by Counts in 1925.[8] About twenty years later Deeg and Paterson[9] and Welch[10] did similar studies. There was little change in rankings in the twenty-year period. Tuckman[11] found similar results in Canada. Kunde and Dawis[12] found that rankings by German and Philippine youth were highly correlated with the rankings obtained by Deeg and Paterson in the United States, the correlations being .91 and .94 respectively. However, there were some interesting differences in the rankings of specific occupations. Baudler and Paterson[13] and Tuckman[14] found that women's occupations were ranked in a similar hierarchy.

Canter found that rankings of occupations by social status and rankings by mean intelligence scores were highly correlated, suggesting that "when a subject is asked to rank occupations for

[8] G. S. Counts. Social status of occupations. *Sch. Rev.*, 1925, 33, 16–27.
[9] M. E. Deeg & D. G. Paterson. Changes in social status of occupations. *Occup.*, 1947, 25, 205–208.
[10] M. K. Welch. The ranking of occupations on the basis of social status. *Occup.*, 1949, 27, 237–241.
[11] J. Tuckman. Social status of occupations in Canada. *Canadian J. Psychol.*, 1947, 1, 71–74.
[12] Thelma Kunde & Rene Dawis. Comparative study of occupational prestige in three Western cultures. *Personnel Guid. J.*, 1959, 37, 350–352.
[13] L. Baudler & D. G. Paterson. Social status of women's occupations. *Occup.*, 1948, 26, 421–424.
[14] J. Tuckman. Rankings of women's occupations according to social status, earnings, and working conditions. *Occup.*, 1950, 28, 290–294.

social status, he probably focuses upon perceived intelligence requirements of the respective occupations, albeit somewhat unconsciously."[15] It may be questioned that subjects are able to estimate intelligence levels of occupations, however. Folsom and Sobolewski[16] found that rankings of occupations for social status and for estimated yearly income by high school students, were also significantly correlated. They do not report the accuracy of the estimates of income, however. Although the relative income levels may have been relatively accurately estimated, there is reason to believe that high school students have erroneous perceptions of the actual incomes. That other factors than income enter into prestige rankings of occupations seems to be clear from an examination of those rankings. But while all the factors entering into the rankings of occupations are not clear, there seems to be no question that a hierarchy of jobs or occupations exists, and that the various perceptions of this hierarchy are an important element in occupational preference and choice.

While it might be suspected that ignorance of the nature of specific occupations might enter into rankings, the providing of information by including descriptions from the *Dictionary of Occupational Titles* made little difference in rankings in a study by Tuckman.[17] There were, however, differences in a few specific occupations. Also, the variability of the rankings of a number of occupations increased when job descriptions were substituted for job titles, indicating that the definitions did influence the rankings of some individuals.

Studies of the prestige rankings of youth have sometimes been taken as support for unrealistic vocational aspirations. However, they seem to reflect the values of our culture. And while there seems to be agreement regarding the average ranks assigned to various occupations, there are no doubt wide individual differences. These differences are important in dealing with individual students.

[15] R. R. Canter. Intelligence and the social status of occupations. *Personnel Guid. J.,* 1956, **34**, 258–259.

[16] W. W. Folsom & E. L. Sobolewski. Income and social status of occupations. *Personnel Guid. J.,* 1957, **36**, 277–278.

[17] J. Tuckman. Rigidity of social status rankings of occupations. *Personnel Guid. J.,* 1958, **36**, 594–597.

In an interesting study of occupational perceptions, Grunes[18] had students make groupings of occupations which belonged together, each subject making as many groupings on differing bases as he wished. She found seven overlapping clusters of the fifty-one occupations. There seemed to be little difference between the students' perceptions of skilled and unskilled workers, but sharp differences between perceptions concerning white-collar jobs and manual work. There were some differences in perceptions when the students were classified into three social class groups. The lowest socioeconomic group saw little difference between the professions and business occupations, while the highest group made less distinction among the various mechanical and manual jobs.

Individual differences are present also in the ordering of occupational values. Dipboye and Anderson[19] had ninth- and twelfth-grade boys and girls from urban, suburban, and semi-rural areas rank the following factors in the order of their importance in choosing a job: interesting work, security, salary, advancement, working conditions, relations with others, benefits, prestige, and independence. While boys ranked them in the order given, girls gave relatively more importance to working conditions, relations with others, and advancement, and less importance to salary. Lines of agreement conformed more according to grade than to sex. College-bound boys and girls differed more than the noncollege-bound.

Singer and Stefflre found similar results in another study. High school seniors were more concerned with an "interesting job," "fame," and "profit" than adults, and less concerned with "independence."[20]

These results are of value in understanding the perceptions of high-school students regarding occupational values, but it is still important to recognize differences among individuals in the counseling situation.

[18] Willa Grunes. On perception of occupations. *Personnel Guid. J.*, 1956, 34, 276–279.

[19] W. J. Dipboye & W. F. Anderson. The ordering of occupational values by high school freshmen and seniors. *Personnel Guid. J.*, 1959, 38, 121–124.

[20] S. S. Singer & B. Stefflre. Age differences in job values and desires. *J. counsel. Psychol.*, 1954, 2, 89–91.

Counseling Use of Occupational Information

While students apparently have some general perceptions about occupations and the world of work, anyone familiar with them will recognize that these perceptions are often vague, if not erroneous, and that there is a lack of specific information. Students often have little if any idea of the wide variety and range of occupations, or of the requirements and preparation for specific occupations. Unless encouraged to survey the field and plan for the future, many students would make no preparation for entering the world of work, but would leave it to chance or to local and current opportunity. It does little good for a school to have an extensive testing program aimed at determining the abilities and potentialities of students if attention is not given to assisting students to develop opportunities for their use. The counselor working with students on problems of vocational choice and development must be able to help the student acquire a picture of the ways in which he can best utilize his assets and abilities.

There have been a number of discussions of ways of incorporating occupational information into the counseling process. Yet there have been few attempts to analyze its use in relation to systematic approaches to counseling. Brayfield in 1948 noted that, despite the "early recognition of the importance of occupational information in counseling, . . . one searches the literature almost in vain for any systematic consideration, on other than a techniques level, of the use of occupational information . . . discussions of basic principles underlying their application are conspicuous by their absence."[21] He proposed a distinction among three uses of occupational information in counseling. The first was the *informational*, where the client needs only information to make or confirm his choice. The second is *readjustive*, which applies to counselees who have set inappropriate goals. Presumably the presentation of accurate information leads the

[21] A. H. Brayfield. Putting occupational information across. *Educ. psychol. Measmt*, 1948, 8, 485–495. Reprinted in A. H. Brayfield (Ed.) *Readings in modern methods of counseling*. New York: Appleton-Century-Crofts, 1950. Pp. 212–220.

counselee to re-evaluate his choice or goal. A third use is *motivational*. This use is designed to arouse an interest in vocational planning. Christensen's four functions—the instructional, the instrumental, the distributional, and the therapeutic[22]—are somewhat similar to those of Brayfield.

Baer and Roeber expand the list of uses to include the following:

Exploratory Uses: Extensive study of occupations.
Informational Uses: Intensive study of a few occupations.
Assurance Uses: Confirmation of client's choice.
Adjustive Uses: Assisting client in gaining insight necessary to change attitudes.
Motivational Uses: Arousing interest in educational and vocational planning.
Holding Uses: Keeping client in counseling until he gains insight into real needs.
Evaluative Uses: Checking the client's knowledge and understanding.
Startle Uses: Determining client's certainty or uncertainty regarding his vocational choice.[23]

Hoppock in his recent book has brought together fifty-three quotations from forty-eight authors on the use of occupational information in counseling. He summarizes the views in a series of twenty-one statements:

The counselor encourages the client to express his own feelings about occupational information.
The counselor encourages the client to keep his plans flexible.
The counselor introduces occupational information when the client is ready for it.
The counselor suggests occupations for his client to consider.
The counselor imparts occupational information to the client.
The counselor and client together examine occupational literature.
The counselor arranges occupational tours for his clients.
The counselor refers the client to a course in occupations; if there is no such course, the counselor organizes one.
The counselor encourages tryout experiences.
The counselor refers the client to other sources of information.

[22] T. E. Christensen. Functions of occupational information in counseling. *Occup.*, 1949, **28**, 11–14.
[23] M. Baer & E. C. Roeber. *Occupational information: its nature and use.* Chicago: Science Research Associates, 1951. Pp. 425–426.

Clients with low intelligence or low reading comprehension are not referred to the library.

The counselor should be sure that his information is accurate and adequate.

The client should be informed regarding the accuracy and adequacy of the information he is considering.

The counselor helps the client to test reality by considering opportunities and requirements for employment in any contemplated occupation.

Diagnosis of the client's aptitudes precedes or accompanies the presentation of occupational information.

When two occupations are both appropriate to a client's aptitudes, occupational information is used to help the client choose between them.

The counselor does not prescribe occupational choices.

The counselor uses occupational information to arouse the interest of the client in the problem of choosing an occupation or in specific occupations or to further education.

The counselor uses occupational information as a means of holding the client for further counseling.

The counselor uses occupational information to minimize his own role and to increase the reliance of the client on himself.

The counselor uses occupational information to facilitate placement.[24]

Hoppock goes on to indicate the place of occupational information in the counseling process as he views it. He points out that it is not the purpose of counseling to recruit clients for particular occupations, nor to direct them from other occupations, nor to select students for college. It is not the purpose of counseling to substitute the judgment of the counselor for that of the client, no matter how confident the counselor is that he knows best. "What the client decides and when he decides it are his business." Thus, "occupational information is used in counseling for the same basic purpose for which the counselor uses any other kind of information. The purpose is to help the client to clarify the goal that he wants to reach and to move in the direction in which he wants to go, so long as the goal and the means of obtaining it are not injurious to others."[25]

This point of view is essentially client-centered. Let us then

[24] Hoppock, *Occupational information, op. cit.,* Chapter 10.
[25] *Ibid.,* p. 148.

turn to a consideration of the principles and problems of utilizing occupational information in a client-centered framework.

Occupational Information in Client-Centered Counseling

Client-centered counseling is a systematic approach, as has been indicated in the preceding chapters. Its methods and techniques are implementations of its philosophy and basic attitudes. As has been indicated, the belief that testing and the giving of information are inconsistent with the client-centered approach is a misconception, based on the belief that the techniques used with clients with personal-adjustment problems are the only techniques which are client-centered. Information may be given in vocational counseling without violating the basic philosophy and attitudes of client-centeredness. The questions are when and how information, specifically occupational information, is incorporated in the counseling process. The following points appear to be consistent with client-centered principles.

1. *Occupational information is introduced into the counseling process when there is a recognized need for it on the part of the client.* This need may be directly expressed, or it may be apparent to the counselor. In the latter case the counselor makes known the existence and availability of information which the client may then decide to obtain and use.

Two problems may arise in regard to this principle. First, the request for information by the client may be, or appear to be, premature. There may be lack of "readiness" for the information on the part of the client; he may not have an adequate understanding of himself or his aptitudes and abilities, or there may appear to be some personal problems present which would interfere with the use of the information. In such a situation, should the counselor withhold information? The client-centered point of view would agree with the conclusion of Baer and Roeber in this situation: "Even though the counselee seeks occupational information without adequate information concerning himself, he is in a real sense ready for information the moment he seeks it."[26] The counselor starts with the client where he is, with his immediate problem. He is sensitive, however, to the

---

[26] Baer & Roeber, *op. cit.*, p. 420.

attitudes and feelings of the client which may lead to the discussion of other problems.

A second problem which arises is the situation where the client may appear to be in need of occupational information, but does not request it or manifest any interest or desire in obtaining it. Should the counselor impose it upon a reluctant client? Again, the client-centered counselor would not. In a school situation, where the client is referred to "straighten out his thinking" in connection with an unrealistic occupational choice, this may be difficult to do and to defend. But while it is possible to impose occupational information on students in courses or groups, where it may or may not "take" (see the next chapter), it is generally agreed that counseling is a voluntary activity on the part of the client, that he has a right to decline it, and that forcing it is ineffective. On a practical basis, then, it is not justifiable to impose information on a resistant client. And doing so may also destroy the chances that the client may later recognize the need for information and seek it from the counselor.

2. *Occupational information is not used to influence or manipulate the client.* Some of the uses of occupational information which have been proposed either overtly or implicitly condone the use of such information to put pressure on the client to abandon an apparently unrealistic goal. Hale suggests the use of visual aids and sensory techniques (placement in a work situation or simulated situation) as methods of dissuading clients from unrealistic goals.[27] The counselor does not protect the client from reality, but accepts the assistance of reality. Tryout experiences may be a valuable aid in vocational choice, and the counselor may help the client obtain such experiences. But there is a line between objectively providing the client with information and reality experiences and pressuring or manipulating the client toward a predetermined outcome of the "counselor knows best" variety.

Hoppock states that client-centered counseling is inescapably limited in that "it functions solely within the client's perception of reality. If the client's perception is false, if he is dealing intellectually and emotionally with misconceptions of his own abili-

[27] P. P. Hale. Dissuasive tools in counseling. *Personnel Guid. J.*, 1953, 31, 451–452.

ties and limitations, or with mistaken conceptions of his occupational opportunities and requirements, he may make decisions and plans that are wholly unrealistic. If pertinent facts to correct the client's misconceptions are not readily accessible to him, if nothing in his experience or in his counseling suggests to him that his perception is false, he may take actions that are wholly logical in terms of his perception, but that are almost certain to lead to failure, frustration, and further maladjustment."[28] This is a misconception of client-centered counseling if it means that such counseling is not concerned with changing the client's perceptions. It is perhaps the strength of client-centered counseling that it provides a situation which is most conducive to the change of perceptions. An essential condition for such change is the absence of threat. It is important that information be presented in a nonthreatening manner and context. The information should therefore be impersonal and be presented by the counselor without judgments of its implications, thus avoiding the threat which is involved in evaluation.

In the vocational counseling process, the counselor may use his knowledge of occupational information to bring to the attention of the client possibilities which, though apparently appropriate, have not occurred to the client. He might, as Strang points out, raise such questions as "Have you considered journalism as a profession?"[29] He uses occupational information and its tools to assist the client in exploring occupational possibilities.[30] In other words, the counselor provides information where it is important and helpful to the client who is engaged in the process of choosing an occupation, and works in much the same way as described in current textbook discussions of vocational counseling. The guiding principle, however, is that the counselor avoids any evaluation or evaluative uses of information. He presents *information*, directly and as it arises from the combination of items of information, including the combination of information about the client (e.g., test scores) and about the occupational environment. But it

[28] Hoppock, *Occupational information, op. cit.,* p. 114.
[29] Ruth Strang. Use in counseling of information about vocations. *Sch. Rev.,* 1945, **53**, 526–529. Reprinted in A. H. Brayfield (Ed.) *Readings in modern methods of counseling.* New York: Appleton-Century-Crofts, 1950. Pp. 208–211.
[30] C. J. Lindley. Occupational exploration. *Occup.,* 1950, **29**, 267–270.

is always treated as objective information, not interpretations or judgments or recommendations.

It must be remembered that the client is not only free to make his own choice, but also free not to come to a decision. There is no one time when the student must make a definite choice. He may continue to explore, in counseling and outside of counseling, for a considerable period of time. It is not necessary that every senior, before his graduation, make a definite vocational choice.

The matter of influencing the client is also relevant to the problem of the counselor's role in recruitment for occupations in which there are manpower shortages (see Chapter 2). Hoppock's terse comments are a sufficient answer to this question: "The counselor is not a recruiting officer, and he should never permit himself to be one. . . . Under the seductive blandishment of the recruiters, the client needs one competent person whom he can trust to put the client's interest first and to help him think clearly about what *he* wants to do. The counselor who permits any other interest to creep into his activities has ceased to be a counselor."[31]

The use of information, or any other technique, for the purpose of directing the client to a specific goal, violates the principle of self-determination inherent in the client-centered method—and indeed most other methods—of counseling. It opens the way for the biases and prejudices of the counselor to enter the counseling situation. To achieve a purpose—his purpose—the counselor may, without being clearly aware of it, select the information he presents to favor his purpose, or slant its presentation to achieve his purpose.

3. *It would appear that the most objective way to provide occupational information, and a way which maximizes initiative and responsibility on the part of the client, is to encourage the client to obtain the information from original sources, that is, publications, employers, and persons engaged in given occupations.* This approach to the use of occupational information is rather widely recommended and practiced. In principle it seems to be a highly desirable method. It not only capitalizes on the responsibility of the client, but it avoids the subjectivity, selection, bias, and error

[31] Hoppock, *Occupational information, op. cit.*, p. 158.

which may be introduced by the counselor. It is also good pedagogy.

There are, however, some difficulties involved, so that it is not always possible or desirable to refer the client to printed sources of occupational information. The material must be suitable to the client, in terms of reading level, as well as being nontechnical in nature. Much occupational information is prepared and written for counselors and is not useful to clients. Brayfield and Reed in 1950 found that almost two-thirds of the occupational materials they studied ranked at the "very difficult" reading level (Flesch formula), and another 32 percent ranked as "difficult" reading.[32] More recently, Watson, Rundquist, and Cottle applied the Flesch and the Dale-Chall formulas to materials from the *Occupational Outlook Handbook* (1957 ed.) and to three samples of occupational information from each of twelve publishers of occupational information.[33] They found that the *Handbook*, which is widely used in high schools, is college-level reading, because of sentence length and the large number of difficult words. The authors suggest that this may not be limiting, since the *Handbook* is primarily intended for counselor use. Nevertheless, it is nontechnical, and in other respects would be, and might be expected to be, useful for client reading. Of the other materials, using the Flesch formula, none fell below the eighth and ninth grades in reading level, and few (14 percent) fell exactly at this level. Only 19 percent were at the tenth- to twelfth-grade levels. Thus two-thirds of the material was at the college, or graduate, reading level. Using the Dale-Chall formula the results were similar, with 3 percent of the materials at the seventh- to eighth-grade level, 18 percent at the ninth- to tenth-grade level, 52 percent at the eleventh- to twelfth-grade level, and 27 percent at the college level. Since many students are retarded in reading level, it is apparent that much occupational information material is not useful for many, if not most.

This suggests that counselors cannot turn clients loose in an occupational library without assistance. There are also other reasons

[32] A. H. Brayfield & P. A. Reed. How readable are occupational information booklets? *J. appl. Psychol.*, 1950, 34, 325–328.

[33] D. E. Watson, R. M. Rundquist & W. C. Cottle. What's wrong with occupational materials? *J. counsel. Psychol.*, 1959, 6, 288–291.

why this cannot be done. Much of the printed occupational information has faults or deficiencies which do not recommend its use by students or clients. These deficiencies include datedness, inaccuracies, biases, and incompleteness.

There are also items of occupational information which may not be accessible to clients, or not accessible with a reasonable amount of effort or inconvenience. Local occupational information may not be easily available, since it changes rapidly and is not permanently recorded.

All this suggests that the counselor must provide some occupational information in the counseling interview. In order to avoid the inaccuracies of a faulty memory and bias, the counselor should review the sources prior to the interview. Better yet, in some situations at least, is the suggestion of Callis, Polmantier, and Roeber that the counselor read the information aloud with the client.[34] The discussion can then supplement the printed information and clear up any misinterpretations or misunderstandings.

4. *The client's attitudes and feelings about occupations and jobs must be allowed expression and be dealt with therapeutically.* As we have indicated before, vocational choice is not entirely a rational process. There are affective or emotional elements involved. These go beyond emotional reactions to information about the client himself. Occupational information may be reacted to emotionally; the client's attitudes and feelings about the social status and prestige factors in occupations are important.

The recognition that every individual seeks and needs psychological satisfactions from his job or occupation means that vocational choice is not a simple matching of abilities and job duties. The client's interests and personality are important and must be related to the psychological and social aspects of jobs and occupations.

The concept of vocational choice as an implementation of the individual's self-concept is pertinent here. The self-concept influences the way in which one perceives the world of work and particular occupations. As Rusalem points out, "it is not what exists 'in reality' in a vocation which enters into occupational

[34] R. Callis, P. C. Polmantier & E. C. Roeber. *A casebook of counseling.* New York: Appleton-Century-Crofts, 1955. P. 197.

thinking, but what comprises the individual's personal perceptions of it."[35] Information, including occupational information, has various meanings to different individuals; it is reacted to in terms of these individual perceptions and meanings, in terms of how it relates to the individual's concept of himself. Because information has emotional significance, it is not enough that it be given, or "imparted," to a client. The client's reactions must be considered, and worked with. Again, therefore, we see that the vocational counselor must be prepared to work therapeutically with feelings and attitudes, and must be able to understand emotional reactions and attitudes to (apparently) objectively presented information. Information which is inconsistent with the self-concept may be rejected, ignored, forgotten, or not even apparently heard or registered. In such instances, intellectual reasoning or argument is not likely to be effective. A therapeutic counseling approach will be more effective.

The operation of emotional factors in occupational choice is sometimes subtle and not clear to the counselor, or even to the client himself. As Hoppock notes, "because of the difficulty, sometimes perhaps the impossibility, of bringing all emotional needs and desires to the conscious intellectual level, the client will sometimes make what is for him a wise choice, although it may appear unwise to everyone, including himself. Strong feelings are sometimes a better guide to action than strong intellects."[36]

Summary

Freedom of choice of an occupation requires that the individual have adequate information about the various possible alternatives. It is the purpose of occupational information to provide sources of such information. While occupational information should be included in the instructional programs of the school, this is not sufficient. It is necessary that the counselor make available to or assist the client in obtaining the specific occupational information which he needs.

[35] H. Rusalem. New insights on the role of occupational information in counseling. *J. counsel. Psychol.*, 1954, **1**, 84–88. Reprinted in H. B. McDaniel, *et al.* (Eds.) *Readings in guidance.* New York: Holt, 1959. Pp. 318–323.

[36] Hoppock, *Occupational information, op. cit.,* p. 160.

If the choice of an occupation is an implementation of the self-concept, it should be apparent that information about the world of work has psychological implications. An important aspect of jobs or occupations is the relation of the work and the work situation to the personality and psychological needs of the individual. However, the psychological and sociological aspects of work are not adequately known; we have much information about the physical demands of jobs, but little about the personality requirements.

The counselor, in his use of occupational information, must recognize that it is not always perceived objectively by the client; his perceptions are influenced by his attitudes and feelings about work in general and specific kinds of work. It is therefore necessary for the counselor to be alert to affective reactions to occupational information, and when they occur to handle them therapeutically. It goes without saying that in vocational counseling the counselor does not use occupational information to attempt to direct the client into a particular field of work, but that he uses it when the client evidences a need and desire for such information in his exploration and consideration of various occupational choices. The principles of using occupational information in client-centered counseling were discussed.

SUGGESTED READINGS

Baer, M. F., & Roeber, E. C. *Occupational information: its nature and use.* (2nd ed.) Chicago: Science Research Associates, 1958. A revision of a standard text in occupational information. It does not, however, deal as extensively with the use of occupational information in the counseling process as did the first edition.

Hoppock, R. *Occupational information.* New York: McGraw-Hill, 1957. While not as comprehensive or as detailed and complete as Baer and Roeber or Shartle, Hoppock's book emphasizes the counseling use more than either of the others.

Norris, Willa, Zeran, F. R., & Hatch, R. N. *The information service in guidance: occupational, educational, social.* Chicago: Rand McNally, 1960. A new text in occupational information which emphasizes the place of information in the counseling and guidance program.

Shartle, C. L. *Occupational information.* (3rd ed.) Englewood Cliffs, N.J.: Prentice-Hall, 1959. One of the standard texts in the field, but less oriented to high school counseling than Baer and Roeber.

Thomas, L. *The occupational structure and education.* Englewood Cliffs, N.J.: Prentice-Hall, 1956. This is an excellent source of sociocultural economic information, important in understanding our occupational structure. It discusses the influence of educational practices upon this structure.

United States Department of Labor, Bureau of Labor Statistics. *Occupational outlook handbook.* Rev. Bull. No. 1255. Washington, D.C.: Government Printing Office, 1959. Summary reports on over 600 occupations and 30 major industries, including pertinent facts about the job as well as trends and outlook.

United States Department of Labor, Bureau of Labor Statistics. *Occupational Outlook Quarterly.* Washington, D.C.: Government Printing Office. This is a quarterly publication which began publication in 1957, intended to supplement the *Occupational outlook handbook* by keeping information on a current level.

CHAPTER 11

GROUP ACTIVITIES
IN GUIDANCE

It seems to be generally agreed that individual counseling is the core or most essential aspect of a guidance program. Other activities, such as the teacher's guidance activities, the counselor's consultations with teachers, and group activities are considered supplementary or supportive.

Hoppock recently has protested what he feels is a neglect or underestimating of group procedures. He suggests that "group guidance, not individual counseling, is the one indispensable part of the guidance process," and feels that "dollar for dollar of investment, and hour for hour of counselor time, we can be of more service to students, relieve more individual suffering, contribute more to individual success and satisfaction by means of group guidance than by means of individual counseling."[1] Most students, according to Hoppock, do not need the confidential, private relationship of individual counseling. Rather, many need some of the things which can be obtained from group counseling, such as the knowledge that a student is not alone in facing his problem and of how he is seen by others in comparison to how he sees himself.

Super asks and answers the question

. . . is it at all likely that group guidance can meet the needs of the great majority of students and adults, leaving individual counseling for special cases only? I think the answer to this question must be in

[1] R. Hoppock. Current concepts and status of group procedures in secondary schools. Presented at the National Defense Education Act Summer Guidance Institute, University of Missouri, Columbia, Mo., June 29, 1959.

the negative, for while group methods can do a great deal of preventive work, and can even do a great deal of creative work, I think it will always be true that most people can benefit from opportunities to discuss their attitudes, aspirations, and plans with a sympathetic listener who has special skill in clarifying issues and who has a perspective on problems and opportunities such as come only with professional training and experience. A good program of group guidance services should forestall the development of some problems, should assist in the growth of better integrated personalities, improve personal, social, and occupational orientation, and finally should render people better able to make effective use of personal and vocational counseling services when and as they are needed.[2]

While Hoppock admits that we do not have sufficient evidence for abandoning individual counseling for group counseling, we have some evidence of its value, and perhaps we do not have any more evidence of the value of individual counseling. He points out that in most schools counselors have insufficient time to do adequate individual counseling, and that they are unable to see every student individually, except perhaps for a few minutes a year.

Most people would not agree with Hoppock to the extent of deemphasizing individual counseling. We need more, not less, of such counseling, for more students. There are many kinds of problems which many students cannot or will not discuss in groups. On the other hand, there are some aspects of educational-vocational counseling that can be handled more economically, and perhaps as effectively, in groups than in individual interviews. The purpose of this chapter is to suggest some of these aspects and ways in which they can be provided in the school.

Group guidance includes a wide variety of activities, making it difficult to formulate a definition. Often it is nothing more than the giving of occupational information to groups of students. Usually it is limited to this activity and instruction in occupational information. It includes instruction consisting of units in various

[2] D. E. Super. Group techniques in the guidance program. *Educ. psychol. Measmt,* 1949, 9, 496–510. Reprinted in G. F. Farwell & H. J. Peters (Eds.) *Guidance readings for counselors.* Chicago: Rand McNally, 1960. Pp. 345–361. Also reprinted in H. B. McDaniel, *et al. Readings in guidance.* New York: Holt, 1959. Pp. 338–346.

standard subject-matter courses and separate courses in occupational information. But it does and should refer to more than this. It also includes group counseling, where small, informal groups of students meet to work on specific problems of vocational choice or more general problems of personal and social adjustment. This chapter will consider all these aspects of group guidance. It will not, however, include discussion of other group experiences which have guidance aspects, such as student participation in school administration, student government, the school assembly, school clubs, career conferences, and home-room activities.

Group Vocational Activities in the Elementary School

Vocational choice does not occur until high school or later. But the preparation for such choice begins much earlier. The process of vocational development may be said to begin almost at birth. The child's personality and interests, which influence later vocational choices, begin their development at this time.[3] There has been recognition of the responsibility of the schools for assisting the child in understanding or clarifying his conceptions of his abilities, aptitudes, and interests, as well as in facing and solving his personal and emotional problems. To be sure, not enough service has been provided in these areas. Such counseling is usually left to the teacher, with inadequate services being provided by trained counselors. There appears to be an attitude that, while trained counselors are necessary at the secondary school level, they are not essential in the elementary school. This is sometimes justified on the basis that vocational counseling is not appropriate at this level, so counselors are not needed. Teachers are assumed to be able to handle such counseling as is necessary, with some consultation with specialists and referral of severe problem children to a psychological or psychiatric clinic. This approach, minimizing the need for and importance of professional counseling services at the younger ages, is inconsistent with our knowledge concerning the development of personality

[3] (1) Anne Roe. Early determinants of vocational choice. *J. counsel. Psychol.*, 1957, 4, 212–217. (2) Leona E. Tyler. The relationship of interests to abilities and reputation among first grade children. *Educ. psychol. Measmt*, 1951, 11, 255–264.

problems and disturbances. The genesis of such problems usually is in early childhood, and more attention to disturbed and maladjusted children at this time would reduce the need for special counseling services later, when in some cases little can be done because it is too late.

Be that as it may, there is at least recognition of the fact that personality problems exist in elementary-school children. But when it comes to vocational development, there appears to be a neglect which seems to be the result of a failure to recognize the importance of this period in the process of vocational choice. Since no specific choices are required at this time, it is assumed that vocational counseling is not needed, and vocational counselors are thus not necessary. Perhaps the identification of counseling with, or limiting it to, vocational counseling, is a basic reason why it is felt that counseling services are not necessary in elementary schools.

But while vocational choices are not being made, vocational preferences are being developed. The child is growing up in a world in which work is a central interest, and he is surrounded by a confusion of different jobs and attitudes toward work and occupations. Children need help in facing this world of work, and in developing a realistic picture of its opportunities and possibilities. That they are interested in work has been shown. Bennett points out that children's responses to the question "I'd like to know what I'm going to be when I grow up" indicated that about 40 percent were concerned about this question from the fourth to eighth grades.[4] Children develop a spontaneous interest in occupations between the ages of 5 and 10 years.

The neglect of formal attention to this area does not mean that nothing is happening. The child does develop perceptions and feelings about jobs and work. But these are haphazard and are influenced by the unwitting examples and attitudes of those around him, including his teachers, and by incidental references in textbooks. Some children do not know what their fathers do for a living; others know little beyond the job title. Many have negative attitudes toward the jobs held by their parents, derived from the parents' attitudes. Some of the negative attitudes, in-

[4] Margaret Bennett. *Guidance in groups.* New York: McGraw-Hill, 1955. P. 246.

cluding shame, arise as a result of attitudes expressed by other children and teachers in school.

Lifton found that the knowledge of teachers about occupations was inversely related to the distribution of jobs, with knowledge of the professions being greatest.[5] A survey of textbooks indicated that in the primary grades there was an emphasis on service occupations in references to work, with a rapid shift in the upper grades to the professions. Thus a distorted picture of the world of work is received. With the emphasis on professions, is it any wonder that students, when asked what they want to do, appear to be unrealistic in their choice of professional jobs?

Lifton found, in a search for available books for use in elementary schools, that there is a gap between the early primary grades and junior high school, with little at the third- to sixth-grade levels. There is thus a need for materials, and for activities, at the elementary-school level which will acquaint students with the occupational environment. Some materials are beginning to be made available. Lifton has contributed a series of materials in the form of a game to one of the encyclopedias for children.[6] A social-studies series on the third-grade level is available.[7] Lifton has also developed a booklet for use in the third to fifth grades.[8] The teacher's manual contains a list of books useful to teachers.

Teachers must utilize these materials, however. Lifton's manual contains suggestions for the incorporation of his booklet in classroom teaching. At the elementary-school level such materials are perhaps best integrated into the curriculum as units, or distributed throughout the curriculum. The latter is more difficult, though perhaps more effective. It requires that the teacher keep in mind the importance of vocational information and capitalize upon opportunities to utilize it. Other activities, such as visits to ob-

---

[5] W. M. Lifton. Vocational guidance in the elementary school. *Voc. Guid. Quart.*, 1960, 8, 79–81.

[6] W. M. Lifton. Ask yourself. In *Our wonderful world.* (18 vols.) Chicago: Spencer Press, 1957.

[7] Alta McIntire & Wilhelmina Hill. *Working together.* Chicago: Felton Publishing Company, 1954.

[8] (1) W. M. Lifton. *What could I be?* Chicago: Science Research Associates, 1960. (2) W. M. Lifton. *Introducing the world of work to children. Teacher's manual for "What could I be?"* Chicago: Science Research Associates, 1960.

serve people at work, talks by representatives of occupations, and films and other audio-visual aids are useful, though they have been criticized as superficial and sometimes misleading.

A recent report illustrates the incorporation of a unit on occupations for a fourth grade. The reports prepared by the children indicated that they learned many new things about work, including the nature of their fathers' work, and the importance of various occupations. They developed respect for other people and the work they do. It was felt they became more realistic about their future goals. The author summarizes as follows: "This unit may not have drastically changed the vocational plans of these fourth graders. It did, however, make them more aware of their future and how much planning it entails. It helped the children to work toward the goals of all good teaching: critical thinking, respect, and understanding."[9]

Hoppock lists the following purposes in presenting occupational information to elementary school children:

1. To increase the child's feeling of security in the world.
2. To encourage the natural curiosity of young children.
3. To extend the occupational horizons of the child.
4. To encourage wholesome attitudes toward all useful work.
5. To begin developing a desirable approach to the process of occupational choice.
6. To help students who are dropping out of school and going to work.
7. To help students who face a choice between different high schools or high school programs.
8. To show children who really need money how they can get it. . . .[10]

The goal of the elementary school is not the development of occupational choices by students. In fact, it should attempt to avoid the premature selection of an occupation, which, although based

[9] Janet Kaye. Fourth graders meet up with occupations. *Voc. Guid. Quart.*, 1960, 8, 150–152. Two other recent discussions of occupational information in elementary grades are: (1) L. A. Grell. How much occupational information in the elementary school? *Voc. Guid. Quart.*, 1960, 9, 48–53. (2) Goldie Kaback. Occupational information in elementary education. *Voc. Guid. Quart.*, 1960, 9, 55–59.

[10] R. Hoppock. *Occupational information.* New York: McGraw-Hill, 1957.

on inadequate foundations, may become involved with the self-concept and be tenaciously held and defended against desirable change. The function of the elementary school is to provide the student with some knowledge and understanding of the occupational environment and with some beginning understanding of his own aptitudes and interests, as a background and preparation for later stages of vocational development.

The Junior High School

While vocational counseling as such, involving individual counseling, is not a part of the primary school, it should be available at the upper elementary level, or the junior high school (seventh to ninth grades). Almost a third of the students leave school at the end of the eighth grade; in some schools and communities a larger proportion leave. Those who continue are faced with choices of a high-school curriculum. While group guidance can be of assistance, many of these students still need individual counseling by trained counselors, and should not be dependent entirely upon teachers for such assistance.

Eighth graders have different problems and require different methods and materials. The Educational Testing Service became interested in the needs of students at this level, in response to the expressed interest of educators in materials for assisting students about to enter high school. The Educational Testing Service Guidance Inquiry was initiated to develop materials for the use of classroom teachers without specialized training or experience in guidance. The resulting materials have been published for use in the eighth or ninth grades.[11] They are for use as a unit comprising about thirty classroom periods, focusing on self-appraisal for educational and vocational planning. The materials were tried out and evaluated by ten teachers in seven different communities with eighth- and ninth-grade students. The teachers' and students' responses were favorable. However, the materials are still in an experimental stage and have not been adequately evaluated.

Gribbons reports an evaluation of the use of this unit by seven

[11] M. R. Katz. *You: today and tomorrow.* (2nd exper. ed.) Princeton, N.J.: Educational Testing Service, 1958.

teachers in five communities.[12] The materials were used in two social-studies classes, an English class, a foreign language class, and three guidance classes, and occupied from twenty-six to forty-two class meetings over periods of from six to fourteen weeks. Samples of students from each class were interviewed, before and after the unit was presented, and each student was rated on six areas of vocational and educational planning. These areas were (1) awareness of factors to consider in curriculum choice; (2) awareness of factors to consider in occupational choice; (3) awareness of abilities and inadequacies in relation to making curriculum and occupational choices; (4) awareness of interests and their relation to occupational choice; (5) awareness of values and their relation to occupational choice; and (6) independence of choice. Students made significant gains in all of these areas. Students in classes conducted by teachers with training in guidance did not gain more than students in classes conducted by teachers with no training in guidance. The study indicated that before the course the students were not sufficiently advanced in vocational thinking to make educational and vocational decisions; the author suggests that "perhaps schools should be organized to permit postponement of curriculum choices until the end of the ninth grade. This extra time, accompanied by individual and group guidance and other curricular experiences, might well result in far fewer unwise educational and vocational choices."

The Secondary School

The Educational Testing Service publication was discussed above because it appears to be most appropriate just before the student enters high school. Where a junior high school is part of the educational system, it might perhaps best be used in the ninth grade.

At the high school level a recently developed device for use with groups is "Your Educational Plans."[13] While it is more like

[12] W. D. Gribbons. Evaluation of an eighth grade group guidance program. *Personnel Guid. J.*, 1960, 38, 740–745.
[13] S. A. Stouffer. *Your educational plans.* Chicago: Science Research Associates, 1959.

a group test than a teaching unit, it may be useful both to the student and to the counselor as a basis for individual counseling. It is organized as a self-report questionnaire centering upon the student's educational and vocational aspirations, self-rated school record, family status and characteristics, educational level of parents and best friend, and attitudes of parents and the best friend toward the student's plans for college training. With scores on an intelligence or achievement test, the materials are sent to Science Research Associates for scoring on twenty-two variables. The results help the counselor in identifying students in need of counseling because of unrealistic plans for attending college, or who perhaps should be going to college but are not planning to go. This is a narrow view of vocational choice and counseling. The instrument has not been used sufficiently to evaluate its worth. It would appear to be useful in some cases, but it is questionable whether it should be used with all students—as is apparently expected by the author.

Group instruction in occupational information has long been provided in secondary schools, either as part of standard subjects or, increasingly, as a course organized specifically for the purpose.

Hoppock gives several reasons for teaching occupational information in groups: it saves time; it provides a background of related information that contributes to individual counseling; it gives the counselor an opportunity to know his clients better; it focuses collective judgment on common problems; it provides some assurance that the problem cases will not monopolize the counselor's time; it can be provided without increasing the school budget; it may permit a part-time counselor to spend full time on guidance, and thus to become more competent (since the counselor is relieved of teaching another subject); it keeps the counselor up to date on occupational information; and counselors recognize the need for such a course.[14] Hoppock assumes that a qualified counselor will teach the course; very often the person teaching it has no special training or preparation in the field. The nature of the course and the way in which it is taught also influence its value and outcomes.

[14] Hoppock, *Occupational information, op. cit.,* pp. 176–178.

Brayfield distinguishes two approaches to such courses.[15] The first he designates as the *standard approach*. Its point of view is that the acquisition of information about the world of work is the starting place for vocational counseling, and its subject matter is occupational information per se. Its methodology is classroom and textbook centered. Workbooks and careers booklets are frequently used. The assumptions, perhaps implicit, are the following: (1) The individual who has been formally exposed to occupational information will make more appropriate vocational choices than those not exposed. (2) The individual will make specific application of the content to his own situation with a minimum of individual assistance. (3) The individual completing such a course will develop attitudes and skills which will carry over as new problems of vocational adjustment arise.

Brayfield refers to the other major approach as the *sociopsychological* or *self-appraisal and careers* approach. The basic point of view is that the acquisition of knowledge about the self is the proper starting point for vocational planning. The subject matter is a balance between psychological study of the individual and of occupational information. Emphasis is placed upon both classroom and community. The providing of individual counseling is an essential part of this approach. Its assumption, in addition to assumptions one and three of the standard approach, is that the number of individuals making appropriate choices will increase as individual counseling is provided as a supplement.

The second approach is becoming recognized as the preferred one, although in many schools occupational information continues to be taught as a course separated from counseling. The standard or traditional course might be designated as the "shotgun" approach, where information is thrown out in hope that some of it will strike a target, that is, that some of the students will be in need of it, prepared to use it, and receptive. While it may seem to be economical to broadcast information in this way, it may be wasteful if it is useful to only a very few of the students. Unlike the elementary-school level, where a broad knowledge of the

[15] A. H. Brayfield. Putting occupational information across. *Educ. psychol. Measmt.*, 1948, **8**, 485–495. Reprinted in A. H. Brayfield (Ed.) *Readings in modern methods of counseling.* New York: Appleton-Century-Crofts, 1950. Pp. 212–220.

basic aspects of the world of work is needed, the secondary-school student needs more specific information and needs to relate that information to himself—his interests and aptitudes.

Several studies of the outcome of courses in occupations have been made. Hoppock's summary of the conclusions of research in the area includes the following:

Courses in occupations measurably increased the subsequent job satisfaction and earning power of the students who went to work and the academic success of the students who went to college.

Courses in occupations measurably increased the range of occupations in which students were interested, their interest in specific occupations, and reduced the amount of [un]employment.

Courses in occupations increased the ability of students to answer questions about occupations by as little as 0 and by as much as 217 percent.

Courses in occupations, with emphasis upon local opportunities for employment, brought occupational choices into closer harmony with employment opportunity but failed to bring them in closer harmony with measured abilities. Psychological testing plus individual counseling brought occupational choices into closer harmony with the measured abilities of the students but failed to bring them into closer harmony with employment opportunity.[16]

It is difficult to evaluate the effects of courses because of the differing methods, content, and contexts of the teaching. Most studies indicate that there is acquisition of occupational information, though this did not occur in the study of Kefauver and Hand; in this study a course given in the ninth grade produced practically no measurable results as evaluated in the tenth, eleventh, and twelfth grades.[17] But is increase in general occupational information a desirable or sufficient goal?

Other studies have shown more pertinent results, however. Cuony and Hoppock report on a follow-up of students who had taken a course in Job Finding and Job Orientation as seniors.[18] Compared to a group who had not taken the course they were

[16] Hoppock, *Occupational information, op. cit.,* pp. 326–327.

[17] G. N. Kefauver & H. C. Hand. *Appraising guidance in secondary schools.* New York: Macmillan, 1941.

[18] E. R. Cuony & R. Hoppock. Job course pays off again. *Personnel Guid. J.,* 1957, **36**, 116–117.

better satisfied with their jobs, had greater combined annual earnings, and had experienced less unemployment five years after graduation. The students in both groups had individual counseling services available. The students in the course asked for and received more counseling than those in the control group.[19] This is one of the few studies involving follow-up and ultimate criteria. Sinick and Hoppock have reviewed the recent research.[20]

Two earlier studies are of particular significance because they include an evaluation of individual counseling in comparison with group guidance, although they were conducted with college freshmen. Stone compared the effects of one year of college alone, a year plus a course in vocational orientation, a year plus individual counseling, and a year of college plus the orientation course plus individual counseling.[21] Criteria were appropriateness of occupational choices (as judged by counselors) and social adjustment. The first three groups showed no improvement in appropriateness of vocational choices; in fact, the percentages of poor occupational choices increased. But the fourth group, with the course and individual counseling, showed a reduced percentage of poor occupational choices and improved in social adjustment. The group with the course had more occupational information and made somewhat more realistic choices in terms of levels of occupations, although they were not rated as more appropriate.

Hoyt found that thirty-four hours of counselor time in group sessions with twenty-five students achieved as good results as thirty-nine hours spent in the individual counseling of fourteen students, all college freshmen.[22] The criteria were improvement in realism of vocational choices, certainty of vocational choice, and satisfaction with the vocational choice.

More recently Hewer reported a study similar in some respects

[19] E. R. Cuony & R. Hoppock. Job course pays off. *Personnel Guid. J.,* 1954, 32, 389–391.

[20] D. Sinick & R. Hoppock. Research on the teaching of occupations: 1956–1958. *Personnel Guid. J.,* 1959, 38, 150–155.

[21] C. H. Stone. Are vocational information courses worth their salt? *Educ. psychol. Measmt,* 1948, 8, 161–181.

[22] D. P. Hoyt. An evaluation of group and individual programs in vocational guidance. *J. appl. Psychol.,* 1955, 39, 26–30.

to the two referred to above.[23] She compared freshman students in a class designed to assist students in the choice of a vocation with students who applied for the course but were assigned to individual counseling. She found no differences in satisfaction with vocational choice, certainty of choice, and realism of choice, as judged by four counselors. However, judgments of realism of vocational choice were not very reliable.

This study is of interest because of the procedure used in the class. The groups were small, consisting of eight students. In addition to lectures, the case-study or case-conference method was used. Each student was the object of discussion by the group for one class session. The group did not know which one of them was being discussed. The leader supplied information about the student, including the results of a battery of tests. In later classes, as the result of the demands of the group, the students being discussed identified themselves and contributed information.[24] This case-conference method has been utilized in high schools.[25]

Group activities have been used for many purposes in relation to guidance. We have been concerned here with their use in direct relationship to the vocational counseling process. Such use varies from precounseling orientation[26] and the presenting of occupational information in a formal classroom situation to vocational counseling in small groups. The values of these approaches vary. Research indicates that usually there are positive results. Most counselors feel that group activities supplement or facilitate individual counseling. It is possible that in many instances group activities can do more than this. There are many normal, well-adjusted students who may need nothing more than the aid provided by a formal course in occupations to make an adequate

[23] Vivian H. Hewer. Group counseling, individual counseling, and a college class in vocations. *Personnel Guid. J.*, 1959, 37, 660–665.

[24] T. Volsky & Vivian H. Hewer. A program of group counseling. *J. counsel. Psychol.*, 1960, 7, 71–73.

[25] G. S. Du Bato. Case conference on occupations. *Voc. Guid. Quart.*, 1959, 7, 257–259.

[26] (1) M. D. Salinger. Is precounseling orientation worth while? *Voc. Guid. Quart.*, 1957, 5, 148–150. (2) H. Richardson & H. Borow. Evaluation of a technique of group orientation for vocational counseling. *Educ. psychol. Measmt*, 1952, 12, 587–597.

occupational choice and vocational plans. There are no doubt others who need additional help, such as can be given in a smaller group counseling situation, utilizing the case-conference approach or a similar method. These group approaches thus can help many students who do not require individual counseling, who probably would not request individual counseling, and who might not be offered the opportunity for individual counseling by a busy, over-loaded counselor. But individual counseling should be available for those students who desire and need it.

Group Counseling for Personal Adjustment

As in the vocational area, group approaches in the personal-social area range in variety from instruction in the regular cur-riculum to intensive group counseling in small groups, from the dispensing of information to attempts to develop or change atti-tudes or personality and to improve interpersonal relationships. Included are units and courses in life problems, life adjustment, and human relations. The goals of personal, social, and emotional maturity and adjustment are part of the goals of the curriculum, as well as of student personnel services. We shall limit ourselves here to ways in which the curriculum may be supplemented by the activities of guidance personnel, including teachers func-tioning in guidance.[27]

We use the term *group counseling* in this chapter to designate a particular kind of group activity. It is distinguished from in-struction in that the major concern of the latter is the imparting of information. Counseling is concerned with attitudes and feelings. Thus we have used the term *counseling* in discussing the assisting of a student in the area of vocational choice, either by indi-vidual or group methods, because of the influence of the stu-dent's feelings and attitudes about himself and jobs in the process of vocational choice. In group activities in the vocational area, there is a continuum from activities concerned only with giving

[27] A description of a program for training teachers to introduce the appli-cation of principles of human relations into the curriculum will be found in R. H. Ojeman. The human relations program at the State University of Iowa. *Personnel Guid. J.*, 1958, **37**, 199–206. Reprinted in J. Samler (Ed.) *Basic approaches to mental health in the schools*. Washington, D.C.: American Personnel and Guidance Association, 1959.

information to those concerned with the attitudes and feelings of the student. There are some activities which are concerned with both.

The same situation exists in the personal-social area. Our concern here is with counseling, with group activities which involve attitudes and feelings of students about themselves and others, rather than with imparting information to groups. The term *group therapy* is one which is sometimes used to refer to group methods of dealing with attitude and personality problems. There is no clear line which can be drawn between group counseling and group therapy. For our purposes we use *group counseling* to refer to work with the more or less normal individual on a relatively short-term basis, such as a school semester. *Group therapy* refers to work with more seriously disturbed individuals, usually over a longer period of time. There is no basic difference between the two, however, with no separate sets of methods or techniques being used in each situation.

Group counseling and group psychotherapy have been relatively recent developments. The group approach is being widely used at present, but it has only recently been tried in the schools. This is due in large measure to the lack of preparation in its use on the part of school counselors. It appears to be an approach particularly suited to adolescents, to whom peer reactions and attitudes are so important, and who are often so uncertain about what these attitudes and values are.

Because it is little used in schools, there are few reports of group counseling activities in the area of personal adjustment. The few reports which have been made deal with its use with special groups. Axline reports an experience with thirty-seven second graders who were poor readers or nonreaders, in which nondirective group and play therapy was utilized, with no specific remedial reading instruction.[28] At the end of a semester many of the children had made large gains in reading scores. Bills found similar results using play therapy with a group of eight third graders with reading retardation.[29] These children were emo-

[28] Virginia M. Axline. Nondirective therapy for poor readers. *J. consult. Psychol.*, 1947, 11, 61–69.

[29] R. E. Bills. Nondirective play therapy with retarded readers. *J. consult. Psychol.*, 1950, 14, 140–149.

tionally maladjusted. In another study, Bills found that nondirective play therapy did not result in improvement in reading in adjusted retarded readers, however, suggesting that where reading retardation is associated with maladjustment it may be improved by group therapy.[30]

Caplan utilized group counseling with 17 boys, 12 to 15 years of age, with records of long-term, frequent conflict with school authority, who had been referred by teachers as unruly, antisocial, unteachable, or incorrigible. Counseling lasted for a semester on a weekly basis. Compared to a control group, more of the boys having group counseling showed greater congruence between the self-concept and the ideal self-concept. The counseled boys also showed improvement in citizenship classes.[31]

Driver and Froelich found improvement in interpersonal relations and in accuracy of self-knowledge, respectively, with group counseling.[32] Froelich found no difference between those counseled individually and those provided with group counseling. Group counseling has been used with underachievers with favorable results; these studies will be reported later (Chapter 14). It may be mentioned here that improvement in personal aspects of adjustment occurred in some of these studies.

Up to this point, we have been dealing with group counseling by professional counselors. Intensive, formal group counseling or group therapy requires an adequately trained counselor. But in some respects every class constitutes an opportunity for the development of some aspects of group counseling. It was stressed in Chapter 6 that the teacher should maintain a therapeutic class atmosphere. It is not necessary that the teacher be trained in group therapy to do this, but it is necessary that the teacher have a good understanding of the basic principles of good human relationships. Programs of training discussed in a recent publication of the American Personnel and Guidance Association are

[30] R. E. Bills. Play therapy with well-adjusted retarded readers. *J. consult Psychol.*, 1950, 14, 246–249.

[31] S. W. Caplan. The effect of group counseling on junior high school boys' concepts of themselves in school. *J. counsel. Psychol.*, 1957, 4, 124–128.

[32] (1) Helen I. Driver. Small group discussion. *Personnel Guid. J.*, 1952, 30, 173–175. (2) C. P. Froelich. Must counseling be individual? *Educ. psychol. Measmt*, 1958, 18, 681–689.

providing such training for many teachers.[33] Two of the reports in this publication are particularly pertinent to group activities of teachers trained in the principles of human relations.

The Merrill Palmer School in Detroit offers a two-semester Seminar in Interpersonal Relations for teachers, counselors, and principals. The purpose of the seminar is "to help the individual teacher express and explore the values, meanings, and dynamics of personal and professional experience, to achieve self-awareness, and to develop sensitive, understanding, responsive attitudes in relations with children and parents." These attitudes are expressed in both individual and group relationships. Teachers in the seminar work with students in groups on a regular basis of one or two periods a week, sometimes more. Varying degrees of structure are used, and sometimes materials such as drawings or student journals are part of the group activity. Usually, however, the meetings consist of free discussions, particularly in the upper grades, though "it was only after several sessions that teachers were able to convince groups that every expression would be held in the strictest confidence."[34]

Another program of training, which was conducted as a project, is reported by Seeley. Selected teachers were trained for a year in human relations. Part of the training consisted in conducting "Human Relations Classes" in schools. These were designed "to afford 'normal' children in everyday classrooms a regular exposure to . . . 'free' discussion . . . to aid the child to understand himself, his peers, and the rest of the world in which he lived, at least in its most immediate bearing on his self-definition and his most general and profound feelings." They were based on "the belief that people (in this case, children) really free (externally) to talk about anything will finally talk about everything, but also, in the curious circling way such communication has, will concentrate

[33] J. Samler (Ed.) *Basic approaches to mental health in the schools.* Washington, D.C.: American Personnel and Guidance Association, 1959.

[34] C. E. Moustakas. A human relations seminar at the Merrill Palmer School. *Personnel Guid. J.*, 1959, **37**, 342–349. Reprinted in J. Samler (Ed.), *op. cit.* For a more detailed discussion of the program, see (1) C. E. Moustakas. *The teacher and the child.* New York: McGraw-Hill, 1950, and (2) C. E. Moustakas. *The alive and growing teacher.* New York: Philosophical Library, 1959.

on those matters that have for them vital psychodynamic import."[35] The sessions were conducted weekly, by a teacher (or project staff member) from outside the school, in several classes from the fourth to twelfth grades. The description of the group discussions is fascinating. The reactions of some of the teachers conducting the groups are also interesting—surprise at the lack of problems of discipline or control, at the emotional involvement of the children, at their active participation, at the content of their discussions. Some teachers were uncomfortable about the lack of logical problem-solving—the "waste of time" in coming to a point, taking hours for what a good teacher could tell them in ten minutes, the jumping about from topic to topic, and leaving things unfinished.

Seeley denies that this was therapy. But it is clear that it was group counseling, if not group therapy. Those conducting the groups were trained, at least to some extent. It is important to recognize that in both the projects discussed, the teachers were trained. Yet they were not trained as counselors or as therapists. The two accounts open up the enormous potential of teachers with training, such as that given in these programs, to work with groups of children on their personal-social-emotional problems. The response obtained clearly indicates the interest of students in such an experience. While in the project by Seeley the group leaders were from outside the school, in the Detroit program they are not. There is often, as suggested by Moustakas, some difficulty in the children accepting the teacher as an accepting, nonjudgmental counselor who will respect their confidences, but a trained teacher can succeed in having them do so.

This approach to working with students in groups seems to be the most promising and most practical way in which all students can be given the benefits of group counseling. It requires training of teachers, and if it were to be accepted as generally desirable, it would suggest that teacher-training would need to be modified, or perhaps a year would need to be added to teacher-training programs to include such instruction. The major problem would appear to be the likelihood that not all teachers would have the aptitude for functioning as group counselors. Those who do, how-

[35] J. R. Seeley. The Forest Hill Village "Human Relations Classes." *Personnel Guid. J.*, 1959, **37**, 424–434. Reprinted in J. Samler (Ed.), *op. cit.*

ever, might be used for several groups. Counselors could also participate in such group counseling, and should be available for consultation by teachers and for individual counseling of those students who would be found to need or desire it as a result of the group discussions. To the writer, this approach offers promise as a way in which adequate counseling services can be made available to all our students.

Summary

While individual counseling is the core of the guidance program, there are situations in which various kinds of group activities may be useful.

The school's contribution to vocational development may be assisted by the use of group vocational activities beginning in the elementary school. These include the providing of occupational information through units and courses in the regular curriculum, and through special courses or group sessions. The teacher here can make a significant contribution to the guidance program of the school. Differing approaches to group guidance in the secondary school were also considered.

In addition to group activities directed toward familiarizing students with occupational information and the world of work, or even of assisting them in learning about their aptitudes, abilities, and interests, there is a place in the school for group counseling for personal adjustment. Here also there is a place for the teacher who is trained in group counseling. Two programs for preparing teachers for group counseling were described. It is suggested that this is perhaps an area in which trained teachers, supervised by the counselor, may make a major contribution to the needs of students for counseling.

SUGGESTED READINGS

Bennett, Margaret. *Guidance in groups.* New York: McGraw-Hill, 1955. Perhaps the standard text in group activities in schools.

Hobbs, N. Group-centered psychotherapy. In Rogers, C. R. *Client-centered therapy.* Boston: Houghton Mifflin, 1951. A description of client-centered group counseling.

Hoppock, R. *Occupational information.* New York: Mc-Graw-Hill, 1957. This book incorporates a revision of the author's "Group Guidance, Principles, Techniques and Evaluation" published in 1949.

Lifton, W. M. *Working with groups: group process and individual growth.* New York: Wiley, 1961. A concise treatment of the dynamics of groups.

Super, D. E. Group techniques in the guidance program. *Educ. psychol. Measmt.,* 1949, 9, 496–510. Reprinted in Farwell, G. F. & Peters, H. J. (Eds.) *Guidance readings for counselors.* Chicago: Rand McNally, 1960. Pp. 345–361. Also reprinted in McDaniel, H. B., *et al. Readings in guidance.* New York: Holt, 1959. Pp. 338–346. An organized summary of the place of group techniques in guidance, concise yet comprehensive.

Warters, Jane. *Group guidance: principles and practices.* New York: McGraw-Hill, 1960. A systematic presentation of principles and techniques of group guidance in the school.

Willey, R. D. & Strong, W. M. *Group procedures in guidance.* New York: Harper, 1957. A comprehensive survey of group activities in the school.

CHAPTER 12

PERSONAL COUNSELING

Discussion of individual counseling in the personal-emotional-social area has been postponed until now so that it could be seen in better perspective. Various terms have been employed to designate this aspect of counseling. Personal counseling, personal-adjustment counseling, and therapeutic counseling are some of the designations used. No one seems to be better or more widely used than the others. The writer has preferred the term *therapeutic counseling*, but it is open to the objection of tautology, since all counseling is—or should be—therapeutic. As was indicated in an earlier chapter, there seems to be a need for an adjective to designate counseling which is primarily concerned with, or focused upon, problems of a personal, emotional, or social (interpersonal) nature, rather than upon educational or vocational problems. *Personal counseling* seems to be as good a term as any, and has been adopted here.

As in dealing with other areas of guidance and counseling, our purpose is not to present methods and techniques for the counselor. This is the function of other courses and texts, rather than the introductory course. We are concerned here with the place of personal counseling in a counseling and guidance program in the schools. There are differences of opinion about whether individual counseling on personal problems should be a part of the counseling and guidance services offered in schools. What are the responsibilities of the schools in this area?

Personal Counseling as a Nonschool Function

There are those who feel that personal counseling is not a service which should be provided by the public schools. Those who feel this way may do so for various reasons; some of these reasons may be briefly discussed.

One of the reasons frequently given is that if school counselors offered counseling on personal-social-emotional problems, counselors would spend all their time working on a continuing basis with a few problem cases. Thus, the majority of students would receive little if any of the counselor's time. Sometimes it is questioned whether anything is achieved by spending so much time on problem cases, since so little improvement seems to result.

This objection appears to be based on the lack of counseling services, and the belief that with an inadequate number of counselors their time would be better spent working with problems other than the personal problems of students. It is recognized that such problems exist, but they may be considered as less important than other problems, as not amenable to counseling, or as depriving other students of the counselor's time. There is considerable feeling that school counselors should serve *all* the students. Whether to see every student for only a few minutes a year is better than to counsel a few students frequently over a long period of time may be questioned. At any rate, both extremes are undesirable. The basic problem seems to be lack of time, or an inadequate number of counselors, to provide sufficient service to all students, some of whom may require much more time than others.

Another reason sometimes given for not providing personal counseling is that this is not the responsibility of the schools. It is suggested that, while such services are desirable, they should be provided by other agencies in the community. This objection seems to involve the identification of such counseling with psychotherapy. It is felt that psyotherapy, like medical treatment, is not a matter for the schools. This reasoning fails to recognize, however, that there are many students who need and could benefit from counseling of a relatively extensive or long-term kind. They need more help than can be given by teachers, relatives, or friends. Yet they do not need intensive psychotherapy of the kind provided by psychologists or psychiatrists. Although such psychotherapy could help them, there are not enough psychologists or psychiatrists to serve all those who have mild or moderate personal problems. Moreover, the use of such specialized personnel in these cases would be an inefficient use of their time. There are few, if any, places where these students could obtain help.

One source of help sometimes suggested, and sometimes available, is the school social worker, visiting teacher, or visiting counselor. Where such personnel are available they can and should be used. But they have other duties and are not sufficient in number to provide all the service which is necessary and desirable.

There are some who feel that there has been too much emphasis on personal counseling in some schools. They feel that vocational counseling has been neglected. Tooker seems to feel this way when he states as the second requirement of counselor training that "the school counselor should be at least as well prepared in the area of vocational and educational guidance as he is in personal guidance."[1] It may be the case in some isolated instances that school counselors, while trained in personal counseling, are not trained in educational-vocational counseling. In most cases the reverse is true, however. It may also be the case in rare instances that there is some justification for the complaint that the school counselor is interested only in therapeutic counseling and not in educational counseling. But we are not suggesting that educational-vocational counseling be abandoned or decreased, and that only personal counseling be provided in the schools. It is only being suggested that in addition to adequate vocational counseling, personal counseling should also be available.

Some feel that because of the current manpower situation (i.e., a shortage of technical and scientific workers) vocational counseling is of primary importance, and school counselors should give all their time to that type, giving up the counseling of students on problems of personal adjustment. The National Manpower Council, for example, has recommended that "school officials use their guidance staffs primarily for vocational guidance purposes and when extended resources of staff and funds permit,

[1] E. D. Tooker. Counselor role: counselor training. *Personnel Guid. J.*, 1957, 36, 263–267.

also for counseling students with personal adjustment problems."[2]

A third objection to the school providing such service is that school counselors are not qualified to engage in personal counseling. Unfortunately, this is all too frequently the case at the present time. Too many counselors have had little, if any, training in any kind of counseling. Most of those who have had training have been rather narrowly trained. Certainly no one who is not qualified, who has not had training, should engage in such counseling. Counselors with the training described and recommended in Chapter 5 would be qualified for all types of counseling. Too often persons who have been trained only as teachers or administrators are assigned to counseling duties.

It is curious that many of those who feel that school counselors should not engage in personal counseling are often in favor of teachers doing such counseling. This solution of the problem is inadequate for a number of reasons, however. Teachers, by the very nature of their professions, are less well prepared for personal counseling than counselors, and as pointed out in Chapter 6, they do not have the time or private facilities to counsel their students. Moreover, it is just in the areas of personal problems that students are usually less able to confide in their teachers, and would prefer to talk with someone else.

Personal Counseling as a Responsibility of the Schools

The general basis for the concern of the school with the personal adjustment of its students was presented in Chapter 1. This concern has been generally accepted, and the total program of the school, the curriculum and personal services, expresses this concern. The counseling and guidance services discussed in this book are clearly attempts to assist students in the area of personal adjustment as broadly defined. Where such services seem to be clearly related to achieving the objectives of intellectual development and vocational adjustment, they seem to be recognized and accepted as services which the school has a responsibility to provide. When it comes to the objective of psychological adjustment or mental health, questions arise concerning how far

[2] National Manpower Council. *A policy for skilled manpower.* New York: Columbia University Press, 1954. P. 27.

the responsibility of the school extends. A question arises as to where a line can be drawn, or where the line should be drawn.

Most of the reasons given above for the school not providing personal counseling assume that problems of a personal-social-emotional nature can be separated from educational and vocational problems. It should be clear from the discussions in the preceding chapters that this is not possible. While there are some cases in which distinctions can be made, and while it is desirable to have terms to distinguish the focus or emphasis of counseling in particular cases, it is not possible to separate clearly or sharply the various kinds of problems faced by students. Educational and vocational problems have emotional aspects, sometimes minor, but sometimes significant. We have seen that good vocational counseling requires attention to the emotional reactions, attitudes, and feelings of the student. As Blum and Balinsky point out, "A vocational counselor should also be able to counsel with personal matters that impinge on vocational adjustment."[3] We cannot say, therefore, that vocational counseling requires less training than does personal, or that it requires an entirely different kind of training. Good vocational counseling requires no less training for counselors than does good personal. The fact that school counselors are not adequately trained for personal counseling thus implies that they are not adequately trained for the vocational type.

Bordin and Wrenn, in a review of counseling in schools, noted that "the trend is toward expecting more and more psychological sophistication of those who counsel, while not materially reducing emphasis upon the knowledge needed of the social, vocational, business or industrial, and educational structure within which the individual functions. There is a merging of traditional vocational guidance with concern for the emotional and motivational aspects of behavior which characterizes psychotherapy."[4] Blum and Balinsky say essentially the same thing: ". . . counseling is therapy. In many instances it is exceedingly difficult to separate the counseling aspects from the therapeutic aspect. It is precisely

[3] M. L. Blum & B. Balinsky. *Counseling and psychology.* New York: Prentice-Hall, 1951.

[4] E. S. Bordin & C. G. Wrenn. The counseling function. *Rev. educ. Res.,* 1954, **24,** 134–146.

because of this belief that we recommend that psychological training be given prior to the administration of vocational guidance."[5] Bennett, Seashore, and Wesman voice the same conclusion as follows: ". . . we have become even more convinced (after reading case reports) that educational and vocational counseling can no longer properly be considered as independent of personal counseling. Counselors not only need to know the curriculum, psychometrics, and the requirements of various careers, but they also must understand the psychodynamics of human behavior."[6]

It will be remembered from our discussion of the functions of the schools that the schools have some responsibility for the personal and social development of the individual. Insofar as personal problems interfere with the cognitive learning of the student, the school has a direct interest in the student's personal adjustment. The extent to which services are provided in this area depends on what services are available from other community agencies. Often there are few, if any, other resources. In those instances where private or community services exist, they are usually inadequate to serve more than the more seriously disturbed individuals. The school is not only justified in providing, but has a definite responsibility to provide, individual services in the area of personal adjustment. Such services may also include the group counseling services discussed in the last chapter. They may be provided in part by school psychologists, school social workers or visiting teachers, and, in some instances, by child-guidance centers operated by a school system. Also included should be personal counseling services provided by school counselors.

As was indicated above, there are many persons with personal problems of a relatively minor nature who could benefit from counseling, but who do not need the services of a psychiatrist or psychologist. An adequately trained counselor can help many of these people. This is particularly true of students in our schools, who may be in the beginning stages of the development of personal problems. Assistance given at this time may require

[5] Blum & Balinsky, op. cit., p. 15.
[6] G. K. Bennett, H. G. Seashore & A. G. Wesman. Counseling from profiles: a casebook for the Differential Aptitude Tests. New York: The Psychological Corporation, 1951.

less time and work than if it is postponed until the problem has become more serious. Counseling services to children may have great preventive value. Early counseling may prevent the development of serious mental or emotional disturbance later in life. It is frequently pointed out by mental-health experts that much adult emotional disturbance could have been prevented by adequate mental-health services earlier in life. While it is important that teachers be aware of the principles of good mental health, and apply them in their relations with students, it is the counselor who, in many schools, is the only person whose chief concern is with the mental health of the individual student. The school is the institution which has access to and responsibility for more of our children for a longer period of time than any other. This gives it a unique opportunity, and responsibility, for identifying and assisting those students with beginning problems of personal adjustment which, if not recognized and dealt with, may lead to serious maladjustment in adult life. The adequately trained counselor is qualified to engage in personal counseling with these students. Students with more serious problems will, of course, be referred to available, appropriate services for treatment.

The answer to the objection that there are not enough trained counselors is to provide more well-trained counselors. The National Education Defense Act of 1958 is an attempt to stimulate the training of an adequate supply of counselors. Unfortunately, it tends to increase the number of partially trained, rather than fully trained, counselors (see Chapter 5).

Objectives of Personal Counseling

The goals of counseling are often difficult to define. Perhaps it is for this reason that the stated objectives of counselors are often very limited or narrow. Counselors, as well as clients, too often think of the objective of counseling as answering specific questions, solving particular problems, or removing or reducing specific symptoms. But counseling should do more than this, if it is really to be of much value to the client. It should be concerned with more than the immediate situation. We have suggested this in our discussion of vocational counseling, particularly in the discussion of career patterns. The same concern with the total life span of the individual should be present in counseling involving problems of personal adjustment.

But when it comes to expressing the goals, we find that no one has succeeded in doing so in very clear or explicit terms. Mental health is often proposed as the goal of counseling activities, both group and individual. But what is mental health? How do we know whether a person is mentally healthy? There has been increasing concern with this problem—with recognition that mental health is more than the absence of mental illness. The concept of *positive* mental health has been proposed by Jahoda, who has reviewed and analyzed various attempts to define it.[7]

Adjustment has long been used as a criterion of mental health and a goal of counseling. But there has been increasing dissatisfaction with this concept. It seems to be a static condition which is to be achieved and then maintained. It seems to involve aspects of conformity. One must always ask, "Adjustment to what?" Adjustment to, or conformity to, certain situations may be undesirable. If everyone were adjusted, change and progress would cease. The advances in civilization appear to have been made by nonconformists, who have been unadjusted to the age in which they lived. The concept of adjustment would seem then to result in a narrow definition of mental health in which there would be little room for individuality and individual differences.

Adjustment is sometimes considered synonymous with happiness, contentment, satisfaction, etc. But these depend to a great extent on one's environment. The acceptance of unfavorable conditions with satisfaction or happiness does not appear to be a healthy or desirable goal—it may be unhealthy, or even, in extreme cases, evidence of serious emotional disturbance.

Integration is another term sometimes used to define mental health. Definitions of personality integration are, however, usually vague, and thus difficult to apply. They usually stress the internal state of the person, rather than his adjustment to the environment. Thus, an individual may be integrated within himself

[7] Marie Jahoda. *Current concepts of positive mental health.* New York: Basic Books, 1958.

and at the same time in conflict with his environment. The concept has probably arisen from an effort to avoid classing as mentally unhealthy everyone who is in conflict with his environment, and is in this sense unadjusted. It includes a unifying outlook on life, a sense of identity, and a resistance to the stress of unfavorable environmental happenings. In contrast to the concept of adjustment, then, it emphasizes the individual and his internal state of being.

Another criterion of mental health which has long been recognized in the diagnosis of severe mental disturbances is that of reality-orientation. Jahoda analyzes this into three aspects, which she designates autonomy, perception of reality, and environmental mastery.[8] The first includes independence and self-determination, self-direction, or self-control, in distinction to outer-control. The autonomous individual is also self-contained, with resources within the self for his satisfactions.

A healthy perception of reality is characterized by the relative freedom of perception from distortion by the needs or desires of the individual, and by sensitivity to and empathy with other people, or the ability to perceive and interpret the attitudes and intentions of others.

Environmental mastery includes adequacy in the various areas of living, such as in love and other interpersonal relations, in work, and in play. It also involves adequacy in meeting the demands and requirements of various situations requiring problem-solving activity and adaptation, and the choosing, modifying, or creating of an environment most suitable to the individual.

These criteria mainly emphasize characteristics of behavior which may be observed by others. They are in a sense mainly external criteria, although references are made to internal states of the individual. Mental health can be viewed from another frame of reference, however, that is, in terms of how an individual perceives, and feels about, himself.

Attitudes toward the self have thus been proposed as a basis for evaluating mental health. Such attitudes as self-acceptance, self-confidence, self-reliance, and self-esteem or self-respect are con-

[8] *Ibid.*, pp. 43–64.

sidered to be evidence of mental health. One's attitudes toward oneself are included in the self-concept. A positive self-regard, or self-esteem, is a requirement of mental health. Negative self-regard is a characteristic of poor mental health. Positive self-regard does not require that the individual be satisfied with himself in all respects. It includes the acceptance of shortcomings, without their overshadowing his assets and strengths.

The development of the self is a second major criterion from the internal frame of reference. Such terms as self-actualization, self-enhancement, self-realization, growth and becoming, have been used to designate this development. The central idea is that the person, or organism, strives to realize its potentialities, and to the extent that it is successful in doing so it is mentally healthy. Self-actualization includes the development of satisfying relations with others, which involve concern with and respect for others.

All of these criteria or characteristics of mental health perhaps have some value, but no one is probably sufficient by itself. From the point of view of this book the last two would appear to be most satisfactory. However, the others are not necessarily inconsistent with these. They represent a different way of looking at the individual, that is, from the outside observer's point of view. It is probable that the individual who is considered to be mentally healthy from the internal frame of reference would manifest behavior which would be more or less consistent with the external criteria.

It is difficult to summarize all the criteria in a single statement, however. Jahoda sees most of the criteria as being consistent with the goal that "an individual should be able to stand on his own feet without making undue demands or imposition on others."[9] The writer has elsewhere suggested a similar goal, that of responsible independence.[10] These concepts perhaps summarize mental health from an external point of view. The concept of self-actualization, with all its implications, is an expression of the same goal or criterion from the internal frame of refer-

[9] *Ibid.*, p. 80.
[10] C. H. Patterson. *Counseling and psychotherapy: theory and practice.* New York: Harper, 1959. P. 62.

ence. Self-esteem is perhaps the key element in mental health, from this point of view.

Some have been concerned that the goals of independence and self-actualization are anarchistic or antisocial. There seems to be some confusion with what has in the past been termed self-expression, which has often been nothing more than the encouragement of self-indulgence at the expense of or in disregard of others. But this is not to be confused with self-actualization or self-enhancement. The enhancement of the self, the development of self-esteem, is intimately related to the attitudes and opinions, the esteem, of others. The individual is dependent on the esteem of others for his own self-esteem, and upon the cooperation of others for his self-enhancement. Thus, genuine self-esteem and self-enhancement cannot exist without regard and concern for others. Healthy independence, then, is, as noted above, a *responsible* independence.

Methods of Personal Counseling

If the goals of counseling, and the criteria of good mental health are as described above, then there are certain implications for methods and techniques of counseling. The importance of self-esteem, and its relation to and dependence upon the esteem of others, suggests that the counselor should respect or esteem the client. The goal of self-actualization implies that counseling should facilitate this process, to free the client from the blocks or obstacles which prevent him from achieving his potential. The development of responsible independence suggests that the counseling situation should allow the client to take responsibility for himself and his decisions, from the beginning of the counseling process.

It should be apparent that the approach to counseling outlined in Chapter 7 is consistent with these goals. The basic principles discussed there are applicable to the counseling of students with personal problems. These principles are the basis of client-centered counseling. The student who is interested in detailed consideration of the practice of personal counseling will find it in the suggested readings given below. No one should attempt to work with problems in this area, however, without adequate training, which should include a period of supervised practice.

Summary

In addition to offering counseling to students in the educational-vocational area, the school should offer assistance to students with their personal-social-emotional problems. We have designated this as *personal counseling*.

Not everyone agrees that the school should engage in counseling of students with such personal problems. Some feel that school counselors should limit themselves to working with the educational-vocational problems of students. It is pointed out that many counselors are not qualified to counsel in the area of personal problems; some feel that this is psychotherapy, and that it is not the school's function to provide psychotherapy.

But there are many problems, and many students with problems, which do not require the services of a psychologist or psychiatrist, even if these services were available in adequate quantity. Moreover, it is often difficult to determine where vocational problems end and personal ones begin. The importance of emotional aspects of educational and vocational development and choice have been indicated in the preceding chapters. Counselors cannot, if they would, limit themselves to the rational aspects of vocational choice. The counselor must therefore be trained and qualified to work with the personal or emotional problems of the average, more or less normal, student. While in the past counselors have perhaps not been adequately prepared to do this, current counselor-training programs, recognizing the impossibility of compartmentalizing the problems of the individual, are preparing counselors to function more broadly as general counselors.

The goals of personal counseling were considered, and the development of a responsible independence proposed as a desired outcome, an outcome consistent with, and combining self-esteem and self-enhancement with, respect for and concern about others. The techniques of personal counseling were briefly discussed in Chapter 7.

SUGGESTED READINGS

Combs, A. W., & Snygg, D. *Individual Behavior: a perceptual approach to behavior.* (rev. ed.) New York: Harper, 1959. A systematic approach to understanding behavior from the phenomenological, or internal, frame of reference.

Jahoda, Marie. *Current concepts of positive mental health.* New York: Basic Books, 1958. A review and integration of various concepts of mental health.

Patterson, C. H. *Counseling and psychotherapy: theory and practice.* New York: Harper, 1959. An attempt to prepare the student of counseling for the problems involved in the practice of client-centered counseling.

Porter, E. H. *Introduction to therapeutic counseling.* Boston: Houghton Mifflin, 1950. A very useful book to assist the beginning counselor in analyzing his methods and techniques.

Rogers, C. R. *Client-centered therapy.* Boston: Houghton Mifflin, 1951. The basic exposition of the client-centered point of view in counseling by its originator.

CHAPTER 13

SOME PROBLEMS IN
COUNSELING IN SCHOOLS

There are some particular problems which arise in counseling in schools, as compared with counseling in other institutions or settings. These problems may involve the setting in which the counseling is provided, the nature of the student—or client—population, or a combination of both. Some of these problems will be discussed in this chapter. While they have received some attention in the periodical or journal literature, they have not, to the writer's knowledge, been considered in a textbook for counselors.

The problems we shall consider are those in which students are involved. Some concerning the relationship of the counselor to the school and its administration were referred to in Chapter 3. Here we are concerned with problems of relationships of the counselor to clients and potential clients. Most relate to student attitudes toward counseling and the counselor.

There seems to be no doubt that the adolescent has problems. The period of adolescence, in our society at least, is one in which the young person faces many demands, some of them conflicting, and must make many decisions which will affect the future. It is the period during which he is expected to become increasingly independent of his family; yet he is not allowed complete independence. He faces the problems of developing relationships with his peers at an adult level. Interpersonal relationships between the sexes become important. The problems of further education and vocational choice become paramount. Research indicates the existence of many problems in adolescent youth—problems which youth themselves will admit, though more often anonymously than as their own problems.[1]

Thus it might be expected that the demands for help with their problems would be great. Yet experience indicates that adolescents infrequently request such help. Even when they are aware of the existence of problems, they often do not seek help, and even refuse it when it is available or offered. This reluctance of adolescents to seek counseling or psychotherapy has been noted by many counselors and therapists. Blos notes, for example, that "few adolescents come for treatment of their own accord, but are by some outside agent brought to the therapist."[2] Willey and Strong lament that ". . . pupils do not come voluntarily and do not willingly discuss problems of real concern to them. The counseling which has been done by the average counselor has often been undertaken under pressure, and the 'permissive' atmosphere imperative to effective counseling has been disregarded."[3]

It cannot be assumed, as is sometimes done, that students do not need counseling, or even that they do not want counseling, because they do not request it or clamor for it. What are the reasons for this failure of adolescents to seek help for the problems which they face? Perhaps an examination of these reasons will be of value in reaching more students with counseling services, and lead to practices by counselors which will encourage more students to seek their help. When does the student seek assistance, and whom does he seek as a helping person?

Attitudes of Adolescents Toward Seeking Help

An interesting study by Holman gives some insight into the attitudes of adolescents toward seeking assistance for their problems.[4] She studied twenty juniors in a Rochester, New York, high

[1] See, for example: H. Bell. *Youth tell their story*. Washington, D.C.: American Council on Education, 1938.

[2] P. Blos. The treatment of adolescents. In Marcel Heiman (Ed.) *Psychoanalysis and social work*. New York: International Universities Press, 1952. P. 227.

[3] R. D. Willey & W. M. Strong. *Group procedures in guidance*. New York: Harper, 1957. P. 29.

[4] Miriam Holman. Adolescent attitudes toward seeking help with personal problems. *Smith Coll. Stud. Soc. Wk.*, 1955, **25** (3), 1–31.

school, ten boys and ten girls, selected to be representative of high-school juniors. Eighteen were 16 to 17 years of age, one was 15, and one 18. All were individually interviewed, using a combination of focused and unstructured methods. They were asked what problems they would seek help with. The answers, classified in six categories, are given in Table 4.

TABLE 4.   Problems for Which Help Would be Sought by
10 Boys and 10 Girls, Junior High School

| Problems | Number of Group Stating Problem | | |
	Boys	Girls	Total
Difficulties in school	7	7	14
Difficulties with parents	6	3	9
Vocational planning	2	1	3
Boy-girl relationships	1	5	6
Money and jobs	3	1	4
Miscellaneous	1	2	3

SOURCE: Miriam Holman. Adolescent attitudes toward seeking help with personal problems. *Smith Coll. Stud. Soc. Wk.*, 1955, **25** (3), p. 12.

They were then asked if they, or others whom they knew, had problems in specified areas. The replies are tabulated in Table 5.

TABLE 5.   Areas of Problems of Study Group and Their Acquaintances

| Problems | Number of Group Recognizing Problem | | |
	Boys	Girls	Total
Vocational-educational planning	10	10	20
Difficulties related to school work	10	10	20
Money and jobs	10	9	19
Difficulties with parents	9	9	18
Difficulties with siblings	7	10	17
Personal appearance	7	10	17
Boy-girl relationships	6	10	16
Relationships with same sex	5	6	11

SOURCE: Miriam Holman. Adolescent attitudes toward seeking help with personal problems. *Smith Coll. Stud. Soc. Wk.*, 1955, **25** (3), p. 13.

It is apparent that students admit to, or feel that others have, many more problems than they are willing to seek help with.

The students were then asked whether they would want to discuss problems in each of these areas with someone. The answers were classified in three categories: would, would not, and qualified. Table 6 shows the results of this question.

TABLE 6.   Willingness to Discuss Problems with Someone

Problems	Would Discuss		Would Not Discuss		Qualified	
	Boys	Girls	Boys	Girls	Boys	Girls
Vocational-educational planning	8	10	0	0	2	0
Difficulties related to school work	0	1	6	8	4	1
Money and jobs	2	7	6	2	2	1
Difficulties with parents	4	2	5	4	1	4
Difficulties with siblings	0	1	8	9	2	0
Personal appearance	10	8	0	2	0	0
Boy-girl relationship	7	7	2	2	1	1
Relationships with same sex	0	5	10	4	0	1

SOURCE: Miriam Holman. Adolescent attitudes toward seeking help with personal problems. *Smith Coll. Stud. Soc. Wk.*, 1955, 25 (3), p. 17.

The interview materials, including the discussion of qualifications of answers, suggested that the willingness to discuss problems was related to their seriousness. The students indicated they would *not* discuss more serious problems. Whether or not a problem would be discussed seemed to depend on the type of problem, its severity, the expectation of help, and the manner in which the expected help would be given. The latter refers to whether the student would be understood, and not condemned or looked down upon. The interviews also indicated several factors which would deter the students from seeking help: (1) Fears of revealing themselves to others, opening the way to being blamed for having a problem or for not being able to solve it alone. (2) Fears of bringing out something about themselves which they did not want to know, such as that the problem was more severe than they realized, was insoluble, or that they needed psychiatric help. (3) Fears in relationship to the helping person—that he might not be competent to help, that the information would be used to their detriment, or that the helping person would not be interested in them. (4) Fear of loss of independence. These fears have obvious relevance to the counselor's functioning.

The study seems to indicate that there is little resistance to discussing problems which are not personal and which are common to all teenagers, such as educational-vocational problems. But problems of a more personal nature, such as conflicts with parents or boy-girl relationships, are too individual and personal to take to school personnel. The author in her summary states that "a theme running throughout this study has been their fear of being thought of as different. This they seemed to see as a 'defect' within themselves for which they would be blamed, criticized, or rejected."[5]

The importance of the peer group is apparent. Adolescents do not want to seek assistance if it endangers their status with their peers—if it suggests to their peers that they are different, have problems which they cannot solve themselves, or are weak or dependent.

Perceptions of Counselors and Counseling Services

Part of the failure of adolescents to seek assistance seems to be due to not knowing where particular kinds of assistance are available. If students or potential clients do not perceive counselors as providing counseling assistance with personal problems they will not come to the counselor for such assistance. A number of studies indicate that school counselors are not perceived by students as a source of assistance with personal problems.

Grant studied the perceptions of high-school seniors in nine schools regarding the areas in which the counselor could provide assistance.[6] They were asked to choose three persons in order of preference from whom they would like assistance or with whom they would discuss educational planning, vocational planning, and personal-emotional problems. Suggested responses were classified as counselor, other school personnel, and nonschool people. Students listed the counselor as their first choice for assistance in educational and vocational planning. In the personal-emotional area they did not perceive the counselor as being able

---

[5] Holman, *op. cit.*

[6] C. W. Grant. How students perceive the counselor's role. *Personnel Guid. J.*, 1954, **32**, 386–388.

to give acceptable help. Almost three-fourths of their first, second, and third choices were of nonschool people, about 20 percent were other school personnel, and only 5 percent of all choices were of the counselor. The persons listed most frequently for assistance in the personal-emotional area were friends, parents, and doctor, in that order.

Another study by Jenson concerned the sources from which students would seek help for various kinds of problems.[7] A 20

TABLE 7.   Student Preference for Different Individuals to
Help Them with Certain Kinds of Problems

Problem Areas	Par-ents	Coun-selors	Teach-ers	Deans	Friends	Misc.
	Preference (in percent) for					
A. Desire to know more about real abilities, interests, ambitions, personality, etc.	27	28	19	7	15	4
B. Desire to discover most promising kinds of school activities and work	20	38	22	9	8	3
C. Finding out how to make progress toward selected goals in school and work	18	36	28	13	4	1
D. Desire to learn how to get along better with friends and others, at school, at home, or in the community	28	27	13	7	22	3
E. Help in developing more confidence in ability to make "good" decisions about problems which bother now and those which may pop up in the future	34	30	14	9	9	4
F. Help in learning to do the things known to be "best" for me and society but which are not easy to do	29	30	17	9	9	6

SOURCE: R. E. Jenson. Student feeling about counseling help. *Personnel Guid. J.,* 1955, 33, 500.

[7] R. E. Jenson. Student feeling about counseling help. *Personnel Guid. J.,* 1955, 33, 498–503.

percent sample of 8000 students who had talked to a counselor in seven high schools was asked to rank in order of first, second, and third choices those to whom they would go for help. The list included parents, counselors, teachers, deans, friends, and others in the community, such as doctors, lawyers, ministers, and Scout leaders. Table 7 presents the results of the survey. No one source was preferred above all others for any of the areas. Counselors were preferred above teachers, but ran about equal with parents in several areas. While there seemed to be no discrimination against counselors in the choice of a person with whom to discuss problems, it is noteworthy that they were chosen only about a third of the time. The list of problem areas does not clearly single out peronal or emotional problems, so it is not clear whether a difference would exist in this area.

Other studies indicate that in some situations the teacher is preferred to the counselor as the person to whom a student with a problem would go. A survey of counseling services in Illinois secondary schools indicated that students would go to the teacher much more frequently than to the counselor with their problems.[8] In answer to the question, "If you had a problem with which you needed help but which was not directly connected with your school assignments and you had to select someone from your school staff, to whom would you turn for help?" first and second choices were obtained, with the following results:

	First Choice	Second Choice	Blank
My class advisor	150	141	909
A counselor	181	107	912
A club sponsor	24	35	1141
Dean of boys	52	77	1071
Dean of girls	97	108	995
My homeroom teacher	212	161	826
My teacher of _____	274	200	726
The principal	126	193	881
Others (listed)	70	97	1033

SOURCE: Allerton House Conference on Education. *Counseling services in the secondary schools of Illinois*. Urbana, Ill.: College of Education, University of Illinois, 1959, p. 44.

[8] Allerton House Conference on Education. *Counseling services in the secondary schools of Illinois*. Urbana, Ill.: College of Education, University of Illinois, 1959.

However, the report notes that in many schools adequately trained counselors were not available; the results might be different where they are present on the staff.

These studies may give a more favorable picture than actually exists in many situations. They ask the student to choose from among a list the persons to whom they might go for help, and some, as in Jenson's study, deal with students who have been to a counselor. A study conducted at the University of Illinois[9] asked 1096 juniors in 39 high schools of 500 or more students the following question: "When you want to talk over your plans with someone, to whom do you usually go?" Table 8 shows the results.

TABLE 8. Persons to Whom 1096 High School Juniors Would
Go to Talk Over Plans

	No One or Self	Family	Friends	Member of School Staff	Others
Percent of girls	2	68	21	7	2
Percent of boys	7	68	12	11	2

SOURCE: J. T. Hastings, P. J. Runkel, Dora Damrin, *et al. The use of test results.* Cooperative Research Project No. 509, U.S. Office of Education. Urbana, Ill.: Bureau of Educational Research, 1960 (mimeo).

Only 9 percent mentioned a member of the school staff. However, when they were asked: "Is there anyone *in school* with whom you talk over your plans and problems?" the results were more favorable to the school (Table 9). About 45 percent of the students mentioned members of the school staff. In contrast to

TABLE 9. Persons in School with Whom Students
Talk over Plans and Problems

	No One	Friends	Counselor	Teacher	Others
Percent of girls	26	29	30	12	3
Percent of boys	30	23	31	12	5

SOURCE: J. T. Hastings, P. J. Runkel, Dora Damrin, *et al. The use of test results.* Cooperative Research Project No. 509, U.S. Office of Education. Urbana, Ill.: Bureau of Educational Research, 1960 (mimeo).

[9] J. T. Hastings, P. J. Runkel, Dora Damrin, *et al. The use of test results.* Cooperative Research Project No. 509, U.S. Office of Education. Urbana, Ill.: Bureau of Educational Research, 1960 (mimeo).

the Allerton study mentioned above, students named counselors about two and a half times as frequently as teachers.

In answer to the question: "Have you ever gone to a guidance counselor to talk over plans and problems?" about two-thirds of the students in schools with more counselors, one-half in schools with few counselors, and one-fourth in schools with no counselors reported having done so. Apparently teachers functioning as counselors, or perhaps as "advisers," were included by students as counselors. There is thus evidence that where more counselors are available, more students utilize their services. However, responses to the question: "What led you to consider the occupation you have chosen?" raise a question about the nature of students' contacts with counselors. Over 80 percent referred to their own thinking or reading, and only 23 percent mentioned school. Only about a fourth indicated that they had learned about the requirements for the occupation from counselors or teachers. There was no relationship to the number of counselors in the school. The authors conclude that much of the students' vocational knowledge is acquired outside the counselor's office.

A member of the school staff to whom referrals may be made for help on personal problems is the school nurse. One study reports 75 percent of 607 school nurses surveyed stating that mental health problems were referred to them, while 57 percent reported referral of social adjustment problems. In this study, however, about 40 percent of the schools represented had no organized guidance program with a full-time director.[10]

Although the results of studies vary, they seem to agree in indicating that the counselor is often not perceived as a source of help with problems which students face. Many students apparently would not go to a counselor for assistance with educational or vocational problems. Perceptions of counselors by students may be at variance with the roles or functions of counselors. However, it is also possible that the perceptions of students are accurate. In many situations counselors do little if any counseling among their many other duties. If the counselor spends most of

[10] Ruth Klein. The school nurse as a guidance functionary. *Personnel Guid. J.*, 1959, 38, 318–321.

his time keeping attendance and tardiness reports, handling disciplinary problems, making out class programs, and perhaps teaching a few classes, he will not be perceived by students as being helpful with their problems, whether educational-vocational or personal-emotional.

The problem of discipline and counseling, touched upon in Chapter 3, is relevant here. Although there has been some attempt to rationalize the integration of disciplinary functions and counseling functions in the same person, this seems to be more a matter of attempting to accept and adjust to an existing situation, rather than any real belief that the functions should be performed by the same individual. Actually, most of the discussion along these lines (see the References in Chapter 3) essentially emphasizes that discipline should be therapeutic. This is, however, entirely different from saying that discipline is therapy, or that discipline should be handled by counselors. Professional opinion is almost unanimous against the counselor being responsible for discipline in the school.

The perception of the counselor as a disciplinarian is perhaps one of the reasons why students hesitate to confide in him or discuss some personal problems with him. Even the view of the counselor as being identified with the administration precludes the discussion of some problems with him. The Allerton House Study and the study of Jenson referred to above indicated that deans and administrators were unpopular as counselors, ranking low in the list of those with whom students would discuss their problems.

Even where counselors are not charged with the handling of discipline, they are often perceived by the teaching staff as a source of help in disciplinary problems, and students with such problems are often referred to them. While this is not necessarily undesirable, and while such students may be helped, the practice of emphasizing this kind of referral creates a problem in teacher-counselor relationships, and may result in the students perceiving the counselor as limited to working with such students.

Finally, the problem of involuntary counseling is related to conceptions of the counselor. Counseling can only occur with the cooperation and desire of the client. This does not mean that the counselor should see only those students who voluntarily ask for counseling services. Students who are referred may accept counseling and continue voluntarily. But if all or most of the students a counselor sees are referred, he may be thought of as providing services *only* to those who are referred by someone else. Students may then hesitate to request counseling voluntarily. Further, since involuntary counseling is not as likely to be effective, the value of the counselor's services may be devaluated if he sees only students who are sent to him on an involuntary basis.

The problem of combining teaching with counseling has already been referred to in Chapter 4. Here it is appropriate to mention that where the only counselor who is available to a student is also a teacher, the student may prefer to keep his personal problems to himself, rather than discuss them with such a counselor, who may be identified as an authority or judgmental figure, regardless of how the latter may perceive himself or even attempt to function in another role. Schools which have no one other than one of its teachers to whom a student may go may in effect be depriving students of counseling services.

All of these problems of the perceptions of the roles and functions of the counselor affect the ways in which counseling services will be utilized. They must be given serious consideration in the organization and administration of counseling programs if counseling services are to be utilized by all the students who can benefit from them.

Confidentiality of Information

An important factor in a counseling relationship is the matter of confidentiality of information. We have referred briefly to this earlier in connection with the counselor's relationships with the administration (Chapter 3) and in connection with test results (Chapter 9). Reluctance of students to consult a counselor is often the result of doubts about the confidentiality of the material discussed in the interview. It will be remembered that in Holman's study one of the fears expressed by students was that information might be used in a detrimental way.

Counselors, as well as administrators, often do not realize the importance of confidentiality. For the professional counselor, the first responsibility is to the client. Professional ethics emphasize this responsibility.[11] Yet, as Arbuckle states, "there are very few school counselors who err on the side of maintaining confidence too much, and there are many who maintain confidence practically not at all."

Arbuckle goes on to note the attitude of some top administrators of teacher-training institutions to whom he spoke on counseling. He states that "a significant number of them apparently felt that a counselor should be expected to reveal any information that he might have on a student to a dean or other administrative officer." Arbuckle continues: ". . . if the counselor himself does not have any concept of his role he will probably see no reason why he should not tell the principal about Mary's plans to run away, about Bobby's sexual deviations, about John's cheating in class. It is likely also, of course, that the number of his clients will rapidly decline and all those who do come in will be extremely wary and come forth with safe and innocuous statements."[12]

The Allerton House Study referred to earlier revealed a similar problem in regard to confidentiality.[13] Twenty-four principals responded to the question: "Is the information which the student gives to the counselor kept absolutely confidential (between the student and counselor)?" Seven (29 percent) replied yes, 14 (58 percent) replied no, and 3 (13 percent) did not reply. Of 128 teachers and counselors responding to this question, *only 19 percent said yes, while 61 percent said no*, and 6 percent did not reply. A further question asked: "If information is not kept absolutely confidential, answer the following: Is this information made available to the principal upon his request?" Of the principals, 16 (67 percent) said yes, 1 (4 percent) said no, and 7 (29 percent) did not reply. Of the 128 teachers and counselors answering the same question, 76 percent said yes, 1 percent said no,

11 See Chapter 3 of the author's *Counseling and psychotherapy: theory and practice*, New York: Harper, 1959, for a discussion of the ethics of counseling.
12 D. S. Arbuckle. Five philosophical issues in counseling. *J. counsel. Psychol.*, 1958, 5, 211–215.
13 Allerton House Conference on Education, *op. cit.*

and 29 percent did not reply. In contrast to these attitudes, 75 percent of the 1200 students felt that information given to the counselor should be kept confidential, while 19 percent felt it should not. Only 24 percent of the students felt it should be released to the principal, 9 percent felt it should not, and 67 percent did not reply to the question. The report points out the serious problem posed for the counselor: "If he is to develop a good counseling relationship, he must keep the confidences of the counseling interview. Students expect this. Too many principals and teachers expect the counselor to break confidences and to discuss confidential information with them." What has sometimes been interpreted as student reluctance or resistance to talk with a counselor, or resistance to discussing his problems, may in many instances be lack of trust in the confidentiality of the counseling interview, and lack of security and confidence in the counseling relationship.

Student Expectations and Counseling Procedure[14]

Several recent studies of student attitudes toward counseling and of client satisfaction with counseling suggest that students prefer counselors who are active and somewhat directive rather than passive or nondirective. One of these studies is that of Forgy and Black.[15] In an earlier study Barahal, Brammer, and Shostrom had concluded, using ratings of client satisfaction, that "client-centered permissive counseling procedures and materials . . . resulted in greater client satisfaction with the counseling process than highly-structured, counselor-centered procedures."[16] But Forgy and Black, in a later follow-up of the same group by a mail questionnaire, found no difference between the client-centered and the control groups in a satisfaction score based on a

[14] Parts of this section are adapted from the following: (1) C. H. Patterson. Client expectations and social conditioning. *Personnel Guid. J.*, 1958, **37**, 136–138. (2) C. H. Patterson. Comments on Goodstein, L. D., & Grigg, A. E. Client satisfaction, counselors, and the counseling process. *Personnel Guid. J.*, 1959, **38**, 25–26.

[15] E. W. Forgy & J. D. Black. A follow-up after three years of clients counseled by two methods. *J. counsel. Psychol.*, 1954, **1**, 1–8.

[16] D. G. Barahal, L. M. Brammer & E. L. Shostrom. A client-centered approach to educational-vocational counseling. *J. consult. Psychol.*, 1950, **14**, 256–260.

check list. In fact there was "a suggestion that the traditionally counseled group actually felt more satisfied with their interviews." They conclude that, while it is possible that there was an immediate, but temporary, difference in favor of the client-centered group, it is more likely that the original ratings obtained by Barahal, Brammer, and Shostrom were contaminated. If this were so, then the original study cannot be accepted as indicating preference for client-centered procedures.

Another study by Grigg and Goodstein, using a mail questionnaire, found that "those clients who see their counselors as taking an active role, making suggestions, and helping with specific plans, are more likely to report a favorable outcome for their counseling experience than those clients who see their counselor as a passive listener." Also, "Clients who feel that their counselor takes an active interest in them and is not playing a passive role of merely an interested listener tend to report greater counseling satisfaction." The results of the study were interpreted as indicating a preference for "a more active, somewhat more directive role."[17] Maher and Rogers also found that college sophomores and seniors preferred more directive counseling procedures.[18]

These studies dealt with college students. Studies with high school students have yielded similar results, however. Maher found that junior and senior high school students preferred the more directive counseling procedures.[19] Sonne and Goldman, in a study of high school seniors' preferences, based on listening to two brief, mock taped interviews, found that students preferred the more directive over the client-centered interview.[20] The authors raise

[17] A. E. Grigg & L. D. Goodstein. The use of clients as judges of the counselor's performance. *J. counsel. Psychol.*, 1957, 4, 31–36.

[18] T. P. Maher & Mary E. Rogers. The attitude of college sophomores and seniors toward counseling procedure with reference to certain personality factors and personal problem frequency. Paper presented at the Annual Convention, American Personnel and Guidance Association, Philadelphia, Pa., April 11–14, 1960.

[19] T. P. Maher. *The attitude of high school juniors and seniors toward counseling procedure with reference to certain personality factors and personal problem frequency.* Educational Res. Monogr., Vol. 16, No. 6. Washington, D.C.: Catholic University of America, 1952.

[20] T. R. Sonne & L. Goldman. Preferences of authoritarian and equalitarian personalities for client-centered and eclectic counseling. *J. counsel. Psychol.*, 1957, 4, 129–135.

a question regarding the applicability of the client-centered approach to high school students:

There has been some feeling among high school guidance workers that methods of counseling developed primarily for college students may not be equally applicable to the younger group. This opinion has been heard especially from junior high school counselors.

The present study raises some questions particularly as to the applicability of a client-centered counseling approach to high school seniors, since the majority of our subjects quite clearly prefer the eclectic interview. Of course, it must be emphasized that the expressed preference of the subjects cannot be accepted as *prima facie* evidence of the effectiveness of counseling methods with them . . .

At a mean age of seventeen years, three months, our subjects may be in need of a more dependent counseling relationship than would a college or adult sample and therefore show this preference for the eclectic interview to a greater extent than would older groups.

It should be noted that college students also have been found to prefer to be dependent in the counseling relationship, so that the question of the applicability of client-centered counseling may be raised at that level also.

Before the results of such studies are accepted as a basis for abandoning the client-centered approach with students, however, a number of factors must be considered. Not all of these apply to all studies, of course. Some of them are not applicable to the studies referred to above, but do apply to other studies which have contributed to the suggestion.

1. It must be emphasized that these are studies of client preferences, not of the effectiveness of counseling. This is recognized by Sonne and Goldman. However, some authors appear to equate preferences, or satisfaction of clients, with effectiveness of counseling. While satisfaction of the client with the counseling process may be a partial criterion of counseling effectiveness, it is not the total nor even the major criterion. Satisfaction with the process must be distinguished from satisfaction with outcomes or results, also. Counseling can be a painful process, yet the results may be considered worth the pain involved.

While the studies cited above are concerned with client satisfaction or preference, other studies have attempted to compare the effects and effectiveness of different approaches. Several of these seem to show that the client-centered method is less effective in certain respects than a more directive method.[21] These studies are subject to criticism, however, often being affected by some of the factors considered below.

2. The concept of client-centered counseling involved in some studies is a misrepresentation of the method. The client-centered approach as conceived and practiced is often a passive approach, in which the counselor does little more than reflect content, often in a rigid, wooden manner. It is easy to believe that students would be dissatisfied with such an approach to counseling.

3. This concept is particularly erroneous when it is applied to educational-vocational counseling. It is not to be wondered that students, and clients, do not like a counseling method in which techniques appropriate for personal problems are applied to vocational problems. The problem used by Sonne and Goldman was the falsification of a parent's signature on a report card. Not only was it not a voluntary counseling situation, but one in which the student, a guilty wrongdoer, would more likely be submissive, dependent, and receptive to a counselor who would actively help him out of the difficulty.

4. In some studies (e.g., Sonne and Goldman, and Maher) the students were not expressing preferences based on experience in counseling, but were reacting to contrived situations.

5. In some studies (e.g., Ashby, et al.) the counselors to whom clients were exposed were not trained or experienced counselors. A beginning client-centered counselor often appears to be passive and unresponsive and may behave in a way such as to discourage a client.

6. In some studies (e.g., Ashby, et al.) not only inexperienced counselors have been employed, but the counselors were required to use a method or technique which was not their preferred or natural approach. The counselor was thus attempting to play a role. In some cases, the same counselor used two approaches, or played two roles. It might be expected that one approach would be preferred to another, that one would be more natural than

21 For example: J. D. Ashby, D. H. Ford, B. G. Guerney, Jr. & Louise F. Guerney. Effects on clients of a reflective and a leading type of psychotherapy. *Psychol. Monogr.*, 1957, **71**: No. 24 (Whole. No. 453).

another, or that one would be more skillfully used than another, thus vitiating the comparison of results.

7. While there seems to be some evidence that students—at least some students—appear to prefer to be dependent in the counseling relationship, there is evidence that students—or again at least some—prefer to be independent. The study by Holman suggested some evidence of this preference for independence. The studies of Maher, and of Maher and Rogers revealed that preferences moved progressively, with age and grade, toward a less directive approach. It is recognized that the child is dependent, and since being dependent has advantages, the growing child hesitates to give up being dependent. At the same time he desires to become independent, to enjoy the advantages of independence. Thus there are conflicting tendencies toward dependence and independence, and it is during adolescence that this conflict reaches its height. As the individual progresses through adolescence toward maturity, however, the conflict lessens, dependence attracts him less, and independence more. One goal of development and a main characteristic of maturity is independence.

While it thus appears that it has not been demonstrated that the client-centered approach is less effective than others, there does seem to be some evidence that it is preferred less than a more directive approach by some students. The question to be answered is the following: Should counselors adapt their methods to the apparent preferences of students? In other words, should they, in effect, abandon independence as the goal of counseling, and accept lesser goals, such as the satisfaction of the client with the process or methods?

The goal of independence is not only the goal of client-centered counseling but of other approaches to counseling and psychotherapy as well. Psychoanalysis does accept, or create, a dependency relationship, but it then brings the client through this phase, so that the psychoanalysis is not complete or successful until the client becomes independent of the analyst. The value, or necessity, of the dependency may be questioned; the resulting task of overcoming it may be a reason why psychoanalysis is so time-consuming.

Not only is independence a goal of many approaches to counseling, it is essentially the goal of the education and training of the young by the school, the family, and other institutions of society. However, it appears that society is not entirely consistent in accepting or working toward this goal. Like psychoanalysis, it seems to encourage, foster, or perpetuate the dependency of the young. The success with which this is done is illustrated by the attitudes of young people as studied by Remmers and Radler.[22] Seventy-five percent of the high-school students polled felt that "obedience and respect for authority are the most important virtues that children should learn," while almost 50 percent felt that "a large mass of the people are not capable of determining what is and what is not good for them." Fewer than half claim to think things out for themselves and act on their own decisions, and only a fourth admit that they often disagree with the group's opinion. The influence of the peer group is apparent in enforcing conformity. This situation contributes to, if it does not create, the adolescent rebellion and struggle for independence. Horney refers to the conflict between dependence and independence in our society, and attributes much neurotic maladjustment to it.[23] Roeber phrases the situation nicely: "The adolescent is constantly experimenting with and fluctuating between adult-like independence and child-like dependence."[24]

Our society also fosters an attitude of deference to and dependence upon specialists. The doctor, the lawyer, the engineer, and the teacher are people who do things to us or for us, or who tell us what to do and/or how to do it. The relationship is one of dependence, of reliance on authority. Similar attitudes are developed toward psychiatrists, psychologists, and counselors. The latter is also often a teacher or former teacher, and is identified with the teacher. Sonne and Goldman recognize this cultural

[22] H. H. Remmers & D. H. Radler. (1) Teenage attitudes. *Scientific American*, 1958, **198** (6), 25–29. Reprinted in G. F. Farwell & H. J. Peters (Eds.) *Guidance readings for counselors*. Chicago: Rand McNally, 1960. Pp. 320–331. (2) H. H. Remmers and D. H. Radler. *The American teenager*. Indianapolis, Ind.: Bobbs-Merrill, 1957.

[23] (1) Karen Horney. *The neurotic personality in our time*. New York: Norton, 1937. (2) Karen Horney. *Our inner conflicts*. New York: Norton, 1945. (3) Karen Horney. *Neurosis and human growth*. New York: Norton, 1950.

[24] E. C. Roeber. Vocational counseling for adolescents. Veterans Administration Department of Veterans Benefits, Information Bulletin, Vocational Rehabilitation and Education, I B 7–135, August 9, 1959.

influence on the preferences of students when they suggest that "in our culture in general, or in the particular subculture from which the subjects were drawn, a relatively dependent relationship between a psychological helper (whether a professional counselor or not) and a counselee may be the norm." They further note that "the experience which these subjects have had with counselors is likely to have been of a sort more similar to that of the eclectic than that of the client-centered interview . . . Thus their preferences may be an indication of a learned standard of counseling."[25]

The preferences and expectations of students are then culturally conditioned. This attitude of dependency is, however, inconsistent with the goals of society for the individual, and of the good mental health which is the goal of counseling. Most counselors and therapists, and most methods of therapy, recognize the necessity for clients to accept responsibility for themselves, to be active in the solution of their own problems. The counseling situation can thus be an opportunity for the student to learn to be independent and to accept responsibility for himself. It would seem to be logical or reasonable that the client begin to accept this responsibility for himself from the beginning of the counseling relationship. The essence of client-centered counseling, and of the approach described in this book, is that the client is given responsibility for himself from the inception of the counseling relationship. Experience indicates that clients can and do adapt themselves to such a counseling relationship when it is offered to them. Danskin's research provides some evidence that when the counselor's role differs from that expected by the client—i.e., when the counselor in dealing with a personal adjustment problem assumes a client-centered approach—a good working relationship can be developed.[26]

It is to be expected, of course, that not all clients will be able to accept responsibility for themselves. That a client desires and is able to do so is an hypothesis. It would be unfortunate, however, if this hypothesis were to be abandoned for all high-

[25] Sonne & Goldman, *op. cit.*

[26] D. G. Danskin. Roles played by counselors in their interviews. *J. counsel. Psychol.*, 1955, 2, 22–27.

school and college students without testing it in each individual case. To do so would be to abandon the ultimate goal of counseling before even beginning the relationship.

Adolescent behavior may be variable, inconsistent, impulsive. On the one hand, in some respects or at some times, the adolescent may behave in a very dependent manner, while on the other hand he strives to be overly independent. The variability of behavior and attitudes makes it difficult for the counselor to respond. The counselor may be confused, even irritated. It is difficult to understand the volatile, changing person. It is often suggested that the adolescent needs someone to become dependent upon.[27] It is perhaps more accurate to say that he needs someone upon whom he can depend. Counselors are often exhorted to adapt to the fleeting wishes of the client—to allow him to become dependent if he desires this, to be authoritative or firm if he seems to need this, etc. But a counselor who behaves in this way is variable, inconsistent, confusing to the client. He is not dependable, or trustworthy. In other words, the counselor's response to the volatility and variablity of the adolescent client should be first, of course, to understand him from moment to moment, period to period, but second, he should be stable, consistent, trustworthy in his behavior. The client's expression of dependency, or desire for dependence, is accepted and understood; but it need not be met by the counselor. The counselor allows verbal expression of dependency, but does not permit himself to become the object of dependent behavior on the part of the client. In other words, dependency needs or desires are recognized and dealt with in counseling, but a dependent relationship is not encouraged or permitted to develop.

Many adolescents do not talk to adults easily. Josselyn states that "The adolescent characteristically is secretive about himself and his feelings. Most of the time it is extremely difficult for him to verbalize how he does feel. Furthermore, he is timorous about exposing himself to others even if he can put his feelings into words." However, "Suddenly he may bare his soul (or so it seems), revealing his ambitions, his feelings of guilt, and his conscious awareness of the nature of many of the conflicts with which

[27] Irene M. Josselyn. *The adolescent and his world.* New York: Family Service Association of America, 1952. Pp. 48–52.

he is struggling."[28] Sometimes the feelings may be distorted, either intentionally or without awareness on the part of the adolescent. Roeber also refers to this vacillation or unpredictability: "While vacillating with respect to independent-dependent behavior, the adolescent may also fluctuate between secretiveness and extreme verbosity. If he can accept the counselor and can feel that the counselor understands him, the adolescent may become highly verbal. On the other hand, however permissive the counselor may be, the adolescent may be so afraid to talk, i.e., to make an error, to say too much or to hurt someone's feelings, that he talks very little."[29] The temptation is strong, in cases where the adolescent is uncommunicative, for the counselor to take command. But this is not necessarily desirable, and may prevent the adolescent from taking responsibility for himself or from accepting the counselor.

Implications for the Counselor

The problems discussed above are of course by no means all the problems faced by counselors in schools. They do include some of the major ones, however. These problems have some implications in terms of the organization and offering of counseling services if such services are to reach all or most students who could benefit from them.

1. The counselor, and school administrators and staffs, should be concerned about the counselor's roles and functions. The duties he is assigned, the definitions of his position, and the perceptions which the staff have of him and his functions—all influence the perceptions which students have of his services and of what it is appropriate for them to discuss with him.

2. Since the perceptions which students have of the counselor and his functions are often incomplete or erroneous, attention must be given to defining and clarifying his functions to students. The nature of counseling services, and the kinds of problems which may be discussed with the counselor, must be communicated to students by a continuous offering of counseling services.

3. Since adolescents are hesitant to ask for help with their

[28] *Ibid.*, p. 42.
[29] Roeber, *op. cit.*

problems, efforts should be made to make it easy for them to see the counselor on a voluntary basis, if possible without its being known to their peers. It is apparently easier for students to request or accept help with educational-vocational problems than with personal problems. The offering of vocational counseling, to all students, perhaps by scheduling an interview with each student early in the year, may give the student with a personal problem an opportunity to discuss it without embarrassment in peer relations—if the counselor is alert to the need of the student to discuss such a problem.

4. It is essential that privacy in the counseling interview and confidentiality regarding the contents of the counseling relationship be maintained if students are to use the counselor for assistance with personal problems. Students are aware, or soon learn, whether they can trust the counselor.

5. The importance of an accepting, nonjudgmental, noncondemning attitude on the part of the counselor is apparent from the studies of reluctance of students to bring their problems to a counselor for fear of being judged or condemned.

6. The desire of some students for independence in solving their problems, and the desirability of encouraging responsibility and independence suggest that the counseling relationship should be one in which responsibility and independence are made possible and encouraged.

7. The fact that many students expect, or desire, to assume a dependent role in counseling, however, suggests that it may be necessary in some instances to structure the counseling relationship verbally so that the student may utilize it in a more independent way. Perhaps in many instances all that is necessary is that the counselor distinguish between counseling and teaching.

These suggestions will not of course solve all the problems involved in counseling in schools. However, the counselor who is aware of the problems, including those touched upon in this chapter, and desires to do something about them, will find other ways in which to help resolve them. There will, however, always be certain problems, perhaps because of the nature of adolescents and the gap between generations, which are difficult for the student to admit to his peers, or which prevent him from seeking help from an adult. To paraphrase Irene Josselyn, counseling the young adolescent is perhaps the most challenging, the most frustrating, the most baffling, the most anxiety-arousing, and the most gratifying experience a counselor can have. Most clients offer one or more of these experiences to the counselor. Rarely is any client, except an adolescent, all of these in one counseling session.[30]

Summary

Because of the nature of the school setting and of adolescents, certain problems arise in counseling in the schools. Some of these problems have been considered in this chapter.

Students often do not seek help from counselors with their problems because they do not perceive the counselor as a source of help for their particular problems. Adolescents also often do not want to admit they need help with their problems, and are reluctant to have their peers know that they are receiving help. They are struggling to be independent, and an expression of this independence may be resistance to accepting help with their problems.

On the other hand, the adolescent is dependent in many ways, and studies seem to show that many adolescents prefer a counselor who allows them to assume a dependent role. Some have suggested that the counselor of adolescents should therefore assume a more directive role.

It is questioned whether this is desirable. Rather, it is suggested that if a goal of counseling—and of education and society as well—is independence, then the counselor should support or encourage the development of independence rather than dependence in the counseling process.

Because of the vacillation and unpredictability of adolescents, their conflict between wanting independence and to be dependent, and their difficulty in confiding in an adult (a difficulty sometimes compounded by the problem of confidentiality), the adolescent is a difficult client for the counselor.

The school and the counselor must make every effort to make

[30] Irene M. Josselyn. Psychotherapy of adolescents at the level of private practice. In B. H. Balser (Ed.) *Psychotherapy of the adolescent*. New York: International Universities Press, 1957. P. 13.

it easy and acceptable for the student to avail himself of counseling services. Some suggestions for doing this were made.

SUGGESTED READINGS

Carter, T. M. Professional immunity for guidance counselors. *Personnel Guid. J.*, 1954, **33**, 130–135. Reprinted in Farwell, G. F., & Peters, H. J. (Eds.) *Guidance readings for counselors.* Chicago: Rand McNally, 1960. Pp. 652–660. A discussion of the problem of privileged communication for counselors.

Hamrin, S. A., & Paulsen, Blanche B. *Counseling adolescents.* Chicago: Science Research Associates, 1950. Chapter 2, "Youth Moves Toward Maturity," and Chapter 9, "Counseling Youth in Emotional Areas," deal with problems of adolescents, including the drive toward independence.

Jersild, A. T. *The psychology of adolescence.* New York: Macmillan, 1957. A textbook on adolescence which emphasizes how the adolescent feels, how he perceives the world, and the importance of self-awareness and self-acceptance in the development of the self.

Remmers, H. H., & Radler, D. H. *The American teenager.* Indianapolis, Ind.: Bobbs-Merrill, 1957. A report of what adolescents think based on polls of 18,000 teenagers.

Strang, Ruth. *The adolescent views himself.* New York: McGraw-Hill, 1957. An analysis, with numerous quotations from adolescents themselves, of compositions by thousands of adolescents on topics proposed by the author.

Williamson, E. G. The fusion of discipline and counseling in the educative process. *Personnel Guid. J.*, 1955, **34**, 74–79. Reprinted in Farwell, G. F., & Peters, H. J. (Eds.) *Guidance readings for counselors.* Chicago: Rand McNally, 1960. Pp. 378–386. Also reprinted in McDaniel, H. B., *et al.* (Eds.) *Readings in guidance.* New York: Holt, 1959. Pp. 236–242. An excellent discussion of the counselor's role in discipline which goes somewhat beyond the conception adopted here.

Wrenn, C. G. The ethics of counseling. *Educ. psychol. Measmt*, 1952, **12**, 161–177. Reprinted in Farwell, G. F., & Peters, H. J. (Eds.) *Guidance readings for counselors.* Chicago: Rand McNally, 1960. Pp. 416–430. A statement of the ethical responsibilities of the counselor.

PART IV

COUNSELING SPECIAL GROUPS

CHAPTER 14

THE GIFTED AND

THE UNDERACHIEVER

In this and the following chapter we shall consider the responsibilities of the counselor with some special groups of students. In the present chapter we shall be concerned with the gifted student and those students who, whether gifted or not, are not achieving up to their potential. In the following chapter, we shall consider students who are handicapped by physical disability or mental retardation. Those with personal, social, or emotional disturbances have been discussed in Chapter 12.

The Gifted

Numerous writers have been pointing out the tremendous waste of talent in America. This waste occurs through the failure to utilize the talents of many able people who, for one reason or another, do not obtain the education and training which would make it possible for them to develop their talents. Large numbers of students who have the ability to do so do not go on to college. Estimates of the proportion of high-ability students who do not go on to college are as high as 50 percent. It is generally agreed that students in the upper 30 percent of the distribution in ability are qualified for college-level training. However, only about 60 percent of this group enter college, and of those entering, only about two-thirds finish.[1] Russell and Cronbach estimate that if every person with the ability to graduate from college did so, we would have nearly 660,000 college graduates per year instead of the actual 270,000. And if every one who could rea-

[1] D. Wolfle. Diversity of talent. *Amer. Psychologist,* 1960, **15,** 535–545.

sonably expect to attain a Ph.D., on the basis of ability, did so, we would have 300,000 such degrees awarded each year, compared to the 8000 which are actually awarded. They correctly point out that "Our scientific manpower problem is not a shortage of talent but a failure to attract enough students into advanced and specialized training."[2]

There are, of course, many reasons why able students do not continue their education. Socioeconomic factors are important in many cases. Wolfle refers to a study which found that 90 percent of those children whose fathers were engaged in professional and semiprofessional occupations, and who were in the upper third of their graduating class, went to college; 80 percent of those whose fathers were in managerial occupations entered college; 70 percent of the children of salesmen, clerks, and service workers went on to college; 60 percent of the children of farmers did so; and only 50 percent of the children of factory workers and laborers, although in the upper third of their class, continued their education to college.[3] Beilin points out that it is not only lack of financial resources which prevents youth from the lower socioeconomic group from attending college. An important factor is the attitude toward education.[4]

In many instances, high-ability youth are not aware of their potentialities, or become aware of them too late to be able to utilize them. Attitudes, goals, and expectations have become fixed, so that even if these students were persuaded to continue their education many would have difficulty, and many would quit or fail before completing college. Preparation for college begins long before high school and requires more than the appropriate sequence of college-preparatory courses.

---

[2] R. W. Russell & L. J. Cronbach. Report of testimony at a Congressional hearing. *Amer. Psychologist*, 1958, **13**, 217–223. In 1958–1959, 385,151 bachelor degrees were awarded and 9360 doctorates, according to the advance report of the U.S. Office of Education, June, 1960.

[3] D. Wolfle. Guidance and educational strategy. *Personnel Guid. J.*, 1958, **37**, 17–25.

[4] H. Beilin. The utilization of high level talent in lower socioeconomic groups. *Personnel Guid. J.*, 1956, **35**, 175–178. See also J. W. Gardner, *Excellence*, New York: Harper, 1961, for a discussion of talent and its recognition and encouragement.

What are the responsibilities of counselors in this matter of making possible the utilization of unused talent? There are several areas with which counselors should be involved.

Discovery or identification of talent. The first step in the utilization of talent is its discovery. While many students with high-level ability identify themselves by their obviously high achievement, others may not be recognized. Moreover, not all students who obtain high grades are talented, since factors other than ability affect grades. There are also talents other than the purely intellectual and these may not show themselves in the ordinary school setting.

It is thus apparent that grades cannot be depended upon to identify the gifted. Can teachers do so by observation and evaluation? Gallagher replies as follows: "The answer of pertinent research is discouraging. Classroom teachers seem prone to make a sizable number of identification errors. First, they identify as gifted many children that individual tests indicate are not gifted. Second and more serious, they do not mention some children whom tests show to be intellectually gifted."[5] Russell and Cronbach refer to a study in which a psychologist asked 6000 teachers to name the "most intelligent" child in each of their classes. Only 15 percent of them were correct in their choices.[6]

Tests have been recognized as an important aid in identifying the gifted. But tests are valuable only when used by those trained in their use, not only in administration and scoring, but in interpreting the results. The use of tests requires a definition of talent or giftedness in terms of test scores. The score suggested varies with authorities. An IQ of 130 or higher is commonly accepted as indicating high-level talent, and 120 or above includes those who are moderately gifted. The former score would select about the top 1 or 2 percent of the population, while the latter would include approximately the top 10 percent. But, as Gallagher notes, "IQ 130 is not always 130."[7] It depends on the test. IQ's on various tests are not equivalent, except possibly an IQ of

5 J. J. Gallagher. *What research says to the teacher.* (Research Series 17.) Washington, D.C.: National Education Association, 1959.

6 Russell & Cronbach, *op. cit.*

7 Gallagher, *op. cit.*

100, since the standard deviations (variabilities) of scores vary. When scores of 120 and 130 are suggested, it is usually with reference to the Stanford-Binet Intelligence Test. In most programs for the identification of the gifted, other tests, usually group tests, are used. When other tests are used, other scores might be selected, if the same proportions are to be included in the groups selected as gifted. Because of such problems as this, a trained counselor or a psychologist should be involved in the process of identifying gifted students. Where doubts or questions arise about a particular score, an individual test should be given.

The existence of other factors affecting the expression of talent, such as poor cultural background, parents who speak a foreign language, atypical educational histories, underachievement, and emotional problems also makes it important that a counselor or a psychologist be employed in making selections of gifted students. The existence of other gifts or talents in addition to high intelligence, many of which cannot be measured by tests or are not easily identified in other ways, requires the assistance of trained personnel for their identification. They include talents in music, art, dramatics, creative writing, mechanical skills, and social relations, including leadership.

Because of these and other factors, it would seem clear that "from the point of view of logic and efficiency the counselor is the staff member who assumes the responsibility for the identification of the gifted."[8] The counselor is the central figure in the Superior and Talented Student Project of the North Central Association of Colleges and Secondary Schools.[9] The purpose of this project, in which one-hundred secondary schools are participating, is to identify superior and talented high-school students, to provide guidance services for them, and to motivate them to make appropriate educational and occupational choices.

Assisting teachers and administrators in fostering the development of talents. Once the gifted have been identified, programs must be developed for their education. This is not the place to enter into a discussion of the various possible programs and

[8] E. McWilliams & J. W. Birch. Counseling gifted children. *Voc. Guid. Quart.*, 1957, **5**, 91–94.

[9] North Central Association of Colleges and Secondary Schools. *NCA Superior and Talented Student Project.* Chicago: NCA STS Project, 1958.

their merits.[10] The counselor, however, can and should enter into the planning of curricula for the gifted, as well as the assigning of students to various elements of the program. He should consult with teachers on aspects of the program for individual students. The counselor, because of his background and training and his individual contact with students, is aware of the needs of students for enrichment of programs, and can tell where programs are succeeding or failing in meeting these needs.

Early identification, followed by the provision of a challenging educational program, are important in developing the potentials of the gifted, and in preventing the problems created by boredom, poor work habits, and dislike of school which arise in many gifted children who are not challenged by schoolwork.

Counseling services. Counseling gifted students is essentially no different from the counseling of other students, as a number of writers have pointed out.[11] There is no reason to believe that the gifted need counseling any more than other students. The concept that intellectual superiority is associated with emotional instability has not been supported. Terman in his study found that the intellectually superior tended as a group to be above average in most other respects.[12]

[10] The following are some sources: (1) W. Abraham. *Common sense about gifted children.* New York: Harper, 1958. (2) R. F. DeHaan & R. J. Havighurst. *Educating gifted children.* Chicago: University of Chicago Press, 1957. (3) J. L. French. *Educating the gifted: a book of readings.* New York: Holt, 1959. (4) N. B. Henry (Ed.) *Education for the gifted.* Fifty-seventh Yearbook of the National Society for the Study of Education. Chicago: University of Chicago Press, 1958. (5) J. Kough. *Practical programs for the gifted.* Chicago: Science Research Associates, 1960. (6) M. R. Sumption & Evelyn M. Luecking. *Education of the gifted.* New York: Ronald, 1960.

[11] (1) Anna R. Meeks. Guidance services for the gifted child in the elementary school. *Gifted Child Quart.,* 1958, **2**, 61–64. (2) Ruth Strang. Guidance of the gifted. *Personnel Guid. J.,* 1952, **31**, 26–30. (3) Ruth Strang. The counselor's contribution to the guidance of the gifted, the underachiever, and the retarded. *Personnel Guid. J.,* 1956, **34**, 494–497. Reprinted in H. B. McDaniel, *et al.* (Eds.) *Readings in guidance.* New York: Holt, 1959. Pp. 264–268. (4) J. W. M. Rothney & N. E. Koopman. Guidance of the gifted. In N. B. Henry (Ed.) *Education for the gifted.* Fifty-seventh Yearbook of the National Society for the Study of Education. Chicago: University of Chicago Press, 1958.

[12] L. M. Terman (Ed.) *Mental and physical traits of a thousand gifted children.* Vol. I of *Genetic studies of genius.* Stanford, Calif.: Stanford University Press, 1925. However, as Gowan points out (J. C. Gowan. Organiza-

On the other hand, the gifted often have difficulty in adjusting to a curriculum devised for the average student and in adjusting to the demands of parents and others, which either fail to take into consideration their intellectual level, or which are unrealistic in some respects or exploitative in nature. The gifted are not, of course, immune from maladjustment. Many gifted children suffer from the same kinds of personal-social-emotional problems as do other children.

While counseling of the gifted is essentially the same as counseling the average student, there are some factors which the counselor should keep in mind.[13]

1. Gifted students, because of their general advanced maturity, are able to utilize counseling at earlier ages than other children. They are able to verbalize, and thus analyze, their problems more easily than other children of the same age. They thus become ready for self-appraisal and self-conceptualization at higher levels, and at an earlier age, than their schoolmates.

2. Although this advancement may lead to earlier vocational choices, the counselor should be cautious about accepting or fostering specific occupational choices at an early age. The gifted child may have a greater realization of his abilities and interests, and of the world of work, but he may not be familiar with all the potential choices open to him, some of which may represent unusual jobs or work in which few people are engaged, and are therefore not well known. For the gifted have more potential choices than the average student; their educational and vocational opportunities are more numerous, or wider in scope. Since the occupations they will enter will more likely be those requiring advanced training, the gifted will have time in which to narrow down their interests to a specific choice, or to a specialization within a profession.

In this connection, the counselor must beware of any tendency to direct the gifted into particular fields, such as science, toward which the counselor may be biased. As Wolfle points out, "We must provide much freedom to our gifted students to change their

---

tion of guidance for gifted children. *Personnel Guid. J.*, 1960, **39**, 275–279), "the able may have special problems, which it takes individual guidance to handle."

[13] Rothney & Koopman, *op. cit.*

plans and aspirations as they go along. We know from experience that many students do change their fields of specialization. We know, too, that many college graduates enter, or switch to, types of work that were not anticipated during college days. In counseling with gifted students on their educational plans, one of our objectives should be to keep the doors of opportunity open. The final decision to accept a particular position or to specialize in a particular area can be made only if many earlier decisions have kept open the doors that lead to the final choice. In educational terms, this means an emphasis on good preparation for higher education and later specialization."[14]

In connection with the educational counseling of the gifted, the providing of information about scholarships is important. It has been estimated that from 60,000 to 100,000 talented students who did not go to college in 1955 for financial reasons could have been recruited to higher education by scholarships.[15] Thistlethwaite suggests that "part of the nation's talent loss may be attributed to lack of student initiative, inadequate counseling, or both, since many of these students do not apply for scholarships or apply only to one or two institutions," while he found that those who made several applications were more likely to receive scholarships.[16]

3. A problem arising in a number of talented students is the lack of orientation toward and motivation for higher education. This is particularly the case in students from the lower socioeconomic classes. Abilities must be developed and trained if they are to be maximally used. The problem is to develop positive attitudes and expectations toward education in these students, and in their parents. There are no magic formulas for achieving this. The early identification of and curriculum planning for the gifted should be an important factor here. But more than this is often necessary. The family may need to be brought into the picture. Wolfle refers to a survey of 7000 students who had received the highest scores on tests of science and mathematics. Many of the

[14] Wolfle, Guidance and educational strategy, *op. cit.*

[15] C. C. Cole, Jr. *Encouraging scientific talent.* New York: College Entrance Examination Board, 1956.

[16] D. L. Thistlethwaite. Counseling high-aptitude students on scholarship opportunities. *Personnel Guid. J.*, 1959, 37, 574–577.

children and their parents were not aware of the abilities possessed by the children. Wolfle suggests that counselors should not only discuss with the child the talents which he has, but should talk with the family in an effort to enlist its interest and support. He writes that "There is no guarantee that these tactics will succeed, but they are certainly more likely to be successful than is the negative policy of not letting the child's family know that he has the ability to profit from advanced education."[17]

4. The counselor must be prepared to work with problems related to the unusual demands and pressures of parents, teachers, relatives, peers, and others. Although on the average, gifted children are socially and emotionally more mature than their age mates, they encounter problems which the average child does not, as well as being susceptible to the problems faced by the average child. A particular problem of the gifted which is important in relation to the waste of talent is that of underachievement, and thus this warrants attention here.

The Gifted Underachiever

The problem of underachievement in gifted students is a real one, although the extent of the problem is not clearly known. Its extent depends on the definition of underachievement. But even under the same definition the number of underachieving gifted students identified varies from study to study. Gowan, using as a criterion a difference of 30 percentile points or more between ability and achievement, reports percentages of underachievers from about 10 percent to almost 50 percent in different schools.[18]

Evidence of underachievement at the college level is clear. One study revealed that almost 30 percent of students in the top decile in ability who go to college fail to achieve adequately.[19] The reasons for underachievement in college are many, including financial difficulties requiring excessive time devoted to employment and worries about financial problems.

[17] Wolfle, Guidance and educational strategy, *op. cit.*

[18] (1) J. C. Gowan. The underachieving gifted child: a problem for everyone. *Except. Child.*, 1955, **21**, 247–249.   (2) J. C. Gowan. Dynamics of the underachievement of gifted students. *Except. Child.*, 1957, **24**, 98–101.

[19] C. A. Wedemeyer. Gifted achievers and non-achievers. *J. higher Educ.*, 1953, **24**, 25–30.

Achievement in high school and later is also related to habits, attitudes, interests, and motivations established at the elementary school level. Personal, emotional, and home problems also are important factors in underachievement in the gifted.[20]

The fact that the underachievement of gifted students is related to personal-emotional adjustment suggests that counseling would be of value. Evidence indicates that counseling is difficult, however, perhaps because of an element of hostility which may be present in such students.[21] Gowan's summary of findings indicating that gifted underachievers tend to be unsociable, self-sufficient, and hard to reach, would also suggest that counseling would be difficult.[22] Both Shaw and Grubb, and Gowan point out that group counseling might be an effective approach to gifted underachievers. There appear to be no reports in the literature of the effectiveness of either individual or group therapy with gifted underachievers.

Studies of group counseling of gifted underachieving adolescents have recently been completed a the University of Illinois.[23] Twenty-nine freshmen in a large midwestern high school were studied. These students ranked in the top 10 percent of their class in intelligence in the eighth grade, but below the ninth decile in grade-point average. The total group was randomly divided into four smaller groups, two of which took part in group counseling while two did not. The counseling consisted of two forty-three minute sessions a week for eight weeks. An eclectic, group-centered approach to counseling was used.

The results of the study indicated that the two counseled groups made greater gains in acceptance of self and others dur-

20 (1) *Ibid.* (2) Gowan, The underachieving gifted child: a problem for everyone, *op. cit.* (3) M. C. Shaw & D. J. Brown. Scholastic underachievement of bright college students. *Personnel Guid. J.*, 1957, **36**, 195–199. (4) Edna G. Sanford. The bright child who fails. *Understanding the Child*, 1952, **21**, 85–88.

21 M. C. Shaw & J. Grubb. Hostility and able high school underachievers. *J. counsel. Psychol.*, 1958, **5**, 263–266.

22 Gowan, The unachieving gifted child: a problem for everyone, *op. cit.*

23 (1) J. W. Broedel. *The effects of group counseling on academic performance and mental health of underachieving gifted adolescents.* Unpublished doctoral dissertation, University of Illinois, 1958. (2) J. Broedel, M. Ohlsen, F. Proff & C. Southard. The effects of group counseling on gifted underachieving adolescents. *J. counsel. Psychol.*, 1960, **7**, 163–170.

ing the eight-week period. Ratings of interpersonal relationships by the investigators, by observers, and by the parents indicated improvement in behavior. On the other hand, counseling did not result in better academic performance as represented by grade-point average. The counseled groups declined in grade-point average slightly, while the noncounseled groups increased their grade-point average slightly. There was also no improvement in achievement test scores by the counseled groups. However, scores on an achievement test administered sixteen weeks after termination of counseling were significantly higher. These results suggest that improvement in personal adjustment did not affect, at least immediately, classroom performance, but did result in greater achievement as measured objectively at a later date.

The investigators report that most of the students questioned whether they were gifted, and that they showed evidence of disturbed behavior prior to counseling and were not the kind of persons one would expect to seek counseling.

Following the completion of this experiment, the two groups which had not received counseling were then counseled. Some of the members of these two groups showed some improvement in acceptance of self and others but the improvement was not significant for the groups as a whole. Grades of students in these groups did not improve during counseling, although their grades the following year improved. In this study, the findings were affected by the fact that one of the two groups appeared to benefit from counseling while one did not. It was felt that, because of the relatively serious disturbance of the students, it would be expecting too much to achieve great changes in an eight-week period. The results of these studies are promising enough to suggest that underachieving gifted students, even though not presumably desirous of counseling may be helped to improved personal adjustment by group counseling. This improvement in personal adjustment may lay the basis for future gains in achievement.

The Underachieving Student

Not only gifted students may be underachievers; the more or less average student may also present a problem in underachievement. As in the case of the gifted underachievers, the discrepancy between potential and achievement may be related to a number of factors. Historically, attention was first directed at deficiencies in the tools or techniques basic to academic proficiency, such as reading or other specific deficiencies. These deficiencies may be of a so-called innate nature or origin, or the result of inadequate training or experience. On the basis of this assumption as to the origin of underachievement, diagnostic studies of specific disabilities, such as in reading, have been stressed. Emphasis was placed on programs of remedial work or tutoring where the deficiency was deemed to be the result of inadequate preparation or training. Training in methods of study has also been used to remedy defects in study habits or skills.

This approach was not found to be effective in many cases. In others, no such specific deficiencies could be found. The factor of interest, or motivation, was then recognized as important in achievement. Drasgow[24] states that in his experience underachievers are usually in the wrong curriculum, and proposes changing them to a curriculum more appropriate to their interests and aptitudes. But what about the underachievers in high school, where there is little if any choice of curricula? And again, what about those cases where interests and aptitudes are consistent with the curriculum being followed?

The importance of emotional factors in underachievement is being increasingly recognized.[25] Students may fail, or achieve below their potentials, because of the presence of personal and emotional problems. This suggests that therapeutic counseling or psychotherapy may be effective in helping underachievers.

Several studies have indicated that interviews by teachers or counselors, dealing with the personal interests or problems of students, are effective in improving achievement of students.[26] Hoehn

[24] J. Drasgow. Underachievers. *J. counsel. Psychol.*, 1957, **4**, 210–211.

[25] (1) K. Feyereisen. Eliminating blocks to learning. *Leadership,* 1948, **5,** 527–535. (2) Barbara Kimball. The sentence completion technique in a study of scholastic underachievement. *J. consult. Psychol.*, 1952, **16**, 353–358. (3) Barbara Kirk. Test versus academic performance in malfunctioning students. *J. consult. Psychol.*, 1952, **16**, 213–216. (4) M. Sheldon & T. Landsman. An investigation of nondirective group therapy with students in academic difficulty. *J. consult. Psychol.*, 1950, **14**, 210–215.

[26] (1) K. W. Bradt & C. P. Duncan. Degree of personal relationship between instructor and student as a factor in course grade improvement.

and Salts,[27] however, found that teacher interviews were not effective. Other studies[28] involving counselors have also yielded essentially negative results, although Calhoun found improvement in grades but none in standardized achievement tests. Group therapy has also been reported as effective in improving achievement.[29] It would appear that the results are somewhat commensurate with the competence and duration and/or intensity of the counseling.

Serene[30] reports an interesting experiment in "motivational counseling," involving one or two interviews with students and one with parents, with positive results. Schoenhard[31] found that interviews with parents in the home did not raise academic achievement, a result which he explained as resistance of the students to parental control. Drews and Teahan[32] report that mothers of high achievers were found to be more authoritarian and restrictive than mothers of low achievers.

A study conducted by a student of the author is pertinent here.[33] Thirty-two members of a class of 220 juniors in a midwest

Amer. Psychologist, 1951, **6**, 368 (abstract).   (2) L. J. Briggs & R. M. Roe. Morale as a function of opportunity to register complaints. Technical Report HRRC-TR-53-4, Human Resources Research Center, Lackland Air Force Base, Texas, 1953.   (3) LaV. H. Richardson & J. D. Perry. Counseling for academic recovery. *J. counsel. Psychol.*, 1956, **3**, 136–139.   (4) A. C. Sherrifs. Modification of academic performance through personal interview. *J. appl. Psychol.*, 1949, **33**, 339–346.

[27] A. J. Hoehn & B. Salts. Effects of teacher-student interviews on classroom achievement. *J. educ. Psychol.*, 1956, **47**, 434–435.

[28] (1) S. R. Calhoun. The effects of counseling on a group of underachievers. *Sch. Rev.*, 1956, **64**, 312–316. Reprinted in G. F. Farwell & H. J. Peters (Eds.) *Guidance readings for counselors.* Chicago: Rand McNally, 1960. Pp. 585–591.   (2) G. M. Guthrie & H. W. O'Neil. Effects of dormitory counseling on academic achievement. *Personnel Guid. J.*, 1953, **31**, 307–309.

[29] (1) C. Gersten. An experimental evaluation of group therapy with juvenile delinquents. *Int. J. Group Psychother.*, 1951, **1**, 311–318.   (2) Sheldon & Landsman, *op. cit.*

[30] H. F. Serene. An experiment in motivational counseling. *Personnel Guid. J.*, 1953, **31**, 319–324.

[31] G. H. Schoenhard. Home visitation put to a test. *Personnel Guid. J.*, 1950, **36**, 480–485.

[32] Elizabeth M. Drews & J. R. Teahan. Parental attitudes and academic achievement. *J. clin. Psychol.*, 1957, **13**, 328–332.

[33] Feriha B. Baymur & C. H. Patterson. A comparison of three methods of assisting underachieving high school students. *J. counsel. Psychol.*, 1960, **7**, 83–89.

high school were identified as underachievers on the basis of discrepancy in class standing on grades and aptitude tests. They were divided into four groups of eight each, matched for aptitude, achievement, degree of underachievement, socioeconomic status, age, and sex. Then one group was provided individual counseling and a second group was given group counseling. The counselor met once with the third group, informed them they were underachievers, and encouraged them to work harder, pointing out the importance of good grades for further education and employment. The fourth group received no help. All groups were given copies of the book *Study Your Way Through School*.[34] Counseling continued for a period of twelve weeks and was conducted in a client-centered manner. All students were given the Brown-Holtzman *Survey of Study Habits* and a Q-sort (a measure of personal adjustment) before and after counseling.

The results indicated that the two counseled groups did not significantly improve their scores on the *Survey of Study Habits*. The two counseled groups combined did show greater positive changes in self-concept. This change was the result of improvement in the students who received individual counseling, however, since those receiving group counseling did not improve. The two counseled groups improved in grade-point average. In this case, the students receiving group counseling seemed to show greater improvement in grades than those receiving individual counseling.

Considering the many factors involved, the results of this study might be considered encouraging. The duration and extent of the counseling were limited; the group counseling consisted of only nine sessions. The group counseling sessions tended to be rather superficial, in the opinion of the counselor. None of the students had requested the counseling; many were not aware that they were underachievers. In spite of these factors, some of the students were benefited. It appears possible that group counseling which does not concentrate on problems of personal adjustment may result in improvement in grades. On the other hand, counseling which involves consideration of personal problems, as in the case of the students given individual counseling,

34 C. Gerken. *Study your way through school.* Chicago: Science Research Associates, 1953.

may, at least in the short run, have little if any effect on grades. In fact, as in the study of gifted underachievers discussed earlier, grades may even decline. The concentration on personal problems may affect application to schoolwork.

It is interesting that the selection of students who were underachievers resulted in the selection of students manifesting personal and social problems, supporting the hypothesis that underachievement is related to general problems of adjustment. Some underachievers, however, appear not to have such general problems. A student may accept, or choose, underachievement in order to gain social acceptance, or in order to concentrate his time and efforts in other areas, such as extracurricular activities. The influence of social attitudes on achievement was expressed by a student in counseling as follows: "That's one problem today with the schools of America—the intelligent person is ridiculed, and the person who may be average or a little below average is the one who gets all the recognition. And that I imagine has frustrated many people of potential ability, just as I think happened to me."

The failure of the attempt to stimulate underachievers in one-session "motivational counseling" is of interest. This group declined in all three measures employed in the study, falling below the control group at the end of the study. The approach used with this group is one commonly employed by parents and teachers who attempt to raise the achievement of students. The results of the study suggest that it may be better to leave underachievers alone, rather than pointing out their failure to achieve adequately and exhorting them to do something about it. Perhaps the failure of underachievers to respond to such exhortations is related to the hostility which appears to be present in able underachievers. Shaw and Grubb write that "it seems reasonable to infer . . . that a basically hostile person would not react favorably to demands for better performance or to higher standards of work, as has been suggested in some quarters."[35]

Underachievement is a problem with a variety of causes, ranging from inadequate previous preparation or instruction, through

[35] Shaw & Grubb, Hostility and able high school underachievers, *op. cit.*

deliberate efforts not to achieve at a high level because of fear of being considered a grind or an "egghead," and preoccupation with family problems, to emotional disturbances and lack of recognition of potentiality. Poor or inadequate background or preparation may be remedied by special instruction or tutoring. The other factors or causes are matters for counseling, rather than instruction or exhortation. More and better counseling services in our schools would undoubtedly lead to the reduction of underachievement and the more efficient utilization of the talent of students. It would not, however, eliminate the problem of underachievement, since this may be the result of factors not amenable to counseling. These include socioeconomic factors, social pressures, and the free but considered choice of the student to accept lower achievement academically in order to achieve better in some other area.

Summary

This chapter is devoted to two special groups of students, the gifted, and the underachiever, including the gifted underachiever.

While counseling the gifted is essentially no different from the counseling of other students, the counselor has certain responsibilities for the gifted, and faces certain problems in counseling with them. The counselor should be involved in the identification of gifted students, and with the development of an adequate curriculum suited to their needs. Special factors to be considered in counseling the gifted were pointed out.

The counselor who is concerned with the problem of the utilization of all the talent of all students will be concerned with the problem of underachievement. Underachievement is related to many factors and causes which must be understood if we are to deal with the problems posed by the underachieving student. While it is desirable, and possible, to help many underachievers through both group and individual counseling, it is probable that not all underachievement can be eliminated, either by counseling or by any other methods. There may always be individuals who may choose not to achieve up to their potentials in the academic area, because they prefer to concentrate their efforts on something else.

SUGGESTED READINGS

Drews, Elizabeth M. (Ed.) *Guidance for the academically talented student.* Washington, D.C.: American Personnel and Guidance Association and National Education Association, 1961. This booklet includes chapters on identifying, motivating, educating and counseling the academically talented, and a bibliography for counselors.

Rothney, J. W. M., & Koopman, N. E. Guidance of the gifted. In Henry, N. B. (Ed.) *Education for the gifted.* Fifty-seventh Yearbook of the National Society for the Study of Education. Chicago: University of Chicago Press, 1958. An excellent brief treatment of the guidance of the gifted.

CHAPTER 15

COUNSELING THE

HANDICAPPED STUDENT

The schools, and therefore counselors in schools, must be concerned with those students who are handicapped in one way or another by physical or mental disabilities. The Committee on Child Health of the American Public Health Association defines the handicapped child as follows: "A child is considered to be handicapped if he cannot, within limits, learn, work, or do the things other children of his age can do; if he is hindered in achieving his full physical, mental, and social potentialities. The initial disability may be very mild and hardly noticeable, but potentially handicapping, or, it may seriously involve several areas of function, with the probability of lifelong impairment."

Children who are handicapped by a physical or mental disability require adaptations of school facilities and instruction. The schools have been increasingly accepting the responsibility for the handicapped child. While the lack of qualified teachers is a problem, special education is still growing rapidly. Special classes, even special schools, have been established for children handicapped by various disabilities.

It may be questioned whether such segregation of the handicapped is desirable. While the child in a special class or school receives individual and specialized teaching, which he needs, he may also be set aside or isolated from other children, whom he also needs for his social development. Isolation, or segregation, may foster stigmatization. Attitudes of other children are affected by the nature and amount of contact which they have with the physically disabled, and if they have none, or very little, they are less likely to understand, and more likely to shun, the disabled child.

The potential dangers of isolation and segregation are being recognized, and the trend is to integrate, insofar as possible, the disabled child into the regular classroom or the regular school. The average school is thus likely to see an increase in the number of disabled students, and these students must be assimilated into the school, and provided with all the services which are provided for the nondisabled child, in addition to the necessary special services. These services, including counseling, are the right of every disabled and handicapped child.

The disabled are not always easily accepted, however. Attitudes of apprehension, even of fear, of dislike, or of uneasiness toward the visibly disabled are common and apparently rather deep-rooted. Many of us do not know how to approach or deal with the disabled. As a result of these attitudes and lack of knowledge of how to treat the disabled, we retreat from them, or avoid them. This may be true of counselors as well as others. It appears that because of feelings of inadequacy with respect to the disabled, counselors often hesitate to work with them. At least there are frequent complaints, which were voiced at the 1960 White House Conference on Children and Youth, that disabled students are neglected as far as counseling services are concerned. Counselors therefore must be concerned about the disabled, and provide counseling services for them. It is the purpose of this chapter to serve as an introduction for the counselor in working with physically disabled and mentally retarded students.

The Physically Disabled Child

It has been estimated that from 10 to 12 percent of school age children, or from 3 to 4 million, have serious disabilities of one kind or another. Accurate figures are not available, and estimates vary considerably, but there is no doubt that the number is large. The National Health Survey indicated that over 2 million children under 15 years of age are affected by blindness, deafness, paralysis, missing or deformed limbs, or other orthopedic handicaps. An estimated 300,000 children and youths are epileptic, from 350,000 to 675,000 suffer from rheumatic fever or its sequelae. Diabetes, cancer, and other disorders affect several hundred thousand children, and some 2 million children have handicapping speech disorders, with some 300,000 of these having associated disabilities such as hearing loss, cerebral palsy, cleft palate, or other congenital disabilities. Some degree of hearing impairment is present in 1½ million children, while 7½ million school children need eye care, of whom about 80,000 are partially seeing and 6,000 blind. About 9 million children are allergic. Other disabilities account for thousands more children.

While the incidence of some disabilities, such as tuberculosis, rickets, and polio, is decreasing, others are increasing. Medical advances have prevented or ameliorated some physical disabilities, but at the same time they have also, by saving the lives of children who would have died at birth or in early infancy, increased the number of children with certain types of disability. We are saving lives, but actually increasing the number of the disabled. Children today are also more likely to have multiple disabilities.

These disabilities constitute handicaps in obtaining an education. Some, such as the orthopedically disabled, require special physical facilities, or buildings accessible to children with crutches or wheel chairs. Others, such as the deaf and the blind, require special methods of instruction. Special education is doing much to provide adequate instruction for the disabled child, although many disabled children are not reached by special education, especially in the rural areas.

But more than special education is needed. The question must be raised, education for what? The disabled person presents problems of adjustment to adult society; a major problem is the earning of a living. Special education is only a means to such adjustment. It must, therefore, be oriented to the goals of adult living. Counselors must be concerned with the outcomes of special education. They must work with special teachers, as well as with the disabled child, to assist in the development of the potentials of the child. Yet, as has been indicated above, counseling services to the disabled child are woefully inadequate. There is often a big gap between special education programs and the absorption of the disabled child or youth into society. Some of this neglect appears to be the result of lack of understanding of the disabled, with its concomitant fears and doubts. It is also true, of course, that the problems of inducting the disabled into society, including the world of work, are greater than in the case of the able-bodied. This may lead to hesitancy in tackling the problems.

The responsibilities of the counselor to the disabled child in school may be discussed under several headings:

Identifying the disabled child. It might appear that there would be no probelm in identifying the physically disabled child. This is true in the case of the severely disabled with visible disabilities. But there are many children whose nonvisible disabilities are unknown to school personnel. Often school officials claim that there are no disabled students in a school. In some instances they are thinking in terms of severe orthopedic disabilities, without considering the hard-of-hearing or partially sighted child as disabled.

Thus, in many situations the school has disabled children of which it is unaware. Health records may be inadequate, or even lacking. While the major responsibility for identifying physically handicapped students is not the counselor's, the counselor should be concerned about their identification in order that adequate personnel and counseling services may be provided. The counselor should therefore work with the school physician, the nurse, and the school administration in setting up and applying procedures for the identification of the disabled student. Wright presents a self-report form which may be completed by students.[1] The utilization of this health survey form in several schools resulted in the identification of about 20 percent of the student body with some degree of physical impairment, about half of whom required special counseling services.

The psychology of the handicapped. The attitudes toward the handicapped are frequently based on feelings that they differ in some essential respects from the rest of us. This feeling is perhaps related to the idea that there is a special psychology of the disabled, and to the feeling of some that all the disabled are psychologically abnormal.

This is not the case, however. Because the disabled differ phys-

[1] G. N. Wright. Wanted—more referrals from high school. *J. Rehab.*, 1959, **25** (1), 22–23.

ically from others, it does not follow that they necessarily differ psychologically. There is no such thing as a psychology of disability. It is, of course, true that there are psychological reactions to disability on the part of those who are disabled but these reactions are varied, and are not necessarily abnormal. It is perhaps also true that the severely physically disabled have more frequent and more serious psychological problems. These problems are often related to the situations which the disabled face because of their disabilities.

But the disabled are essentially the same as the nondisabled. They are human beings, with the same basic needs, desires, hopes, and ambitions. We should think in terms of a child with a disability, not of a "crippled child." The disability is only one aspect of the child, and there are many other abilities and assets present. Many of the problems of the disabled are those with which society faces him, and the psychological aspects of disability are often more in the minds and attitudes of others than within the person himself.

Counseling the disabled with personal problems. The personal problems of the disabled are similar to those of the nondisabled, although they may be more frequent or more severe. The disabled child may have problems with his parents, for example, who may be overprotective or over-restrictive, thus inhibiting the development of independence. In many cases the problem is with the parent, not the child. The counselor may have to work with the parent more frequently than in the case of the nondisabled.

Ideally, parent counseling should be available from the birth of the child, or the onset of the disability. Where it has not been available, or where it has not been utilized, the counselor in the school faces a more difficult problem. But essentially it is the same problem of achieving independence which is faced by the normal child.

Similarly with other problems, such as boy-girl relationships and marriage; there are complications, of course, but the nature of the problem is essentially the same in the disabled as in the nondisabled. Here again, many problems are imposed by the attitudes of others, such as those who feel that the disabled should not marry the able-bodied. The disabled are limited in their contacts, and in their dating activities. Beatrice Wright cites autobiographical accounts of frustrating boy-girl relationships of the handicapped during adolescence, but she comments that such trying experiences are common to adolescents in general.[2] The author has counseled handicapped college students who have experienced the agonies of unrequited love, infatuations, and rejections which were in no way different from similar experiences of the nonhandicapped. It is true, however, that the severely handicapped may be justifiably concerned about their chances for marriage, and, as in the case of one client of the author's, may have a difficult time distinguishing between, on the one hand, the failure to establish heterosexual relationships because of the restrictions imposed by the handicap and others' attitudes toward it, and, on the other hand, failure related to personal attitudes and relationships with others.

There are no special skills, knowledges, or techniques necessary for the counselor who works with the personal problems of the disabled. The methods discussed in Chapter 7 are appropriate here also.

Vocational counseling of the disabled. As in the case of counseling disabled students with personal problems, so the vocational counseling of the disabled is fundamentally the same as the vocational counseling of the nondisabled. The goals of counseling are identical: the attainment of vocational or occupational adjustment, which is characterized by the fullest use of the potentials of the individual in an occupation which is satisfying, which provides the means for economic independence and security, and which contributes to society. Work, with its material, social, and psychological rewards and satisfactions, is just as important and desirable for the disabled as for the able-bodied. The utilization of the skills of the disabled is as important to society as is the utilization of the skills of the average person and the talented.

The vocational counseling process is essentially the same for the disabled. The greatest difference is that the choices of the disabled person are more limited because of the handicaps imposed by the disability. The ideal goal of vocational adjustment for the disabled is participation in an occupation in which the

[2] Beatrice Wright. *Physical disability—a psychological approach.* New York: Harper, 1960. Pp. 189–193.

disability does not constitute a handicap. The disabled individual, in other words, would be able to perform the duties and functions of the occupation without any interference by his disability. This, as is indicated, is an ideal; it cannot always be achieved. Many severely and multiply disabled persons can never compete on an equal basis with the nondisabled, or find an occupation in which their disabilities are not a handicap. The objective in these cases is to utilize as much of the potential of the individual as possible in the most suitable occupation which can be found.

The counselor of the disabled student, therefore, must have some knowledge of the student's disability. It is not necessary that he have an extensive medical knowledge, but that he have a general understanding of the nature of the common physical disabilities. Such more detailed information as is necessary he can obtain from medical reports and consultation with physicians.

The essential information for the vocational counselor consists of the limitations of the disability, in terms of the physical and mental capacities of the students, and in terms of the environmental conditions which should be avoided. The appraisal of physical capacities and of environmental limitations is an aspect of vocational counseling of the able-bodied also, but it is of greater importance in the counseling of the disabled. In the consideration of possible appropriate occupations, the capacities or limitations of the student can be compared with the physical demands of the occupation and its working conditions. A check list form may facilitate this comparison. Such forms have been developed by the United States Employment Service, the War Manpower Commission, and the Veterans Administration. Examples are shown on pp. 272–273. In using the form, the capacities of the student are indicated in the column to the left of the job factor, using the symbol 0 (zero) if the capacity for meeting the activity or working condition is absent or negligible, and an X where there is partial capacity or limitation in capacity. Leaving the space blank indicates no limitation in capacity. For the job-demands columns, each occupation being considered is evaluated in terms of its demands in each job factor where the client's capacity has been determined to be absent or limited. If this capacity or working condition is a requirement of the job, it is marked with an X, if it is not, it is marked with a 0. The result is a list of job factors which are requirements of the job and in which the client has limitations (those factors marked 0 or X in the client-capacities column and X in the job-demands column). The presence of such factors does not necessarily or automatically rule out the occupation being considered. More detailed evaluation should then be attempted. There may be specific jobs in the occupation where the factors are not important, or the job may be easily modified to change or adapt the requirements to the point where the client can meet the job demands.

It is thus apparent that in addition to a knowledge of the disability in terms of its occupational limitations, the counselor of the disabled must have a knowledge of the requirements of jobs and of the nature of the working conditions of jobs. This, again, is something which the counselor of the able-bodied must also have, although it is again perhaps more important in the case of counseling the disabled. It should be noted that although, as has been indicated above, the occupational choices of the disabled are more limited than those of the able-bodied, they are still rather broad except in the case of the very severely and multiply disabled, with whom the counselor in the school is not likely to work. It needs to be emphasized that there are no lists of jobs which are suitable for those who have a particular disability. Individuals with every kind of disability will be found working in a wide range of jobs. Even in the case of such a disability as blindness, one finds few occupations in which a blind person is not engaged. It is important therefore that each disabled person be treated as an individual, and the range of occupational opportunities considered in terms of his specific assets and limitations, not in terms of a disability stereotype.

Opportunities for advanced education for the disabled, like occupational choice, are limited. Most colleges and universities will emphasize that they do not discriminate against handicapped applicants. But this actually applies only to the mildly handicapped. Schools which pride themselves on accepting handicapped students usually are thinking of the mildly or at most the moderately handicapped student. The severely handicapped are excluded, not by a policy of discrimination, but because the physical facilities of the school are not such as to make their attendance feasible or possible. It may be true to some extent also that colleges do not have to deny admission to such applicants, since severely handicapped individuals do not apply, or even consider applying, because of the obvious or apparent inaccessibility of facilities for wheel chair students. We do not know, therefore, how many otherwise qualified students fail to attend college. That there are many may be assumed from the experience of the University of Illinois. Handicapped persons upon first hearing of the university's program for handicapped students often are surprised to learn that such an opportunity exists, and state that they had never thought college training would be possible. The university is forced to exclude over half of those applying for admission because of lack of space in the program. This program at the University of Illinois, which now includes 180 severely handicapped students, over two-thirds of them in wheel chairs, is the largest program of its kind. Southern Illinois University has recently embarked upon such a program. Fortunately, other schools are planning or contemplating programs which will make possible the admission of otherwise qualified disabled students.

Another area in which the counseling process with the disabled may be modified to some extent is in the use of tests. The disabled individual may be handicapped in performance on some tests. There are three conditions which affect the performance of the handicapped on aptitude and ability tests which must be considered in the use of tests with these groups. First, the disability may interfere with the perception of the test problems or materials. The blind cannot see the performance test items, for example, and the deaf cannot hear items presented verbally by the examiner. Second, the disabled student may be unable to manipulate or handle the test materials. Those who have little or no use of their hands cannot perform tasks which require such manipulation. Third, the disabled student may not be able to make the required response indicating answers to the test items. Inability to use a pencil, for example, may prevent marking responses on answer sheets, or a speech defect may make verbal responses impossible.

Many of these difficulties are mechanical in nature and can be overcome by adaptations of test administration. Some apply only

Client Capacities		Physical Activities	Job Demands		
			1	2	3
		Lifting			
		Carrying			
		Pushing			
		Pulling			
		Climbing			
		Balancing			
		Stooping			
		Kneeling			
		Crouching			
		Crawling			
		Reaching			
		Handling			
		Fingering			
		Feeling			
		Standing			
		Walking			
		Treading			
		Sitting			
		Turning			
		Talking			
		Hearing			
		Smelling			
		Near vision			
		Far vision			
		Depth perception			
		Color vision			

Job Demands and Physical Capacities Appraisal

Client Capacities	Working Conditions	Job Demands 1	2	3
	Inside			
	Outside			
	Extreme cold			
	Extreme heat			
	Sudden temperature change			
	Humid			
	Wet			
	Dry			
	Noise			
	Vibration			
	Cluttered floors			
	Slippery floors			
	High places			
	Moving objects			
	Hazardous machinery			
	Danger of burns			
	Electrical hazards			
	Explosives			
	Fumes			
	Odors			
	Toxic conditions			
	Dust			
	Poor ventilation			
	Poor lighting			
	Variety of duties			
	Repetitive work			
	Fast pace of work			
	Following specific instrs.			
	Exacting performance			
	Meeting emergencies			
	Competitive work			
	Working alone			
	Working around others			
	Working with others			

Job Demands and Physical Capacities Appraisal (*continued*)

to particular types of tests, and other tests may be substituted. The literature on the use of tests with the handicapped is concerned mainly with the adaptation, substitution, or development of tests to eliminate these obstructive conditions. In many cases the adaptations in test administration are not great, and do not affect the use of the usual test norms with the handicapped. It is suggested that there has perhaps been too much concern about this aspect of testing the handicapped. With a well-trained and ingenious or resourceful psychologist or psychological examiner, the problems can be resolved with little if any effect on the validity of the test.

But there are some situations in which the testing conditions need to be so greatly altered, that the test can no longer be considered the same as the unaltered test used with the nonhandicapped; and there are other situations in which the conditions, even though greatly altered, do not allow for responses or performance that can be compared with that of the nonhandicapped. A timed test, administered verbally to a blind subject, cannot be compared with the same test given to a seeing subject. A matching test, or even a multiple choice test, is more difficult for a blind subject than for a seeing subject. One cannot arbitrarily add five or ten points to the score of a blind subject and consider the result equivalent to what he would have obtained if he could see.

Some who have been concerned about the use of tests with handicapped individuals have suggested the development and use of special tests with norms for the particular type of handicapped individual. Others have suggested the development of special norms based upon disabled subjects for existing tests. But a moment's reflection will show that the disabled are a very heterogeneous group, with varying types and degrees of disability. How many norm groups should we have? Should we have different groups for different disabilities and different degrees of severity of each? Not only is such a project impossible, but it is actually undesirable. With whom are the disabled going to compete? With each other, or with the general population? If, as is the case in most situations, with the latter, then we should not have special norms. And if tests are developed to meet the requirement of practicability of administration to a group with a particular handicap, then norms for nonhandicapped subjects should be obtained and used. In this case, the handicapped are competing with the nonhandicapped on more or less equal terms.

There is another point which is given very little attention in testing the handicapped, but which is probably as important a factor in the lower scores of the handicapped as is the fact or nature of the handicap itself. This is the restriction of experience of the handicapped as a result of the disability. Our tests are developed and used upon the assumption of a common background of experience; otherwise they measure not aptitude or ability, but achievement. When used with the handicapped, our tests are more often a measure of experience than of aptitude, and the lower scores may thus reflect lack of experience rather than lack of aptitude, at least in part. This factor has been recognized in the case of such disabilities as blindness and deafness, where the limitations of experience are more or less obvious. But it has been overlooked in the case of physical disabilities which restrict opportunity for many of the normal experiences of growing up in our world. Newland points out that "no research evidence has been presented which demonstrates that the basic assumption regarding comparable acculturation has been satisfied."[3]

Psychological tests, then, which even in the case of the non-handicapped are only fallible estimates of aptitude or talent, are even more fallible when used with the handicapped. It is suggested that while in many cases a skilled psychologist may obtain a fairly good estimate of aptitude by the judicious selection and use of tests, there are other cases, usually with the more severely disabled, where the available standardized tests are of little help. The results of psychological testing may be spuriously low, for a number of reasons, but there is no correction factor which can be added to give a true score. The skilled psychologist can, however, make or suggest a revised estimate on the basis of several tests, plus other information available. In working with a severely disabled student, the counselor, unless he is trained and experienced in testing the disabled, will want to make use of the services of a psychologist.

Recognition of the inadequacy of tests in evaluating vocational

[3] T. E. Newland. Psychological assessment of exceptional children and youth. In W. M. Cruickshank & G. O. Johnson (Eds.) *Psychology of exceptional children and youth.* Englewood Cliffs, N.J.: Prentice-Hall, 1955.

aptitudes and abilities of the severely handicapped has led recently to the use of another approach to evaluation. It is not a new approach. It has been used in other situations where tests have not been available. This approach consists of obtaining observations, ratings, or measurements of performance in specially contrived situations designed to bring out the behavior to be evaluated. These specially developed tasks are sometimes called situational tests or work-sample tests, and this method was used by the Office of Strategic Services during the war for the selection of special agents. In the field of vocational counseling of the handicapped, simulated or sample work tasks have been developed to make possible observation of actual performance on a task.[4] This approach has not been extended as yet—and may be difficult to extend—to evaluating academic aptitude. But the logical extension of the method is the actual work-trial approach, involving a tryout in the job or criterion situation. Tests are, of course, designed to substitute for the criterion, because they are usually easier and less time-consuming to use, and are standardized. But there is nothing to prevent the use of a trial on the criterion task or in the criterion situation, except possibly the financial cost which is involved. The desirability of utilizing all available talent, and of enabling the individual to have the personal satisfaction of functioning at his capacity, is sufficient to warrant the use of this approach. In cases of doubt, therefore, the individual should have the benefit of an actual trial in the training or educational situation.

Finally, in the counseling of the disabled, placement is often more difficult. It has been pointed out above that ideally the disabled individual should be placed in an occupation where his disability is not a handicap. But this is not always possible. And in many instances it may not be desirable, in that such occupations as meet this requirement may not utilize the assets of the indi-

---

[4] See, for example: (1) W. M. Usdane. Vocational counseling with the severely handicapped. *Arch. Phys. Med. Rehab.*, 1953, **34**, 607–616. (2) W. C. Gorthy, R. C. Darling, Lucille Tsu Pai & J. Obrien. Vocational evaluation by work sample technique and its dependence upon medical contributions. *Arch. Phys. Med. Rehab.*, 1959, **40**, 238–242. Both of these articles are reprinted in C. H. Patterson (Ed.) *Readings in rehabilitation counseling*, Champaign, Ill.: Stipes Publishing Co., 1960.

vidual, or be consistent with his interests. Placement is thus not always ideal.

Another problem in placing the disabled is the attitudes of employers. Employers are frequently resistant to employing the disabled, for various reasons. They may fear increased accident rates, absenteeism, reduced efficiency of production, increased insurance, etc. These fears are unfounded, as indicated by studies of the disabled.[5] The work of the President's Committee on Employment of the Physically Handicapped, of the Governor's committees of the various states, and of local committees is resulting in improvement in this area, but employer attitudes are not always favorable. Fears and prejudices still persist in many instances, and are not always removed by facts and information.

In working with the older disabled students, the school counselor has, and should use, the resources of the state Divisions or Bureaus of Vocational Rehabilitation. These agencies administer a complete vocational counseling, training, and placement program for disabled youth and adults. Eligibility for the services of the program, in terms of age, varies somewhat among the states, ranging from 14 to 16 years of age. In most instances, however, state rehabilitation counselors are able to begin to work with potential clients prior to the age at which they become eligible for services, or at least they can work with the school counselor in a consulting capacity. Greater coordination between school counselors and state rehabilitation counselors is needed. Each can assist the other in the counseling and vocational rehabilitation of the student. It is important for the school counselor to know of the resources of the state agency, and if the student will be eligible for its services, so that he may work with the student on long-range vocational plans.

A final comment regarding the vocational counseling of the disabled seems in order. Cruickshank makes the following statements:

The guidance of physically handicapped adolescents must be stuctured within the limits of reality. Mental capacity is only one aspect of

[5] For example: M. D. Kossoris & H. S. Hammond. Work performance of physically impaired workers. *Monthly Labor Rev.*, 1948, **66**, 31–33. Reprinted in C. H. Patterson (Ed.) *Readings in rehabilitation counseling, op. cit.*

this important problem. The other aspect is that of physical capacity and physical limitation. . . . Not all intellectually normal physically handicapped children should be advised to go to college. Certainly great care should be taken in advising such young people to enter professional schools. One of the great tragedies in modern society is that of the overtrained, unemployable, physically handicapped adult. Many young people with serious physical handicaps should appropriately have only the enrichment experiences of a liberal arts education. . . . The unemployable physically handicapped person who has a good mind will have extensive enforced leisure time. . . . Society can and will assimilate a large number of physically handicapped workers in the professional and technical fields. However, the field is not unlimited. Guidance personnel in the high schools must recognize the fact and assist young people to recognize it before they meet a succession of discouragements in seeking employment.[6]

These comments may appear to be eminently reasonable. Insofar as not all the able-bodied with sufficient ability should attend college, it is reasonable to recognize that not all the handicapped with college ability should necessarily attend college. And it seems to be praiseworthy to encourage college education for its enrichment experience even though it may not lead to employment or improve employability. And certainly we must face up to reality in our counseling of the handicapped, as well as in our counseling of the able-bodied. But what is reality? Is it something fixed and unchangeable? If we accept it as such, then it will not change. But the reality of one moment or time is not necessarily reality for all time. It is the unfortunate reality of the present that many intellectually able, talented, and trained physically handicapped individuals are unemployed. They are not, however, unemployable. It is society's loss that they are not employed, and in the present concern about the waste of human talent more attention should be devoted to this source of unused and wasted talent. Progress has been made and is being made in the utilization of the abilities of the physically handicapped, but this progress has not come about through the placid acceptance of reality. To be sure there is a risk involved in training

---

[6] W. M. Cruickshank. The exceptional child in the elementary and secondary schools. In Cruickshank & Johnson (Eds.) *op. cit.*, p. 124.

any severely handicapped individual. He may not be employed. However, if he is not made employable through education and training, he will have no chance whatever of becoming employed. The counselor, then, must not be bound completely by present reality. He must not adopt an entirely pessimistic attitude. His responsibility for enabling the student or client to utilize his potential abilities means that he should attempt to make this possible even though there is no guarantee that society will buy, or pay for the exercise of, the talents when they become developed.

The Academically Retarded

The intellectually retarded student needs, and should be provided, counseling services in schools. The counselor should be concerned with the problems of these children, as well as with those of the average or superior child. The special provisions for the teaching of these children are the province of special education.[7] Here we shall briefly consider some of the responsibilities of the counselor for the intellectually retarded child.

Identification of intellectual retardation. There are approximately a million mentally retarded school children. The term *mental retardation* and *mental deficiency* are usually used interchangeably, although there are some who attempt to differentiate them. An adequate consideration of the definition and classification of mental retardation or deficiency is not possible here.[8]

While classification of a child as mentally deficient is, or should be, based upon a thorough evaluation in which intelligence tests

[7] See, for example: (1) Cruickshank & Johnson (Eds.) *op. cit.* (2) S. A. Kirk & C. A. Johnson. *Educating the retarded child.* Boston: Houghton Mifflin, 1951. (3) U.S. Office of Education. *Curriculum adjustments for the mentally retarded.* Bull. 1950, No. 2. Washington, D.C.: Government Printing Office, 1950. (4) J. E. W. Wallen. *Education of mentally handicapped children.* New York: Harper, 1955.

[8] For detailed discussions see the following: (1) Ann M. Clark & A. D. B. Clark (Eds.) *Mental deficiency.* Glencoe, Ill.: Free Press, 1959. (2) M. L. Hutt & R. G. Gibby. *The mentally retarded child.* Boston: Allyn & Bacon, 1958. (3) R. L. Masland, S. B. Sarason & T. Gladwin. *Mental subnormality: biological, psychological, and cultural factors.* New York: Basic Books, 1959. (4) S. B. Sarason. *Psychological problems in mental deficiency.* (3rd ed.) New York: Harper, 1959.

are only a part, it is commonly accepted that mental retardation is characterized by an intelligence quotient of 70 or below. Subdivisions usually made up are: idiot, IQ 25 or less; imbecile, IQ 25 up to 50; moron, IQ 50 to 70 or 75. Another designation being increasingly used is that of untrainable, trainable, and educable, with the IQ's of each group generally corresponding to those given above. Individuals in the first group are almost always confined to institutions. Those in the second are often in institutions, but may live outside in a family setting. Neither of these groups is represented in the ordinary school. The trainable may be represented in special classes or in schools which are being established specifically for them.

The third group, the moron or the educable mentally retarded, is the group with which we are concerned. They are usually in special classes. In addition, we are interested in a fourth group, the dull normal child, whose IQ may be as high as 90. In the school where the more severely retarded are in special classes, these dull normal students constitute the major problem as far as intellectual retardation is concerned.

Since the identification of intellectual retardation is a complex process involving the use of tests, the counselor should have a part in the process. A simple IQ test is not adequate by itself for evaluation. There may be considerable variation among the ability areas, and this variability must be recognized and understood. Attention must be given to special deficiencies, such as reading. Attention must also be given to the influence of cultural and emotional factors which may affect test results, as well as to physical conditions or health. Sometimes such factors may depress test scores to such an extent that mental retardation may appear to be present. Severe emotional disturbances, particularly, may sometimes result in what has been called pseudomental deficiency. Intelligence test scores have been too frequently used to classify children as mentally deficient, sometimes depriving potentially productive mentally retarded persons of opportunities for adequate education, training, and opportunities for employment and independence. An IQ of 70 is not always the same, since there are differences in test score distributions and norms, and even the best tests have errors of measurement. Repeated testing, observation, and study are necessary before an individual is classified as mentally deficient or retarded.

Assistance in curriculum planning and assignment. The differences among the aptitudes and abilities of the child should form the basis for the curriculum provisions for the retarded child. The counselor, who should be aware of these differences and their implications, should therefore be involved in the curriculum planning and assignment of the retarded child. He should also continue to work with teachers to appraise the suitability of the program, and to suggest appropriate changes or modifications. The desirability of grouping, in some or all subjects, must be considered in terms of the total needs of the child and of other children, and in terms of the personnel and facilities of the school.

Special attention should be given to the possibility of the advantages of remedial instruction or tutoring in the fundamental processes, such as reading or arithmetic, and to the possible need for speech therapy.

Counseling services. The intellectually retarded child is usually more difficult to work with in counseling than the superior, or even average, child. This is perhaps primarily because of his lack of verbal facility. Many have felt that the retarded individual is not capable of profiting from counseling or psychotherapy. Others have felt that although some results might be achieved, it would be too slow and time-consuming. Finally, there are those who believe that if the retarded client is to be helped at all, it must be by directive techniques.

However, increasing attention has been given to the counseling and psychotherapy of the retarded.[9] It appears that much the same approaches can be utilized, including the client-centered method, as with the average child. The basic requirement of acceptance of the client as a human being, as a worthwhile and likable person must be met.[10] Perhaps the difficulty of achieving this with the retarded client has been an obstacle in counseling.

[9] C. L. Stacy & M. F. DeMartino (Eds.). *Counseling and psychotherapy with the mentally retarded.* Glencoe, Ill.: Free Press, 1957.
[10] Theodora M. Abel. Resistances and difficulties in psychotherapy of mental retardates. *J. clin. Psychol.*, 1953, 9, 107–109.

Several studies have indicated that counseling or psychotherapy is about as effective with the higher level retarded as with normals.[11] Group approaches to counseling are also useful.[12]

Vocational counseling and placement. Considerable emphasis has been placed upon vocational counseling and placement of the intellectually retarded. At least two reasons for this emphasis are obvious: (1) employment is an immediate objective following the educational program, since few if any have the aptitudes or abilities for advanced training; and (2) the employment opportunities are limited for these students, so that they often need special assistance in locating available, appropriate opportunities. In the past ten or fifteen years a considerable literature has accumulated on the vocational counseling and placement of the mentally retarded.[13]

It appears that the mentally retarded child is often neglected as far as counseling toward vocational adjustment is concerned. Special classes and special programs in the schools are often not geared to prepare the retarded student for independent living in the community. There is often a gap between the educational program and efforts at assisting in the vocational adjustment of the student. Schools frequently have not assumed the responsibility for vocational placement.

This situation has been improving. A 1958 survey of what was being done in the public schools toward assisting older mentally retarded youth into employment found that of thirty-five states providing information, twenty-eight indicated that schools were

[11] For example: (1) S. Nehan. Psychotherapy in relation to mental deficiency. *Amer. J. ment. Defic.*, 1951, 55, 567. (2) F. C. Thorne. Counseling and psychotherapy with mental defectives. *Amer. J. ment. Defic.*, 1958, 52, 263–271.

[12] (1) M. Cotzin. Group psychotherapy with mentally defective problem boys. *Amer. J. ment. Defic.*, 1958, 53, 268–283. (2) R. Kaldek. Group psychotherapy with mentally defective adolescents and adults. *Int. J. Group Psychother.*, 1958, 8, 185–192.

[13] (1) S. G. DiMichael (Ed.). *Vocational rehabilitation of the mentally retarded.* Washington, D.C.: Government Printing Office, 1950. (2) The Woods Schools. *Vocational training and rehabilitation of exceptional children.* Proceedings of the 1957 Spring Conference. Langhorne, Pa.: The Woods Schools for Exceptional Children, 1957. See also issues of the *American Journal of Mental Deficiency* for the past ten years.

accepting this responsibility to some extent.[14] Twenty-nine states indicated that more would be attempted in job placement than was being done. Twenty-seven states reported that orientation of pupils for entry into employment was included in the curriculum of special classes. In response to a question as to adjustments, other than curriculum, which should be made in the school program for mentally retarded youth, more use of guidance services was most frequently mentioned. Twenty-eight states reported some guidance services toward employment. Some problems which were raised included the point at which vocational guidance of mentally retarded children should be initiated, how much prevocational training should be included in the school curriculum, whether schools should make provision for schoolwork programs, and whether schools should make direct job placements.

The school is not alone in its efforts to assist the mentally retarded student in vocational placement and adjustment. In 1943 the mentally retarded became eligible for assistance under the state-federal program of vocational rehabilitation. State vocational rehabilitation agencies are thus available to the school counselor in working with the older retarded student. There is need for greater cooperation between the schools and vocational rehabilitation agencies. Counselors in the schools should become familiar with the state agency and its personnel, and enter into cooperative arrangements for the vocational counseling, training, and placement of retarded youth. The requirements which must be met for the state agency to render services should be known. As stated, these usually include a minimum age, often 14 or 16 years, although consultation and planning concerning a potential client can begin before this age is reached. The applicant must have a substantial physical or mental disability, which interferes with the obtaining of suitable employment, but which is not of a nature or degree to make the applicant unemployable. The

[14] W. K. Barnett. Public school responsibilities for the mentally retarded. In Department of Health, Education and Welfare, Office of Education and Office of Vocational Rehabilitation. *Preparation of mentally retarded youth for gainful employment.* Bull. 1959, No. 28, Rehabilitation Service Series No. 507. Washington, D.C.: Government Printing Office, 1959.

mentally retarded who are in the schools usually qualify under these requirements, but the dull normal individual may not. DiMichael, in a discussion of the issues in the cooperation of the schools and state vocational rehabilitation agencies, outlines a classification guide for such cooperation.[15]

The first category is *the directly placeable group*. These are in the main the dull normal and higher level retarded for whom special education is sufficient for placement from the school. The counselor, assisted perhaps by the State Employment Service or others, is able to assist the student to obtain satisfactory employment. The vocational rehabilitation agency does not enter except in special cases. In these cases the school assumes the responsibility for vocational and prevocational training.

The second category is *the deferred-placeable group*. These youth need services beyond those offered by the school. They may need special counseling, personal adjustment training, prevocational or vocational training, including on-the-job training, before being placed in competitive employment. In these cases the school counselor and the rehabilitation counselor should begin to work together a year or two before the student is scheduled to leave school. "Thus the student's closing years of school are arranged to make for a smooth transition to the rehabilitation agency and its services, leading to employment and a fuller life. When the individual leaves school, the rehabilitation counselor assumes a primary responsibility, with the school counselor assuming a consultative role. The school must willingly invite and encourage the participation of rehabilitation counselors as professional associates."[16]

In this group also, the school assumes responsibility for prevocational and vocational training up to 17 or 18 years of age, or at least to the school-leaving age. This may include a work-school or work-study program, in which the student works part-time and attends school part-time. DiMichael questions the value of work-study programs for the retarded, feeling that the school should offer more help in personal, social, and work-adjustment training.

[15] S. G. DiMichael. Vocational rehabilitation and the mentally retarded: a statement of issues. In *Preparation of mentally retarded youth for gainful employment, op. cit.*
[16] *Ibid.*

The third category is *the sheltered employable group.* These are youth who are capable of partial self-support in a sheltered workshop environment after further preparation following school. This group will include educable students with no prospects for competitive employment because of social, emotional, or physical factors, or more stable "trainable" students with ability for routine independent travel and good social adjustment and favorable family conditions.

The fourth category, *the self-care group,* includes persons who are not capable of engaging in productive employment even in a sheltered workshop. They are usually not eligible for the services of the vocational rehabilitation agency, and there is little the school can do beyond attempting to develop as great self-care and self-sufficiency in them as possible. These children are usually not found in school except in classes for the trainable retarded.

In a report of a study of ninety-seven cases which were assisted in finding employment by state vocational rehabilitation agencies, DiMichael and Terwilliger reviewed aspects of counseling which are significant for school counselors.[17] Twenty-five of the cases, the largest group, were referred by schools to the state agencies. The study indicated that these cases required a great investment of counselor time, requiring from two to fifty counseling interviews (the median being eight) and from one to fourteen interviews with relatives. Interviews with employers were involved for seventy-seven clients, indicating that most of them were unable by themselves to establish effective job contacts and employment arrangements.

Vocational training was provided in fifty-two cases. The authors note that "These results demand attention because the average layman and even the professional person believes there is little or no training required for unskilled and semiskilled jobs. Actually the mentally retarded need organized training to learn beforehand how to do simple jobs." The most frequent type of training was on-the-job training (twenty-two cases). "This may mean that on-the-job training for the retarded is a necessary supplement to academic and vocational work in the schools. In

[17] S. G. DiMichael & W. B. Terwilliger. Counselor's activities in the vocational rehabilitation of the mentally retarded. *J. clin. Psychol.,* 1953, **9,** 99–106.

other words, the schools should not be expected to complete the preparation of the individual for competitive employment. On the other hand, it is also possible that some clients were not provided with effective vocational training in school and needed some 'makeup' through on-the-job training. Experience has shown the great difficulty of persuading vocational high schools to furnish special low-level training for retarded adolescents."[18]

The ninety-seven clients were placed in sixty-nine different kinds of work, classified as follows: service occupations—thirty-two; unskilled jobs—twenty-four; semiskilled jobs—seventeen; clerical and sales—ten; agriculture—seven; skilled work—five; managerial—one; homemaker—one.[19]

A list of special problems involved in the counseling process included the following: personal and interpersonal problems—thirty-six (including mainly undesirable personal attitudes); difficulties in locating suitable jobs—twenty-five; difficulties due to other (mainly physical) disabilities—twenty-one; upsetting family problems—nineteen; slowness in learning job—nineteen. The number of family problems and attitudes is significant. Several studies have indicated that unrealism of parents, or overprotectiveness, are problems in working with retarded youth. The importance of working with parents in the earlier years is apparent. The support and participation of the family was an important positive factor in twenty-four cases. Other positive factors included unusual positive qualities of the client (thirty-nine cases), including strong willingness to work (twenty-two cases), and patience and understanding of the employer (nineteen cases).

The vocational counseling and placement of the retarded constitute problems which the school must face. Preparation for employment must also include orientation to work, which should be part of the curriculum. In-school work programs have tended to be limited and unrealistic in many respects. The emphasis tends to be on teaching specific skills, and sometimes skills which are not in demand in the community. On the other hand, most schools are unable to provide adequate vocational training for

[18] *Ibid.*

[19] See the following for an excellent discussion of placement of the mentally retarded: Anna M. Engel, Employment of the mentally retarded. In DiMichael (Ed.), *op. cit.*

the retarded. It appears that such training in many instances is best left for the postschool period, at least in those cases where the student is eligible for state vocational rehabilitation services, which include on-the-job training as well as institutional or sheltered workshop training.

The school, for its contribution, should concentrate more on training in work attitudes and habits and social skills. Dependability, punctuality, work persistence, as well as training in applying for work are important. Training in independent living and in understanding and handling the financial aspects of employment are also necessary. Peckham[20] found that the reasons why the mentally retarded quit or lost jobs included teasing and ridicule by fellow workers, difficulty in social and vocational sophistication, problems of travel, leaving or staying away from work without notifying employer, problems in budgeting their money, lack of initiative or job responsibility, impulsiveness, and feelings of the family that the job wasn't good enough. Rarely did they lose jobs because of inability to perform the work. The importance of preparation in these problem areas is thus evident.

As Goldstein and Heber note, "The in-school program is most useful when it stresses attributes which may be generalized to any job situation such as the relationship of the worker to the employer and vice versa, concepts of punctuality, socialization, and task completion."[21] The counselor should be involved in the development and conduct of such training, because of his familiarity with the demands of the world of work. Work-school and work-study programs should also utilize the services of the counselor, both in planning and conducting such programs, and in individual counseling of the students enrolled in them.

The counselor should be responsible for the placement of the student in employment, although the actual placement may be made by a placement specialist of the State Employment Service or the vocational rehabilitation agency. Follow-up is also necessary. Many problems arise in the early stages of employment, which can often be remedied relatively easily if they are known

20 R. Peckham. Problems in job adjustment of the mentally retarded. *Amer. J. ment. Defic.*, 1951, 56, 448–453.
21 Goldstein & Heber. Summary of the conference. In *Preparation of mentally retarded youth for gainful employment, op. cit.*

and assistance is available, but which may lead to serious difficulty or discharge if they are not remedied. Counseling services provided to the student during the early stages of employment are thus important in enabling him to adjust to employment. Counseling should also cover other problems of adjustment, including personal and social adjustment. It is desirable that such counseling services, however, be separated from supervisory aspects as much as possible. In cases where the student has established a relationship with the school counselor, the counselor may continue working with the student during on-the-job training or employment which is supervised by the vocational rehabilitation agency, when such an arrangement is acceptable to the agency. The providing of such counseling services recognizes that the school has some responsibility for its students after they have formally severed connections with it.

While the problems of vocational placement and employment of the retarded are many and difficult, the results of effort in this field are encouraging. Kirk summarizes studies in this area as follows:

1. Under ordinary circumstances, the large majority of boys and girls graduating from special classes will obtain and hold jobs, although they tend to change jobs frequently, like other youngsters just out of school. Their record of unemployment, however, is slightly higher than average.
2. The jobs on which they succeed most frequently tend to cluster in the semiskilled and unskilled categories of employment.
3. The mentally retarded succeed more frequently when they have been assisted through training, placement and guidance.[22]

Kirk points out that the studies on which these rather favorable conclusions are based were made in an era when little vocational guidance, training and placement were provided. It would appear that the prospects for vocational adjustment of the mentality retarded would be quite favorable with adequate counseling services supplemented by training and placement services.

[22] S. A. Kirk. Vocational rehabilitation: an educator's critique on past, present and future programs. In The Woods Schools, *Vocational training and rehabilitation of exceptional children, op. cit.*

Summary

Two special groups of students which require special consideration by the counselor are the physically handicapped and the mentally or intellectually retarded. These students present special problems in educational-vocational counseling. Because the counselor often feels unprepared to work with them, they are often neglected.

This chapter attempts to give the counselor sufficient understanding of the physically and mentally handicapped so that he may be able to assist them with their problems. Their problems are essentially the same as those of the rest of us. The differences arise from two sources: (1) their disabilities result in limitations upon their activities and choices, and (2) the attitudes of others toward them impose limitations, and often result in problems which are reactions to those attitudes.

The effects of these differences in the counseling of the handicapped are considered, with special attention to the vocational counseling process. The counselor who specializes in work with physically disabled or mentally retarded students will benefit from some special training in this area. Such training is now offered by a number of colleges and universities as part of training programs for rehabilitation counselors.

SUGGESTED READINGS

Hamilton, K. W. *Counseling the handicapped in the rehabilitation process.* New York: Ronald, 1950. The first, and still a basic, text in rehabilitation counseling.

Lofquist, L. H. *Vocational counseling with the physically handicapped.* New York: Appleton-Century-Crofts. Although oriented toward counseling in a hospital setting, this book presents general principles which are applicable in other situations.

Lurie, W. A., Goldfein, J., & Baxt, R. An intensive vocational counseling program for slow learners in high school. *Personnel Guid. J.,* 1960, **39**, 20–29. A description of a project conducted by the Federation Employment and Guidance Service of New York.

Patterson, C. H. (Ed.) *Readings in rehabilitation counseling.* Champaign, Ill.: Stipes Publishing Company, 1960. A collection of sixty-four articles covering the field of rehabilitation counseling in its various aspects.

Stacy, C. L., & DeMartino, M. F. (Eds.) *Counseling and psychotherapy with the mentally retarded.* Glencoe, Ill.: Free Press, 1957. A collection of forty-nine papers on various means and methods of working with the mentally retarded and their parents.

United States Department of Health, Education, and Welfare. *Preparation of mentally retarded youth for gainful employment.* Bull. 1958, No. 28, Rehabilitation Service Series No. 507. Washington, D.C.: Government Printing Office, 1959. A brief, but good treatment of the responsibilities of the schools in vocational adjustment of the mentally retarded.

Woods Schools. *Vocational training and rehabilitation of exceptional children.* Proceedings of the 1957 Spring Conference of the Woods Schools, Chicago, May 10 and 11, 1957. Langhorne, Pa.: The Woods Schools for Exceptional Children, 1957. A report of a conference which includes several papers by experts in the field of mental retardation.

PART V

RELATIONSHIPS WITH OTHER PERSONNEL AND SERVICES

CHAPTER 16

RELATIONSHIPS WITH OTHER SCHOOL PERSONNEL

The counselor in the school guidance program is only a part of the total program of personnel services to students, albeit in many instances the counselor is the major source of such services. But as part of a larger program, the counselor must be concerned about his relationships with others in the school who perform personnel services to students. In this chapter we shall consider some of the aspects and problems of the counselor's relationships with other school staff members who have pupil personnel functions. Before considering the particular persons with whom the counselor must relate and work, however, we shall consider a basis upon which the counselor may establish his relationships. Because situations vary so much from school to school and from system to system, no detailed blueprints for the integration of services can be given. The number, kind, and qualifications of other personnel workers who are available are important factors, as well as the preparation and training of the school counselor himself.

The Counselor as Integrator of Student Personnel Services

A basis for interrelationships with other school staff members is the concept of the counselor as the integrator of all personnel services to students within the school. With numerous services being provided, by the various personnel referred to later in this chapter, as well as others not mentioned, it is desirable, if not necessary, that there be some coordination of services. It is not conducive to the best interests of the student for several different individuals to be working with him at the same time, with none of them knowing that the others are involved.

It may not always be desirable or appropriate for the counselor to serve in this integrating or coordinating function. In particular situations other members of the staff who are engaged in personnel services may discharge this function. If there is an assistant principal for student personnel services this would seem to be a part of his duties. However, this should be the case only where the assistant principal has had professional training in counseling or student personnel work. This is becoming more prevalent. However, in a large school, where the assistant principal is engaged in full-time administrative duties, it might be desirable that the coordinating function be assigned to someone else.

The visiting teacher when professionally trained might function as the coordinator. However, the fact that the visiting teacher is often engaged in work outside the school for much of the time might be a handicap. Some have suggested that the school psychologist should function as the head or director of pupil personnel services.[1] This suggestion seems to be based on the concept of the counselor or guidance worker as being too inadequately trained in psychology to serve in such a position. As counselors and guidance directors become more adequately trained, along the lines indicated earlier (Chapter 5), there should be less objection to their heading up or coordinating pupil personnel services. Also, of course, in many schools there is no school psychologist, and smaller schools do not need the services of a full-time staff psychologist. There are actually few schools with full-time psychologists, so that it is apparent that someone else will have to assume the responsibility of integrating services within the school. It would appear that in many if not most schools the logical person to integrate pupil personnel services is the counselor.

The integration of services involves two aspects: the adminis-

---

[1] Norma E. Cutts (Ed.) *School psychologists at mid-century.* Washington, D.C.: American Psychological Association, 1955. P. 79. The suggestion appears to refer to a school system rather than to the individual school.

trative and the professional. The administrative aspect includes the designation or assignment of the counselor as the administrative head of pupil personnel services, and the setting up of administrative procedures which will enable him to perform the professional function of integrating services. Record systems and clerical assistance, together with procedures which make the counselor's office a clearing house for all personnel activities, will facilitate coordination.

The more purely professional aspects of integration include continuing consultation with staff members performing personnel services (and teachers are included here) and regularly scheduled conferences for the discussion of professional problems and procedures, as well as discussion of cases, or case conferences.

In the framework of the counselor as the integrator of personnel services to students, we now turn to a consideration of the counselor's relationships with other staff members performing personnel services.

The Counselor and the School Administrator

Fortunate is the counselor who has an administrator who understands the professional nature of counseling. Such an administrator will understand the goals of the counselor, and will accept the need for the establishment of the conditions necessary for professional counseling. He will recognize the necessity of privacy in the interview, and of confidentiality of information and records.

With an understanding administration, which supports a program of professional personnel services, the counselor's task of developing adequate relationships with other school personnel and of integrating personnel services is half-achieved. The organizing of services and the assigning of functions to personnel can be carried out in a manner which recognizes differences in functions. Incompatible functions, such as discipline and counseling, are not assigned to the same staff member. Expectations for the results of counseling and other personnel services are realistic. A climate for teamwork is created, so that effort is not deflected from the student to the problem of developing a basis for working together in a situation where internecine warfare for status may prevail. Attention can be directed to actually seeing students instead of struggling to create the conditions and climate for an adequate program of student personnel services.

Unfortunately, all too frequently one of the major tasks of the counselor is to obtain the understanding and support of the administrator. Often this is a time-consuming process. Until the support and understanding of the administrator are obtained, no adequate program of professional services can be developed. Without administrative support, the counselor is handicapped in developing adequate relationships with the school staff and in integrating their services into the best program for the welfare of students. It is to be hoped that administrators will be exposed in their training to courses which will give them an understanding of the nature and requirements of professional counseling and guidance services. More and more training programs for administrators include a course in counseling and guidance services of the kind for which this book is written. As such administrators increase in number, the framework and climate for the integration of pupil personnel services will be present in our schools.

Relationships with Teachers

Perhaps the most important, and certainly the largest, group of personnel workers with whom the counselor must establish adequate relationships is the teaching staff. Teachers are the closest to students, and thus the source of most referrals. They are the channel through which the counselor as well as other personnel staff must work with students. The assisting of teachers in their teaching function with individual students is second only to serving the student himself as a goal of all personnel services. The success of the counseling program stands or falls on its acceptance, support, and use by teachers.

The counselor is in a difficult situation in regard to his relations with teachers. On the one hand, if he is a former teacher he may be accepted as one of them, and thus not have the problem of gaining such acceptance that he would if he came into the system after graduate training in counseling. On the other hand, if he is a former teacher, but without adequate training as a counselor, he may not be respected as a professional person. While he is "one of us," he is no more than that professionally. Teachers then see the counselor as no better, no more qualified or competent as a counselor, than they are.

The adequately trained counselor must recognize that it will be difficult for some teachers to accept him. He must apply his understanding of human behavior to teachers, and recognize that he may be threatening to them. If teachers feel that counseling is one of their functions, they may feel it unnecessary to have a trained counselor on the staff, and resent someone who is brought in. Some teachers may be envious or jealous of the counselor, who may have a higher salary, and so much "free" time for counseling. They may see him as taking over a position which is felt to be theirs by right.

Teachers often do not recognize the need and importance for confidentiality in the counseling relationship. It is sometimes difficult for teachers to accept the refusal of a counselor to divulge what the student has told in the counseling interview. This is particularly the case where the counselor has just recently been one of them. Cases have been known of teachers quizzing students as to what they discussed with the counselor. It is sometimes hard for the counselor in this situation not to break confidence. Both should heed the code of ethics of the National Education Association, which states: "Respect the right of every student to have confidential information about himself withheld except where its release is to authorized agencies or is requested by law."[2] This is perhaps an argument against appointing teachers to counseling positions in the same school, or for requiring teaching experience in the system for appointment as a counselor.

While the counselor must refuse to discuss confidential information with teachers he must recognize the necessity of cooperating with teachers and assisting them in their relations with their pupils. A brief survey of some of the ways of cooperating with teachers is presented below.

1. Since the teacher is, or should be, the major source of referrals to the counselor, with the possible exception of self-

---

[2] National Education Association. *Code of ethics of the National Education Association.* Washington, D.C.: The Association, 1952.

referrals, the counselor must make such referrals simple and easy. Informal, rather than formal, methods are desirable. If written referrals are necessary for record purposes, the procedure must be kept simple and forms brief. It is perhaps better if referrals can be made without the use of forms. Although it is often suggested that referrals should go through the administration, this would appear to put an obstacle between close contact of the teacher and the counselor. If the counselor is the coordinator of personnel services, it should not be necessary for referrals to go through administrative channels.

2. The counselor should be prompt in responding to requests of teachers for help. Not only should students referred by teachers be seen as quickly as possible; in addition, requests of teachers for consultation should be met without any unnecessary delay. The counselor should be easily and quickly accessible to teachers who want to see him.

3. In their consultations with teachers, counselors must be accepting, and respectful of the teachers as professional persons. There should be no "talking down" to teachers, or unnecessary use of technical or psychological jargon.

4. While it is not ethical for the counselor to reveal confidential information to teachers, it must be emphasized that the teacher who makes a referral is entitled to a report. Teachers are genuinely interested in their students, and have a right to information which would be helpful in understanding and working with them. Such information can be given without giving personal details or the content of the counseling interview. The aim of the counselor should be to help the teacher understand the student, and any information communicated should be for this purpose.

5. Sometimes teachers who consult a counselor about a student may be the problem rather than the student. Sometimes teachers want help on personal problems. This raises the question as to whether counselors should counsel teachers. Undoubtedly many teachers, being human, need and could benefit from counseling. Ordinarily, however, the school counselor is not in a position to engage in such counseling of teachers. Even as teachers are often handicapped in counseling their own students, so is the

counselor handicapped in counseling teachers in his own school. This is particularly the case, of course, where he has been a teacher in the school, and has had little training in counseling. There are situations where the counselor can work with teachers on their personal problems, however. There have been instances where counselors have been helpful to teachers with relatively minor personal problems. In some situations no other source of help for the teacher may be available. In working with teachers on their personal problems, the counselor must be aware of the problems involved, and should discuss the situation, and the conditions under which he can work with such personal problems, with the teacher before embarking upon a counseling relationship.

One way in which the counselor can assist teachers in their personal problems, as well as in their relationships with their students, is through participation in in-service training of teachers. The counselor should take the initiative in developing in-service training in human relationships for teachers, or offer his services in this area if an in-service training program exists. This is an opportunity for the counselor to inform or educate teachers about the nature of his services and his qualifications, and of the ways he would like to be of help to them.

The new counselor in a school or the inexperienced counselor may require time to develop adequate relationships with teachers. Acceptance may not come quickly. A study at the University of Illinois asked counselors two questions about the frequency with which they were consulted by teachers. Tables 10 and 11 indicate

TABLE 10. In the Course of a Year How Many of the Teachers Take Time to Come to You and Request Information about Their Students?

	Percent of Counselors Answering		
Years Counselor Has Been in a School	Less Than Half	More Than Half	Almost All
1–2	60	30	10
3–5	31	45	24
6–11	29	33	38
12–41	37	39	24

SOURCE: Adapted from unpublished data collected by J. T. Hastings, P. J. Runkel, Dora E. Damrin, *et al.* Cooperative Research Project No. 509, U.S. Office of Education.

TABLE 11.   Of the Teachers Who Do Come to You for Information, Approximately How Often Do Most of Them Come?

Years Counselor Has Been in a School	Percent of Counselors Answering		
	One per Semester	Twice per Semester	More Than Twice per Semester
1–2	33	35	32
3–5	17	38	45
6–11	25	27	40
12–41	32	23	45

SOURCE: Adapted from unpublished data collected by J. T. Hastings, P. J. Runkel, Dora E. Damrin, *et al.* Cooperative Research Project No. 509, U.S. Office of Education.

that teachers consult more often with counselors the longer counselors have been in the school.[3]

6. The counselor must recognize the interest of teachers in information that will help them to understand and help their students. One of the kinds of information they desire is that concerning tests. A study of teachers in twenty-eight Illinois schools (more than half of the teachers participated) revealed the following things which the teachers felt were not performed by counselors, but which ought to be performed:

1. Invite teachers to group meetings to learn more about the interpretation of tests.
2. Conduct meetings in which teachers can learn more about the techniques, purposes, and values of counseling.
3. Conduct general faculty meetings to discuss staff needs with regard to the kinds of tests that would be most useful.
4. Conduct small group faculty meetings to discuss the interpretation and use of tests to help solve problems specific to that group (e.g., science department, language department, etc.).
5. Conduct a general faculty briefing meeting after test data are received and discuss the results and possible uses in general terms.[4]

[3] J. T. Hastings, P. J. Runkel, Dora E. Damrin, *et al. The use of test results.* Cooperative Research Project No. 509, U.S. Office of Education. Urbana, Ill.: Bureau of Educational Research, 1960 (mimeo).
[4] J. T. Hastings, P. J. Runkel & Dora E. Damrin. *Effects on use of tests by teachers trained in a summer institute.* Cooperative Research Project No. 702, U.S. Office of Education. Urbana, Ill.: Bureau of Educational Research, 1961 (mimeo). Appendix J, Vol. II.

It appears that teachers wish more meetings and discussions with counselors concerning the counselor's activities and work. Counselors should respond to this desire, and make efforts to keep in close communication with teachers.

The Counselor and the School Psychologist

As suggested above, the school psychologist is in shorter supply than counselors. In 1952 only one-third of the elementary schools in the country had the services of a school psychologist available.[5] Recommendations vary from one psychologist for every 1000 pupils to one for every 3000.[6] It is usually the case that the psychologist is responsible for serving several schools, or a school system. Since he spends only part of his time in a particular school, it would appear that someone must coordinate his services with other school personnel services. While it has been suggested that this person be the principal,[7] it would appear to be better from the point of view of integrating personnel services for the teacher to work with the psychologist through the school counselor. Of course, the psychologist operates in a given school only with the cooperation and approval of the principal.

The relations of the counselor with the psychologist are complicated by the fact that many of their functions are apparently similar. The school psychologist is defined as "a psychologist with training and experience in education. He uses his specialized knowledge of assessment, learning, and interpersonal relationships to assist school personnel to enrich the experience and growth of all children, and to recognize and deal with exceptional children."[8]

In his work he deals with problems of personal and social adjustment, academic deficiencies, physical handicaps, and behavior difficulties, and is concerned with the identification of the gifted and mentally retarded and planning for their special needs.

[5] A. J. Jones & L. M. Miller. The national picture of pupil personnel and guidance services in 1953. *Bull. Nat. Assoc. Secondary School Principals,* 1954, **38** (No. 200), 103–159.

[6] Cutts, *op. cit.,* p. 4.

[7] *Ibid.,* p. 72: "The teacher requests the principal to call the psychologist."

[8] *Ibid.,* p. 30.

Discussions of the functions of the school psychologist[9] include many if not most of the functions of the school counselor as they have been dealt with in this book. Perhaps the use of individual tests by the school psychologist is the main difference.

School psychologists, however, vary tremendously in their background and training, and in their functions in particular schools or systems. In general there are two levels of school psychologists: those trained at the doctoral level, and those at the master's level. State certification requirements are not standardized. Of the twenty-four states providing for certification, six states provide for certification at two levels, and one at three levels. Four require the doctorate, two of these states certifying at a lower level also. Only two states allow certification with a bachelor's degree; most require from one to two years of graduate work or a master's degree. Twelve states require a teacher's certificate, and two require eligibility for a teaching certificate for certification. Ten of the former also require teaching experience.[10]

Titles of those functioning in school psychology vary. School psychologist is the most prevalent, with psychological examiner being next in frequency. But many other titles are used. It is recommended that the title "psychologist" be limited to those with the doctorate.[11]

It is apparent that the counselor must be prepared to encounter individuals providing psychological services with many titles and with varying degrees and kinds of training. Some are well-trained psychologists, with high-level competencies in many areas. Others, however—and perhaps the majority at present—have much less training and are limited in the services they can give. Many will have less training than the counselor who has the training outlined in Chapter 5. Perhaps the only area in which he is adequately trained, or better trained than the qualified counselor, is in individual testing.

[9] *Ibid.*, pp. 30–53: American Psychological Association, Division of School Psychology, Committee on Reconsideration of the Functions of the School Psychologist. *The psychologist on the school staff*. Published by the Division, 1959.

[10] W. L. Hodges. State certification of school psychologists. *Amer. Psychologist*, 1960, **15**, 346–349.

[11] Cutts, *op. cit.*, p. 31.

The relationships of the counselor with the school psychologist will therefore depend on the amounts and kinds of training each of them possesses. The psychologist is a resource person for the school personnel, and for the counselor, in dealing with problems having psychological implications which arise in the school. As suggested above, the counselor is in most cases the logical person to integrate the services of the psychologist with other personnel services. The counselor should make or funnel referrals to the psychologist, or at least be consulted regarding such referrals, so that counseling and psychological services may be coordinated. In any particular situation, the counselor and the psychologist should work out their respective duties and responsibilities in terms of the special training and competencies of each, and in terms of the amounts of time each is able to devote to particular areas and functions.

The School Social Worker

The origin of social work relationships with the schools dates back to the early years of the present century, when social workers in two New York settlement houses felt that a relationship with the teachers of the children they served would result in a better program for the children.[12] More formal programs were developed during the first quarter of the century, and during the last twenty-five years school social work as a specialized field has developed, with formal training programs, legislative support, and a professional organization (the National Association of School Social Workers, now a section of the National Association of Social Workers).

Early emphasis of school social work was with the prevention of truancy and delinquency. This emphasis has decreased, until at present school social workers are interested in all areas of personal and social maladjustment, as well as academic difficulties, physical deficiencies, and even "confusion regarding educational and vocational choices."[13] It is thus apparent that, as in the case of school psychologists, there is a common interest, and

[12] Jean R. Pearman & A. H. Burrows. *Social services in the school*. Washington, D.C.: Public Affairs Press, 1955. P. 5.
[13] *Ibid.*, p. 4.

an almost complete overlap of stated functions, of school social workers and counselors.

School social workers utilize casework methods with children and their families. It is difficult, if not impossible, to distinguish between casework and counseling. However, the school social worker, unlike the counselor, spends much time out of the school, and works with parents in the home, being concerned with problems of parental neglect, overwork of the child in the home, and economic inadequacies and needs. This activity is reflected in the term "visiting teacher," which is often used to designate the school social worker. Another title frequently used is "visiting counselor."[14]

As might be expected, the school social worker is trained in social work and education. The highest standards for employment and certification include certification as a teacher and the completion of a two-year graduate training program in social work. However, as in the case of counselors and school psychologists, requirements vary tremendously. Sometimes a bachelor's degree plus some courses in social casework, counseling, and human development are all that is required in the way of training. In addition to a teaching certificate, teaching experience is often required. Many social workers question these requirements, as do many psychologists and counselors. It has been recommended that school social workers should be employed in the ratio of 1 to about 1000 students, which is about the same ratio suggested for school psychologists.[15]

It is apparent that, as in the case of the school psychologist, the counselor must work out his relationships with the school social worker on an individual basis, in terms of the amounts and kinds of training and skills each has. The activities of the school counselor in the area of personal adjustment, or personal counseling, have been a sore point with some school social workers, who feel that this is social casework, and that the counselor is not

---

[14] In Illinois the title is "Visiting Social Counselor." R. Graham. *The Illinois plan for special education of exceptional children. The maladjusted.* Circular Series "F" No. 12. Springfield, Ill.: Office of Superintendent of Public Instruction [no date].

[15] Pearman & Burrows, *op. cit.*, p. 92.

competent in this area. In many cases, of course, this has been the case. But with the increase of counselors trained in this function, school social workers must recognize this as a legitimate function of the counselor. The school social worker, who usually serves several schools, is unable to provide all the counseling services which are desirable. School social workers have been more frequently used at the elementary-school level than in secondary schools. The reverse has been true of counselors. Social workers have perhaps performed many of the functions of the counselor in the elementary school because there have been so few counselors available. Perhaps the counselor and the social worker can work together as the psychologist and social worker do in many other settings, such as child-guidance clinics, with the counselor working with the child and the social worker with the parents. In many, if not most, instances it is desirable that the same person not work with both child and parent. Many school social workers feel that the focus of their efforts should be with the parents, rather than with the child, particularly in the case of younger children.[16]

Since the school social worker is usually assigned to a number of schools, it would appear that the counselor would be the best representative of the individual school in integrating the social worker's services in the total pupil personnel program. On the other hand, the counselor should work through the social worker in his contacts with social service agencies in the community.

The School Nurse and Doctor

The schools have responsibilities in the area of assisting students to achieve and maintain the optimum level of physical health. This does not mean that the school maintains a medical treatment service or a hospital—although at the college level this is the case. The traditional method of private practice in medical care has been accepted by the schools. The responsibilities of the school in the health field are (1) the protection of students from health hazards, including infection by students who may be car-

[16] J. C. Nebo. Some aspects of social work practice in the schools. In *Social work in the schools.* New York: National Association of Social Workers, 1960. P. 7.

riers of disease, and (2) the detection of remediable physical conditions, the informing of the student and his parents of the existence of the condition, and the providing of assistance to them in obtaining adequate treatment or correction. There is, of course, the responsibility for providing emergency treatment for conditions which develop or appear in the school, such as accidental injuries.

The school nurse and/or the school physician carry out these responsibilities. In addition to these services to the individual student, they also contribute to the health-education program through teaching and assisting teachers in preparing and presenting health-education materials.

Klein reports a survey of the functions and activities of 607 school nurses in 161 public schools in New Jersey.[17] The purposes of school health services included the following: to help prevent and control disease (91.3 percent of the schools); to appraise the health of pupils and school personnel (89.4 percent); to encourage the correction of remediable defects (86.3 percent); to provide a safe and healthful environment (83.2 percent); to counsel pupils and parents concerning findings of health appraisals (82.0 percent). Only 11.2 percent of the schools indicated that a major purpose was to assist in the identification and education of handicapped children.

Health "counseling" of parents is an important health activity of the school. This includes giving information, advice, guidance, and assistance in working out health problems. Parents may be informed of the health needs of their children by home visits (77.6 percent of the schools in the study cited above), by written notices sent home by the children (64.6 percent), by contact with the family physician (45.3 percent), by mail (44.7 percent), or by parent conferences in school (41.6 percent). The study indicated the following major activities of the school nurse in the area of health guidance and education: instruct teachers on handling specific health problems; counsel pupils on personal health problems; organize group conferences with faculty or staff personnel concerning health and disease; assist teachers in activating pupils

[17] Ruth A. Klein. The school nurse as a guidance functionary. *Personnel Guid. J.*, 1959, 38, 318–321.

to acquire healthful habits; counsel teachers about needed adjustments in the physical environment of the classroom for pupils, including the physically handicapped.

Nurses reported the sources of their referrals as follows: 94.6 percent indicated teachers; 94.4 percent, principals; 87.5 percent, parents; 52.2 percent, community agencies; 49.9 percent, psychologists; 47.0 percent, guidance directors; 44.6 percent, superintendents; 40.1 percent, pupils themselves; 39.0 percent, speech specialists; 32.1 percent, reading specialists; 9.1 percent, the janitor; and 0.7 percent indicated the attendance officer.

Perhaps a greater proportion of schools have some kind of nursing or medical service than have counseling services. In schools without counseling services, the school nurse may provide some counseling and guidance services. That this is so and that it is the case also in schools *with* counselors, is indicated by the survey of public-school nursing in New Jersey referred to above.[18] The kinds of pupil personnel problems referred to the school nurse were reported as follows: physical health problems were reported by 95.1 percent of the nurses; home and family problems by 76.8 percent; mental health problems by 75.3 percent; financial problems by 62.2 percent; social adjustment problems by 57.0 percent; sex problems by 53.7 percent; moral and spiritual problems by 35.9 percent; vocational and job placement problems by 17.0 percent; and personal hygiene problems by 1.5 percent. It should be noted that 41.4 percent of the nurses reported that no organized guidance program supervised by a full-time director existed in their schools. Where such a program was reported, 88.6 percent of the nurses stated that they were considered members of the guidance team.

Here again we see almost complete overlap with the kinds of problems handled by all of the other personnel workers. It appears that any kind of problem may be referred to any of the several kinds of personnel workers in the school, and each group seems to feel it appropriate for them to work with all kinds of problems. In some cases, no doubt, certain problems may be accepted because no one else is available to handle them. But it might be suggested that there is a need for better division and

[18] *Ibid.*

integration of services. While the nurse is a professional person, it is doubtful that she is trained for or is competent in dealing with home and family problems, social-emotional problems, or vocational problems. But the nurse is a part of the guidance program in a broad sense, and of pupil personnel services. Her activities should be coordinated and integrated with those of other personnel workers. To the counselor she is a source of referrals, as well as a person to whom to make referrals. An alert nurse, with her opportunities to see pupils, and to see their families and homes, should be able to recognize many cases where the counselor, the school psychologist, or the school social worker could be of help.

Other School Personnel

Other school staff members whose work has implications for personnel work, and with whom the counselor must develop adequate professional relationships, are the special-education teachers, remedial teachers, and the speech therapist. The functions of these staff members are obvious, and their significance to the counselor is also obvious. They are important resources of the school for serving the individual pupil, and thus resources for the counselor in his work with individual students.

A group of teachers with whom the counselor should develop particularly close relationships is the vocational education department. Vocational education teachers frequently complain that counselors do not recognize the contributions of vocational education, and the potential assistance of vocational education teachers to the counseling and guidance program. There is perhaps some basis for this complaint.[19] In some schools counselors concentrate upon the college-bound student, and neglect those who are not in the college preparatory curriculum. Many counselors are not as well prepared for counseling the student who is not college bound. The vocational-education teacher can be very helpful to the counselor in working with these students. Assignment to vocational curriculums should be based upon counseling, and such counseling requires adequate knowledge of the require-

[19] D. A. Davis. Counseling and vocational education. *Voc. Guid. Quart.*, 1960, **9**, 37–40.

ments and opportunities in the technical and skilled or semi-skilled occupations. Selection of a vocational-education curriculum should be determined by positive criteria, not, as is common, upon lack of ability in the more academic areas.[20]

Closely related to vocational education are the work-study programs conducted by many schools. Counselors should cooperate with the coordinators of these programs, who may be called trade and industrial coordinators, or coordinators of distributive and business education. These vocational coordinators have a personnel function, and the counselor should be interested in offering assistance in the selection and assignment of students to employment.

One staff member who is not always considered a part of student personnel services is the school librarian. However, the librarian is of particular importance to the counselor, and she is, or can be, of considerable help to the counselor in his vocational-counseling and his group-guidance activities. Her cooperation is essential for the adequate acquisition, filing, and use of occupational information. An interested librarian can develop and maintain special collections of materials of occupational significance, and can make them available and useful to students. She can arrange for displays, including posters and bulletin board materials, and set up a career shelf or section in the library, and the librarian who is really interested and secure in her position may even not object to placing some of the library materials in the counselor's office or waiting-reading room. The training of the school librarian should include a course in occupational-information materials; the author has had several in his classes in this area, and has found them interested in how they can cooperate with the counseling program.

Problems in Interprofessional Relationships[21]

Perhaps there is no word or concept more used, and overworked, in the field of interprofessional relationships than *team-*

---

[20] C. H. Patterson. Predicting success in trade and vocational school courses: review of the literature. *Educ. psychol. Measmt.*, 1956, 16, 352–400.

[21] This section is in part adapted from the author's paper, Is the team concept obsolete? *J. Rehab.*, 1959, 25 (2), 3–10, 27–28. Also in C. H. Patterson (Ed.) *Readings in rehabilitation counseling.* Champaign, Ill.: Stipes Publishing Company, 1960.

work. But when one examines what is meant by teamwork in actual practice, one is confronted with some confusion. Teamwork means different things to different people. To the psychologist it may mean the reporting of certain findings, their interpretation, and recommendations to other persons working with a client. To the social worker it may mean obtaining and contributing certain kinds of information about the client, and working with the client in certain areas, so that he may be prepared or enabled to benefit from other services. To the nurse, and other paramedical personnel, it may mean carrying out the prescription of the doctor and reporting on the results. To the doctor it often means the cooperation of ancillary workers in carrying out his plans or prescriptions for a patient.

Teamwork has its appeal because it is recognized that no one person or profession can provide all the desirable personnel services singlehanded. The team concept has arisen and been adopted perhaps because of the analogy with group sports activities, a current preoccupation of the American people. This analogy has brought with it the idea that a team must have a captain. It is felt, apparently, that people cannot, or will not, work together unless someone is a captain, a leader, or a director.

While the team concept would seem to be ideal in a multi-disciplinary field such as student personnel work, there is evidence that it isn't too successful in many instances. A number of reasons have been advanced. It has been suggested that the members of the various professions are too individualistic, and that they have not learned to work together during their professional training. Professional jealousies are sometimes blamed, as well as the desire of a member of one profession to control the student.

No doubt these and other reasons have contributed to difficulties in teamwork. But there is perhaps a more basic cause, inherent in the team concept itself. This is the problem of authority, the question of who is to be the captain of the team.

Perhaps the team concept is not the most appropriate one for a group of professionals. Perhaps it should be abandoned. But what would take its place? The need for cooperation, integration, or teamwork, is apparent. Possibly this can be achieved without a captain.

Whitehouse has suggested that teamwork should be a "democracy of the professions." "Teamwork," he says, "is not a collection of opinions from professional consultants each considering the client from his own viewpoint in a static fashion with a master arranger combining these viewpoints into a decision." This is what seems to happen in most situations. But, he says, "the control of the decision cannot be vested exclusively in one person nor does it lie in summing up reports, but in assimilating them."[22]

What are the mechanics of achieving cooperation, coordination, and integration if there is to be no captain? The team is a group of professional equals. No one member is more important than any other. Still if no one is the captain, how can they work together? The analogy of a basketball team may be useful. Although such teams have a captain, it is somewhat of an honorary position. In actual play, action is so rapid that there is no control by the captain, or anyone else. Each member of the team plays his own position, but each works with the others, without the need for direction. Can a team of professionals work together in this fashion? If other groups can work together toward a common goal, without a director, or captain, a group of professionals can do so, providing they can accept the concept of the democracy of the group. A democratic professional group is a group of professional equals.

The term group-centered leadership has been used to designate this application of democracy to group activities.[23] In the group-centered situation, instead of one leader and many followers, co-workers participate as equals in formulating and achieving group objectives. No member is *the* captain, or *the* leader. Any and all members are leaders, at the times when their contributions are important.

This approach to group activity does not result in anarchy or disorganization. There may be a person designated as a leader, who acts as a chairman or moderator or administrator to keep the group functioning as a group. He is not, however, a leader in the usual sense of the term. Such group action is not always

22 F. A. Whitehouse. Teamwork: a democracy of professions. *Except. Child.*, 1951, 18, 45–52.

23 T. Gordon. *Group-centered leadership.* Boston: Houghton Mifflin, 1955.

easily or quickly achieved. There may be a period of apparent disorganization, during which group members become accustomed to functioning as responsible members of the group. Just as there are some who resist authority, so there are others who desire authority, and who must become accustomed to working without it. These include those who are comfortable working under authority, as well as those exercising authority. In a democratic atmosphere, however, the group will learn to take responsibility for itself.

There is some evidence that when groups function in a democratic atmosphere, they are more productive and better satisfied with the results than when they operate under an authoritarian structure. The work of Lewin and his students on experimentally created social climates in the 1930s was the beginning of many studies in school, in industry, and in other situations. In the usual authoritarian situation there is insecurity among the members of the team, a defensiveness or resistance or, sometimes, dependence and passivity. In a group-centered situation these disappear and there is instead a security which stimulates active participation by each individual, leading to greater spontaneity and creativeness. In such a situation mutual trust and respect, and recognition of each other's competence, may develop to a greater extent than usually occurs in a leader-centered group.

A group of professional people can function without the need for external supervision or control. The group itself coordinates or directs the activities and services which the student needs. Continuity of services can be maintained without any particular person directing them. Each professional specialist continues to work with the student for as long as he has something to contribute. At any one time, depending on the needs of the student, one or another of the staff members may have major responsibility for providing particular services. The group itself, through informal contacts and sessions, as well as through formal meetings, coordinates the services and activities provided for the student.

This situation requires that the members of the group accept each other as professional equals, and each as professionally competent in his own field. The counselor must accept the teacher as a specialist in his own right, as a professional colleague. Other staff members who contribute to personnel services should likewise be respected for their contributions. There is no substitute for respect for others in developing a cooperative program. The counselor, as integrator or coordinator of student personnel services, must set the example. His success will depend on his attitudes and feelings about other staff members and their contributions. If he is accepting, understanding, and respectful of others, and modest and adaptable in his own behavior, then he will likely be successful. In his expectations and requests of others, he takes them as they are, where they are, and if they are lacking in knowledge, techniques, and attitudes, he brings them along slowly, more by example than by precept. He suggests or recommends when asked; he does not order or impose his recommendation upon others. His recommendations and expectations recognize the limitations of the situation in which the teacher or other staff member must operate. His communications are simple and are phrased in language which can be understood by the average teacher. He does not talk down, or try to impress with a technical vocabulary. In his relations with colleagues, such as psychologists and school social workers, he recognizes his own limitations, and the overlap between functions in some areas. There is bound to be some overlap among all those who work with people. The individual cannot be cut up into pieces and parcelled out to various professions. The various professions must accept each other's competence in areas where each is trained. Their services are then coordinated, with each contributing what he is best prepared to do. In those areas where several professionals can function equally well, other considerations, perhaps of such a practical nature as time, or which person has already developed a relationship with the student, determine who shall provide the service.

Mutual understanding, acceptance, respect, and a basic concern for the welfare of the individual student will therefore result in collaboration rather than competition among personnel workers in the school. The person serving as administrative head of pupil personnel services has a responsibility for integrating the services into a smoothly functioning program in which the welfare of the pupil is paramount. Our point here is that this integration of professional services should be achieved in a democratic manner. The function of the coordinator is to facilitate the cooperation of professional workers. He provides the administrative structure in which such cooperation can take place, and in which continued intercommunication and democratic discussion is possible. An integrator is a facilitator, or catalyst, of interaction among a group of professional equals, all engaged in activity contributing to a common goal—the individual welfare of the student and the creation of an environment in which he can function at his optimum potential.

Summary

The counselor in the school must work with all other school personnel if he is to function effectively and provide a program of services which reaches all students. He should be particularly concerned with his relationships with other staff members who are providing personnel services.

It was suggested in this chapter that the counselor is perhaps the logical person to integrate or coordinate the personnel services of the school. This involves the establishing of certain administrative procedures and practices. Other staff members in the personnel-services area whose activities and services the counselor may coordinate are the school psychologist, the school social worker or visiting teacher, and the school nurse and doctor.

The counselor must also maintain adequate and effective relationships with other staff members. First among these is the teacher, upon whom he depends for referrals and for implementing many aspects of the total guidance program. Industrial-arts or vocational-education teachers, special-education teachers, remedial teachers, the speech therapist, and the librarian are other staff members whose attitudes and cooperation are important in the provision of an effective program of guidance services.

The problem of working together with other staff members in a democratic team relationship was considered, and a group-centered approach to the integration and coordination of personnel services was proposed.

SUGGESTED READINGS

Cutts, Norma E. (Ed.) *School psychologists at mid-century.* Washington, D.C.: American Psychological Association, 1955. A report of a ten-day conference of school psychologists, presenting the problems faced and the conclusions reached. Insufficient attention is given to the work of the counselor in the school.

Gottsegan, M. G., & Gottsegan, Gloria B. (Eds.) *Professional school psychology.* New York: Grune & Stratton, 1960. A collection of articles covering various aspects of the functioning of the psychologist in the school.

Lee, Grace (E.) *Helping the troubled school child: selected readings in school social work, 1935–1955.* New York: National Association of Social Workers, 1959. Fifty-five papers on the philosophy, description, and development of school social work, the social and emotional problems of the child in school, the practice of school social work, and the education of school social workers.

Pearman, Jean R. & Burrows, A. H. *Social services in the school.* Washington, D.C.: Public Affairs Press, 1955. Designed as a text for us in training school social workers, the book provides an introduction to the work of the visiting counselor or teacher.

White, Mary Alice & Harris, M. W. *The school psychologist.* New York: Harper, 1961. The first comprehensive consideration of the responsibilities and functions of the school psychologist. Chapter 12 deals with "The School Psychologist and Pupil Personnel Services."

CHAPTER 17

EXTRASCHOOL

RELATIONSHIPS

The school is part of the community. It is only one of the institutions of society which is concerned with children and youth. There are also many individuals and organizations outside the school which are interested in children, and in the purposes of the school. Many of these individuals and agencies supplement the services of the school, and are sources of assistance to the counselor and other school personnel services.

As the counselor is, or may be, the integrator of personnel services within the school, so he is, or may be, the person who coordinates the personnel services of the school with those of outside agencies and persons. This, of course, does not mean that he is the only person who has contacts with community agencies related to the schools. But in the area of personnel services he should be the center through which all activities of a personnel nature are routed or cleared. Direct contacts may be made by others, but the counselor as integrator of personnel services to students should be aware and informed of all such activities involving personnel services.

Working with Parents

It may seem peculiar that the matter of working with parents is considered in this chapter, since parents are clearly so closely related to the schools which teach their children. Yet they are not in the school, and are not on the school staff. While their interest is a more personal one than that of most outside individuals or agencies, they are still outside the schools.

Other staff members in addition to the counselor have contact with parents. The principal and other administrative staff members deal with parents on administrative matters. Teachers work with parents in the academic area. Other staff members concerned with personnel services also work with parents, as was indicated in the last chapter. It is suggested here that the counselor, as integrator of personnel services in the school, should be involved in, or informed about, all contacts with parents in the area of personnel services. While the school social worker may work independently with parents, the counselor should be aware of the families the worker contacts.

The counselor has direct contact with parents in relation to the personnel services which he performs. Although there has been some writing concerned with the teacher's relation to parents,[1] there has been, as Berdie points out,[2] very little written about the counselor's relationships with them. This is an area in which counselors are frequently uncertain and at sea. Each works out his own procedures, and practices vary greatly. With no research, and little authoritative discussion, few, if any, definitive statements can be made. There are, however, in the author's opinion, certain principles which should be generally accepted. Their application might clear up some of the confusions and contradictory practices in working with parents.

It is recognized that parents have certain rights in relation to the school. These rights have been succinctly stated by Nebo as follows:

1. To know about all the services of the school and to be involved in any plan for special services to their children in school.
2. To understand the problem of their child as the school sees it, to learn of the child's limitations, abilities, and needs, and to participate constructively in what is being done to help the child.
3. To expect that the school will supply appropriate facilities to

[1] For example: Maria Piers. *How to work with parents*. Chicago: Science Research Associates, 1955.

[2] R. F. Berdie. The counselor and the parent. *J. counsel. Psychol.*, 1955, 2, 185–188. Reprinted in H. B. McDaniel, *et al.* (Eds.). *Readings in guidance*. New York: Holt, 1959. Pp. 361–365.

meet their children's needs and to work with the school to
find them.

4. To expect schools to work with them to prevent serious difficulties from developing in their children.

5. To choose whether or not they will accept a service for their
children and themselves. However, they do not have the right
to make no choice. The school has the responsibility to try to
help the parents understand not only the services offered, but
the alternatives if the service is rejected. In cases of neglect,
one of the alternatives will be referral to an appropriate
agency or the court.

6. To be concerned about their children and to be consulted
about difficulties which their children are having in school.
This right, especially, applies to both parents.[3]

These points all have relevance to the personnel services of the
schools. In the special area of the counselor, Ricks has stated that
"parents have the right to know whatever the school knows
about the abilities, the performance, and the problems of their
children."[4]

The questions arise as to how the parent exercises these rights,
and how the school discharges its responsibilities to parents regarding these rights. And how about the rights of the child?
What does the counselor (or teacher or principal) say to the
parent who asks for his child's IQ? Should test scores be sent
home with the child along with the report card? Should the
child's cumulative record be available for inspection by the
parent? Should the parent be called in for a conference about
the child's personal or social problems? Answers to these questions must be based upon some sound principles of parent-school,
or parent-counselor, relationships. What are some of these
principles?

1. *In general the counselor should talk with parents only with
the consent and/or knowledge of the student.* This appears to be
a reasonable principle, based upon respect for the student as a

---

[3] J. C. Nebo. Some aspects of social work practice in the schools. In:
Social work in the schools: selected papers. New York: National Association
of Social Workers, 1960.

[4] J. H. Ricks, Jr. On telling parents about test results. *Test Service Bull.*,
No. 54, December, 1959. New York: The Psychological Corporation, 1959.

person. Yet it is violated frequently, by teachers and school administrators, if not by counselors. The principle may not be applicable with children in the early elementary grades, or with children too young to be aware of or to realize the nature of the situation. Even at the second-grade level, however, it is doubtful that the parents should be contacted without the child being aware of it. It would appear to be much better to inform him in advance, rather than to have him discover it later, as he inevitably will. The advantage of regularly scheduled conferences of teachers with parents is that the child is aware of them, and in addition knows that all other parents are being seen also. This tends to reduce the threat which is inevitably involved when a child is discussed by his parents and someone else who is significant in his life.

It has been suggested that counselors have regularly scheduled conferences with all parents, usually for the purpose of discussing the results of the school testing program. When this is a regular procedure, students are, of course, aware of it. But their consent has not necessarily been obtained. It may be that parents should have the right to knowledge of the student's performance on regularly administered tests, without the specific consent of the child.

But when it comes to informing parents of the results of tests taken as part of counseling, the situation is different. Here the counselor should not divulge the results without the consent of the student, even if the parents should initiate a request for the information. To be sure, it is not likely that the student would object to his parents having such information, so that obtaining his consent may appear to be a formality. But it is an important formality, and one which may make or break a counselor or the counseling program. There are occasions in counseling when the counselor may feel that it would be helpful for the parent to be brought into the situation, or to be consulted. When this is the case, it should be discussed with the student. The counselor may say: "Don't you think I should talk to your mother?" or "Would it help if I talked to your father?" or "Would you like me to talk to your father?"

It is possible that there are exceptions to the principle of consent, where the welfare of the student or others is involved. In such cases, the counselor may feel he must consult the parents, even without the consent of the student. The student should be informed of the opinion and intentions of the counselor, however, although there may be exceptions to this. A counselor of the writer's acquaintance contacted the father of a student he was counseling when he felt she was becoming too deeply involved with an older man. He had reason to believe the father would not divulge the situation, and the counselor could continue working with the girl without the fear that she would get into difficulty because of lack of parental awareness of what was happening.

2. *The confidentiality of the counseling relationship must be maintained.* The incident just referred to was a violation of the confidentiality of the counseling relationship, which the counselor felt was justified. Only in exceptional circumstances does the counselor violate confidentiality. The importance of confidentiality has been emphasized in other connections; it is important also in relationships with parents. Students often confide in counselors what they cannot tell their parents, and parents have no right to ask or expect the counselor to break confidence with the student. In the case referred to above, the parent had earlier made inquiries concerning what his daughter talked about with the counselor, and had been informed that this was confidential.

The usual purposes of counselor-parent conferences can be achieved without the revelation of confidential information. These purposes are either (or both) (1) to help the counselor better understand the pupil, and (2) to help the parent better understand the pupil. In the first case the counselor is bringing the parent into the situation to obtain the benefit of his knowledge and understanding of the child or student, to learn and understand the parent's point of view—his attitudes and feelings, his hopes and goals for the student. In this kind of conference the counselor is not expected to provide information. In a conference having the second purpose, the counselor has the responsibility of helping the parent understand the attitudes, feelings, desires, goals, and needs of the student. The counselor presumably has developed an understanding on the basis of his counseling, and desires to communicate this to the parent, and to do so without divulging the confidential details upon which his understanding is based. The trained and skillful counselor is able to do this. He does so by avoiding specifics; he does not have to give the data from which his understanding has been developed. The specific problems of the student need not be discussed, particularly the more personal ones. The implications of the problems may be communicated without detailing their nature. In some cases the nature of the conflicting demands, and choices, which the student faces may be depicted. Discussions of vocational choice, or of academic problems, usually do not involve highly personal or confidential material, and here the counselor can be more free in his discussion.

In any event, before discussing specific information with a parent, the counselor should obtain the permission of the student to do so. This does not apply, of course, to information which is more or less public. Nor does it apply to information which is in the general school records, such as results of general testing programs. In this case, however, the information should be handled and communicated in such a way that the student is not misrepresented, placed in a bad light, or stigmatized.

3. *The counselor has an obligation to communicate understandable and usable knowledge to the parent.*[5] If parents are to understand their child and his problems, they must have information which they can absorb and use. This is particularly the case in those situations where, as in educational and vocational choices, the parents must accept or approve the decision, or support the student in his education or training.

Giving information which is not understood is not enlightening or helpful. Unfortunately, perhaps all too much of what counselors tell parents about their children is not understood or useful to the parents because of the language in which it is clothed. How many parents really understand the flood of percentiles, grade-placement figures, standard scores, age scores, and quotients with which they are overwhelmed?

Perhaps one of the reasons counselors fail to communicate meaningful information is that they do not adequately understand what they are trying to communicate themselves. The

[5] The following discussion draws upon the *Test Service Bulletin* cited *Supra.*

counselor must really know the meaning of test scores, their limitations, the probable (or standard) error of the scores, the nature of the norm group or groups, and the characteristics of the statistical devices or terms which he is using before he can intelligently discuss the results of tests with parents. IQ scores should not be reported as such, since they are usually perceived by parents as being fixed, immutable, and somehow infallible. They may be misinterpreted, as in the case of the mother who bragged that her daughter had gotten an almost perfect score on her intelligence test—an IQ of 99! On the other hand, a percentile of 50 or 60 is usually seen as a failing or below average score unless the counselor makes very sure that the percentile system is understood.

Perhaps it is not necessary to use numbers in discussing test results with parents. While the use of ranges is suggested as a way of avoiding an impression of undue accuracy, parents may fixate upon one or the other end of the range, depending upon their attitudes and needs. The use of terms such as upper quarter, middle third, or upper tenth, may be better. Another method is to designate the group in which the student's score places him. Thus, a parent may be told, "Your son scores like students who are quite likely to succeed in college," or ". . . who have a difficult time graduating from college," or ". . . who are usually happy in teaching," etc.

The important thing is that the parents be given as clear and as accurate a picture of the student as possible. The meaning of the information contained in test scores must be communicated, yet without implying more accuracy or certainty than are inherent in the scores.

4. *Parents should be worked with therapeutically, and sometimes in a counseling relationship.* Information which is closely related to oneself is not always accepted at face value. Emotional feelings and attitudes may be aroused. This is often true regarding the information which the counselor provides parents about their children. If it is at all unfavorable, or disappointing, it may not be accepted easily. Resistance to accepting objective information is often called defensiveness, and parents are sometimes criticized for not being able or willing to "face the facts." But being defensive in this way is not resistance, or lack of co-

operation, or inability to face reality—it is a natural reaction to a genuinely threatening situation. The counselor must recognize this, and be prepared to handle such reactions therapeutically, that is, with acceptance and understanding, rather than with argument and reasoning. The comments in Chapter 9 regarding the communication of test results to students apply here.

The counselor must be prepared sometimes to enter a counseling relationship with parents. Parents whose children are in trouble or having difficulty often have problems themselves, and sometimes seek help from the counselor. This is recognized in child-guidance clinics, where parents are seen in counseling or therapy along with the child. A problem arises where the child is being seen in a counseling relationship by the counselor. It is usually not desirable for a counselor to work with two members of a family at the same time. He may tend to relate more closely to one than to the other, to identify with one rather than the other, or even be prejudiced against the other. The two clients may be uncomfortable because of these possibilities, and each may attempt to bring the counselor to his side. It is thus better that someone else work with the parent if the counselor is working with the child, as is done in child-guidance clinics. Here the counselor may find the school social worker a resource, if one is available, or the school psychologist, or perhaps another counselor. Of course if the parent is seriously disturbed, it is not the place of the counselor to attempt intensive psychotherapy.

5. *Parents should be consulted regarding important personnel actions of the school or concerning referral to sources or services outside the school.* The parent has a right to be informed about special treatment of the child in school, such as remedial reading, speech therapy, or any other action of an administrative nature such as placement in special classes or sections. Whether the parent should be notified if a child is being seen regularly by the counselor regarding personal problems is debatable. In the case of the young child, in the elementary school, perhaps such information should be communicated to the parent. It is best if the pupil can tell his parents himself. In the high school or even the junior high school, the need for students to keep such counseling private should be recognized.

If the student requires special services not offered in the school, but available from another community agency, the child should not be referred without the knowledge and consent of the parents. Parents have a right to refuse such services if they desire to do so.

Relations with Health and Welfare Agencies

The school does not and cannot provide complete services to children. Other community agencies exist to give necessary services. One group of such agencies include the health and welfare agencies, both public and private. These include public health and public welfare services, and family welfare agencies. In a large community there are numerous such agencies, often representing different governmental levels, such as city, county, and state. A council of social agencies may coordinate services.

The school should utilize these agencies for the welfare of children who need the services which they offer. Chronically ill, undernourished or underfed, and poorly clothed children cannot be expected to perform up to their potential in school. Someone in the school must have the responsibility for initiating action to bring the health and welfare resources of the community to the assistance of those children who need them. The counselor as coordinator of the personnel services of the school and the community should function in this respect. This means that he should know the resources of the community if he is to utilize them adequately.

The counselor will find the knowledge and experience of the school social worker, if one is available, or the school nurse, invaluable in utilizing community health and welfare resources. In a school which has the services of a social worker or nurse, the responsibility for actual contacts and cooperation with these community agencies may be delegated or assigned to them.

Psychological Service Agencies

Another group of agencies with which the counselor should be familiar and develop mutual working relationships is that which performs services of a counseling or psychological nature. There is, of course, some overlap between the agencies discussed above and those included here. Public welfare agencies which provide casework services are offering psychological as well as material help. But here we are interested in agencies offering primarily mental-health and vocational services.

Child-guidance or mental-hygiene clinics are perhaps the major agencies in the mental-health category. The counselor should be familiar with the nature and extent of the services offered by such clinics. The requirements for eligibility for services, charges, and the time required because of waiting lists should be known. Along the line suggested above in relation to health and welfare agencies, the counselor who has a school psychologist available will want to work closely with him in utilizing community mental-health services. In addition to community clinics—and where such clinics do not exist—a knowledge of other counseling resources is required of the counselor. These include psychiatrists and psychologists in private practice, counseling services offered by churches, the YMCA or YWCA, or by college or university centers or clinics.

A resource in vocational counseling and placement is the State Employment Service, which maintains offices in many communities. In the larger communities the staff includes a counselor, and aptitude, interest, and ability tests are available for administration. Where testing and placement services in the schools are limited, the State Employment Service will, at the request of the schools or of individual students, and as its resources permit, provide testing and placement services to graduating seniors. The State Employment Service and its local offices are a major source of recent local occupational information and employment trends. Its staff members can be helpful in assisting in courses in occupations, providing materials and serving as resource persons and lecturers.

We have already mentioned, in the discussion of the counseling of handicapped students (Chapter 15), the services offered by the State Vocational Rehabilitation Division or Bureau. The school counselor should develop a cooperative arrangement with the state rehabilitation counselor so that long-term planning can be started by the handicapped student. When the student leaves school the rehabilitation counselor can take responsibility, with the school counselor cooperating by providing information from the school records.

Other Relationships

The counselor represents the counseling and personnel services of the school, and in some cases the school itself, to the public and to community organizations. He thus performs, to some extent, a public relations function. He may be asked to talk to PTA meetings, or to service club luncheons. In these contacts with community organizations, the counselor has an important responsibility. He must represent not only his school but his profession. This means that he must be accurate, modest, and responsible in his description of counseling and personnel services. He must not make claims which are beyond the possibility of fulfillment. He must not overemphasize the spectacular or the extreme cases, or misrepresent his functions or achievements. He is not an entertainer, but a professional person.

There is another caution in connection with public contacts. The counselor must avoid devoting too much time to such activities, to the neglect of the school's program. The counseling program is primary, and a program which exists mainly in the mind of the counselor or in his speeches does not help students. Perhaps this danger is not a particularly real one for most counselors. It is doubtful that many possess the talent of public speaking to an extent which would lead to too great demands on their time.

Counselors occasionally are called upon to present their programs to the Board of Education, either in terms of a report, or for the purpose of obtaining interest and support for the program or for its expansion. This again requires responsibility and judgment in the claims made for the values of counseling and personnel programs. It is also a difficult task to reach laymen with an understandable and yet forceful presentation in a brief period of time. While overselling must be avoided, concrete results of the program must be illustrated, since school boards have many demands made on their limited financial resources. An illustration of one approach, using audio-visual materials, is given by Walker and Dimengo.[6]

[6] R. N. Walker & C. Dimengo. Give your board the big picture! *Voc. Guid. Quart.*, 1960, 9, 3–6.

Making Referrals

It has been indicated above that the school is not able to provide all the personnel services needed by its students, and must utilize community resources. The inability of the school to supply all needed services is not a matter of inadequacy—the school is not expected to do so. Its responsibilities in this area are limited.

By the same token, the inability of the counselor to supply all the needs of all students in the area of counseling and guidance is not a reflection upon him. Every professional person has competencies in some areas but not in others. It is a mark of the responsible professional that he recognize when a problem is beyond his competence, and that he make an appropriate referral.

A recent study of a School Committee of a Council of Social Agencies of a large city recommended "that the schools make intelligent use of community resources by a closer relationship between school and social agencies."[7] For maximum or optimum use of such resources by the schools, the committee emphasized the following points:

1. An understanding by the school and the social agencies of each other's functions. This would include: (a) the chief service rendered by the agency; (b) the philosophy of counseling; (c) understanding of social work practice; (d) clientele served by the agency, including any restrictions; (e) scale of fees.
2. A comprehensive referral system. This would indicate channels and procedures of referral.
3. Sharing of information between the school and the agency staff. This would include any information pertinent to the problem or purpose for which referral was made.

Hoyt and Loughary report a study of the use of referral sources by 118 counselors in nonmetropolitan Iowa high schools.[8]

[7] L. M. Sielski. Developing principles of public school and social agency cooperation. *Personnel Guid. J.*, 1956, **35**, 247–248.

[8] K. B. Hoyt & J. W. Loughary. Acquaintance with and use of referral sources by Iowa secondary school counselors. *Personnel Guid. J.*, 1958, **36**, 388–391. Reprinted in G. F. Farwell & H. J. Peters (Eds.). *Guidance readings for counselors.* Chicago: Rand McNally, 1960. Pp. 549–554.

Counselors in metropolitan schools were not included, since these schools had special referral departments in the systems. While the counselors were familiar with 58 percent of the 34 referral categories used in the survey, they had used only 12 percent of them. The list included a number of sources with which counselors might be familiar but would not be likely to have occasion to use directly, however. Some of these were homes for dependent and neglected children, training schools for delinquents, state schools for the mentally deficient, and state mental hospitals. While about 70 percent were familiar with the State Division of Special Education, only 27 percent had used it; 75 percent were aware of the existence of the Division of Vocational Rehabilitation, and 30 percent indicated that they had used it. The agency with which most counselors (86 percent) were familiar, and also used the most (47 percent), was the State Employment Service. It might be expected that counselors would not have much occasion to deal directly with agencies at the state level (most of those in the list were at this level). However, only 20 percent of the counselors reported that they were acquainted with private service agencies and institutions, and only 9 percent had used them. On the other hand, 47 percent were acquainted with local church, civic, and service groups, and 32 percent had used them. The meaning of the results of this study may be questioned, since most counselors would use local agencies, or work through such agencies. The study does not indicate whether the question included indirect usage; it would appear that this was not included, however. On the other hand, in nonmetropolitan areas, local agencies are often few, and it might be expected that counselors would utilize state services more directly. At any rate, the study raises a question about the adequacy of counselors' acquaintance with, and particularly the use of, referral sources.

Making a referral involves more than telling a student or parent to contact or visit a community agency, or call for an appointment. In a few cases this may be appropriate, such as informing students about the placement services of the local State Employment Service Office and suggesting that those interested in employment should register. It is, of course, desirable that the student or parent take as much responsibility as possible in the referral process.

But the matter of a referral involves a number of considerations. First is the necessity for referral. Referrals should not be made if the school can provide the service. The counselor must feel quite sure that the service is really needed. This may be a matter in which consultation is helpful, or it may be the subject of a staff meeting. Often consultation with the agency to whom the referral is to be made is desirable. This is also a way of assuring that the needed service is available, and that the potential client is likely to be eligible for the service.

This is all preliminary to discussing the referral with the student and/or his parents. It is not sufficient to announce to them that a referral is recommended. They may not be prepared for a referral, and may need to be helped to recognize its necessity and value. The student and his parents must be helped to see the problem which requires referral, and how the agency can be of help. Here the counselor must be careful not to misrepresent or oversell the results to be expected.

When referral is accepted, the procedure for carrying it out will vary with the nature of the problem, the situation of the student and his parents, and the preferences or practices of the agency. While it is desirable that the student or his parents take as much responsibility as possible, it must be remembered that this is probably a new and somewhat threatening situation, and they should not be left completely alone. The counselor knows, or should know, the agency and its personnel. It is no more than courteous to offer to make the initial contact or introduction, or arrange for a preliminary appointment.

The following guides to good referrals may be helpful to keep in mind.[9]

1. Get acquainted with the people working in community agencies in your area. There is no substitute for personal respect and friendship in building smooth and effective school-community cooperation. Try inviting them to a faculty meeting to tell of their service and to meet the staff. Visit them at the agency to get the "feel" of their service.

2. Help the agency or specialist by indicating which person

[9] This listing is adapted from the following: *How to make referrals.* Guidance Series. (10th annual ed.) East Lansing, Mich. Michigan State University, College of Education, 1956.

should be the point of contact representing the school. This person will supply additional information as needed, and will receive agency reports which he in turn will share, as seems indicated, with others on the school staff.

3. Try to discover what persons have had contact with the parent or student in regard to the problem, and what results were obtained from these contacts before making a referral. A case conference may result in the early and appropriate use of resources in the school and community, and will also serve to bring together information about the student in usable form, and to coordinate the efforts of the total school. "Let your right hand know what your left hand is doing."

4. Check to see if the school has used all its own available resources in helping the student before looking outside the school for help. Perhaps there are other steps which should be taken before referring the student to an outside agency or specialist.

5. Learn whether a community agency is already working with the family, because a consultation with that agency is the proper first step in considering a referral in such cases.

6. Try discussing an incipient problem with an agency or specialist before its referral becomes urgent. Many agencies are willing to work in cooperation with the school in the area of prevention.

7. All agencies, public and private, have their own eligibility requirements and accepted procedures. Do not expect them to suspend rules for you.

8. It is unwise and impractical to refer a student to community agencies without the knowledge, consent, and cooperation of his parents. Many child-guidance agencies will not accept students for treatment unless parents cooperate fully and are willing to present themselves for help, too. Check on the policy of your local agencies in this regard.

9. When telling students or parents about available services, in the school or in the community, explain both the functions and the limitations of these services. Do not give the impression that any specialist or agency has all the answers and can work wonders.

10. Remember that a parent's great emotional involvement with

his child may make it difficult for him to recognize that a problem exists.

11. Let the student or his parents make their own arrangements for service whenever possible. Do not "spoon feed" the student by being more "helpful" than necessary.

12. Remember that in some cases, however, help may be needed by very immature, dependent, or ill students or parents in arranging an appointment or even in arranging transportation to the agency.

13. Secure a signed consent from the student's parents before releasing information to a social agency. This is a wise precaution in most cases.

14. Share information about the student with the new service working with him, but do not violate the confidence of the student except under very unusual circumstances. In passing along information, distinguish between professional sharing of information and gossip. Facts, not your evaluation of facts, will usually be most valuable.

15. A school can expect a report from a referral agency regarding its general plans for working with a case. A school cannot expect to know the details of treatment, nor to share in confidences given by parents or students to agency personnel.

16. Expect to be asked to work cooperatively with the specialist or agency during the treatment period. In some cases this will be an important part of the treatment.

17. Do not expect immediate help for particular symptoms. Usually basic attitudes and feelings are involved in behavior, and these attitudes and feelings may change very slowly. Do not expect miracles to be worked on cases you refer.

18. *Respect the individual!* The basic attitude in the referrals, as in all counseling, is a fundamental respect for the individual and a fundamental belief that it is best for him to work out his own problems in his own way. Schools and agencies are helpers in this process, not directors.

The follow-through of referrals is an important area. It is not sufficient to make a successful referral, and then forget about the student. It is noted in the guides above that the agency should make a report following the referral. More than this, there should be periodic reports, or periodic inquiries from the school. This raises the question as to who is responsible for such follow-up of referrals. The responsibility would certainly be that of one of the personnel services of the school.

In the suggested organization of such services, in which the counselor would be the coordinator, the responsibility would fall upon the counselor. However, this responsibility may be delegated, or assumed by another member of the staff. The importance of cooperative effort, or teamwork, by the personnel staff cannot be overemphasized. Referrals should usually be a matter of concern to the whole staff, and as suggested above usually involve consultation or discussion in staff meeting prior to the actual decision to refer. It has also been suggested that where a social worker or psychologist is available for a sufficient amount of time, the referral may be handled by one of them. Similarly, if the referral is initiated by such a staff member, it appears desirable that the same person follow through with the case throughout the contact with the referral agency.

In this and the preceding chapter we have outlined the functioning of a program of personnel services within the school and its relationship with outside agencies in a situation where the counselor is the integrator of services within the school and the coordinator of services outside the school. This is, of course, not the only solution. An assistant principal may perform these functions, and where there is an assistant principal for guidance and/or personnel services this would appear logically to be one of his duties. It is frequently recommended that the principal serve in this capacity. However, it is the opinion of the author that (1) the person who acts as coordinator should have professional training in counseling or personnel work, and (2) it should be a full-time person who can keep closely in touch with other staff and outside agencies. The counselor or director of guidance would thus appear to be the most appropriate person. Where there are trained social workers or psychologists available within the school on a full-time basis, there is no reason why such a person could not assume the responsibility of integration and coordination. And where such personnel are available part-time, they may be delegated the function or responsibility of working with out-of-school agencies, each in his particular area.

The important point is that the responsibility be assumed by someone with adequate background and time to carry it out. In the carrying out of the function, it is not only possible, but even desirable, that the assistance and cooperation of other staff members be utilized. The providing of personnel services to students is a cooperative undertaking, in which each person providing a specific personnel service contributes his time and talents cooperatively with others. This is not a place for prima donnas, or for jurisdictional disputes or authoritarian procedures. In the area of helping others there is and always will be considerable overlap of services. But there is room and need for the contributions of all. The essential requirement is that whoever provides a service be competent to do so, and be willing to work with and refer to others where referral is desirable, in the best interests of the student.

Summary

The school is part of the larger community. It cannot, nor should it, offer all the personnel services which the students may need. It therefore depends upon community agencies and facilities for a number of special services to students. It is necessary that the counselor, as the coordinator of personnel services in the school, be familiar with community resources and utilize them effectively. While the actual contact with specific agencies may be delegated to other members of the staff who have responsibilities related to particular agencies, the counselor should keep informed of the contacts of staff and students with community agencies.

Agencies with which the counselor should be familiar are those in the health and welfare fields, child-guidance or mental hygiene clinics, agencies working with the handicapped, including vocational rehabilitation agencies, and employment agencies, such as the State Employment Service. Procedures for making referrals to these various agencies are important, and factors to be considered in making referrals are listed.

One group of nonschool people with whom the counselor must work is parents. Little has been done to help the counselor in this area. Therefore, some principles underlying relationships with parents were suggested.

SUGGESTED READINGS

Berdie, R. F., Grams, A. & Vance, F. *The parent and the counselor.* St. Paul, Minn.: State of Minnesota, Department of Education, 1960. Directed to parents, this pamphlet contains chapters on "Knowing Our Children Better," "Problems Encountered During the High School Years," "The School Counselor," and "The Parent Works with the School Counselor."

Hoyt, K. B. & Loughary, J. W. Acquaintance with and use of referral sources by Iowa secondary-school counselors. *Personnel Guid. J.,* 1958, **36,** 388–391. Reprinted in Farwell, G. F. & Peters, H. J. (Eds.) *Guidance readings for counselors.* Chicago: Rand McNally, 1960. Pp. 549–554. A study of counselor use of referral sources, indicating that rural counselors are not well acquainted with referral sources available to them.

Sielski, L. M. Developing principles of public school and social agency cooperation. *Personnel Guid. J.,* 1950, **35,** 247–248. A report of a study by the School Committee of the Council of Social Agencies of Buffalo and Erie County.

PART VI

IMPROVING SERVICES

CHAPTER 18

IN-SERVICE TRAINING

AND RESEARCH

Every counselor should be interested in improving the counseling and guidance services of his school. No program is perfect; there is always room for improvement. And there is perhaps no such thing as holding the line, or maintaining a level of services by standing still. Without concern about developing better services, the program will fall behind, since new knowledge and new techniques and methods are constantly becoming available. Change is inevitable; the question is whether retrogression or progression occurs. With the pace of current improvements in counseling and guidance and personnel services, one must run in order to keep up with new developments.

There are two major ways in which programs in counseling and guidance may be improved. One is by the development of greater competence in the counseling and guidance staff, so that they may better apply existing knowledge and practices. The second is the study or evaluation of the existing services to determine their effectiveness, and to discover new methods or approaches to achieve the goals of the program. The latter is essentially research. In this chapter we shall consider briefly these two methods of improving services.

In-Service Training

Every professional person has a responsibility to himself, to his clients, and to his profession to maintain and advance his professional competence. Professional growth is necessary if he is to meet this responsibility. Even the well-trained and experienced counselor must devote time and effort to this end. And in a situation where so many of those functioning as counselors are incompletely or inadequately trained, it is incumbent upon everyone to encourage and assist in the continued training of these counselors.

There are a number of things which the counselor on the job can and should do to maintain and enhance his professional competence:

1. The counselor should identify himself with professional organizations. These organizations will include local, state, regional, and national groups. At the national level the National Vocational Guidance Association and the American School Counselor Association, both divisions of the American Personnel and Guidance Association, are professional organizations with which the counselor in the school may affiliate himself. Membership in professional organizations is a way of identifying with the profession as a whole, and associating with other likeminded professional persons. This association offers a means of interrelationship and intercommunication for those in the profession, and provides the counselor a means of identifying with the profession.

2. Professional organizations provide opportunities for members to communicate with each other through the conventions or meetings which they hold, usually once a year. Counselors should attend conventions to keep up with the current developments which are reported in the programs, and to meet and talk with other counselors in informal contacts. The conventions bring outstanding members of the profession to contribute to the program, and offer counselors an opportunity to present to others new ideas, programs, or results of studies or research projects. Administrators should recognize the value of attendance at professional conventions for staff members, and should make it possible for them to attend by granting leave and providing expenses.

3. Counselors should make an effort to read professional literature. This includes both professional journals and books. Membership in professional organizations includes subscriptions to the journals published by them. Members of the American Personnel

and Guidance Association receive the *Personnel and Guidance Journal.* The National Vocational Guidance Association publishes the *Vocational Guidance Quarterly* and distributes it to its members. A journal not published or distributed by a professional association, but one with which the professional counselor should be familiar, is the *Journal of Counseling Psychology.* There are a number of other journals which publish articles related to counseling. Besides the articles, these journals carry announcements or reviews of new books in the field of counseling.

4. Individual counselors, particularly those who have had little training, should take advantage of courses in counseling or psychology offered by local or neighboring colleges and universities. Many courses appropriate for counselors are offered in the late afternoons or evenings, or on Saturdays. The incompletely trained counselor should also devote his summers to professional study until he reaches the minimum level of training outlined in Chapter 5. Administrators should encourage such study by approving leave or allowing the counselor to arrange his hours of work so that he can attend classes.

In addition to the personal efforts of the counselor, the administration should encourage professional development by allocating a budget for this purpose. Such a budget should include money for travel to professional conventions, as suggested above. In addition, standard professional books and manuals should be purchased by the school for the use of the counseling staff. Subscriptions to basic professional publications should be paid for by the school. These books and publications, as well as other professional materials received by the school, should be circulated on a regular basis among the staff for individual reading.

While the individual counselor can do much on his own to advance professionally, the school or school system with a number of counselors should have a program of in-service training for its staff. It should be the responsibility of the administration and the director of guidance and counseling to stimulate and make possible a program of in-service training. Where there are no large schools or systems, the county superintendent should take the initiative or lead in making in-service training possible. A well-trained counselor in the county superintendent's office could assist in organizing and providing in-service training for individual counselors in the schools in the county. An example of a county-wide program is described by Camp.[1]

To be successful, an in-service training program should be organized and developed with the following considerations in mind:

1. A program which is imposed from above or from outside may be perceived as a burden or imposition rather than a help.

2. The program therefore should develop out of the interests and needs of the counselors who are to participate in it. These interests and needs may be clear and obvious, or it may be desirable to make a survey of the felt or expressed needs of the counselors.

3. The counselors for whom the program is organized should participate in its planning, organization, and conduct. Not all counselors need to or should participate actively, but the program should be the responsibility of a committee rather than of a single person. The director of counseling or guidance of the school or system may be the chairman, but he should be assisted by representatives of the group.

4. The program must start at the level of the staff. Where the staff has little formal training, the object of the in-service training program should be to provide the fundamentals of counseling. Where there is heterogeneity among the counselors in their background and training, an attempt should be made to provide a program which will include something of value for all of them. This can be achieved by having a varied program, utilizing several of the methods and techniques to be described later.

5. The program should include both theory and practice. Too often counselors on the job, usually those with the least training, decry theory and desire practical how-to-do-it programs. While techniques and practical procedures are necessary, principles are of more importance. Theories, and the basic principles which develop out of theories, are the bases for practice. They provide the rationale or reason for particular techniques. A professional person is more than a technician. He needs to know not only what to do, but why he is doing it. It is only on the basis of theories

[1] H. H. Camp, Jr. A county studies its in-service counselor training program. *Personnel Guid. J.*, 1959, **38**, 309–313.

or principles that the professional person can know what to do in new or unique situations.

6. The program must be continuous, systematic, and progressive. If results are to be achieved, and the interest and motivation of the participating counselors are to be retained, the program cannot be a hit-or-miss affair, irregularly scheduled, repetitive, with no system or thread of continuity.

7. The program should utilize all the resources available. This would include college or university personnel, and staff members of other community agencies. The special competencies of the staff itself should not be overlooked, either.

8. The administration must support the program if it is to be successful. Administrative support includes assistance in obtaining resources, some financial support for materials and supplies and employment of consultants or lecturers, and released time for counselors to participate in the various activities of the program.

These are some of the things which must be considered in organizing a program of in-service training. What about the techniques and contents of in-service training programs? Here there are many possibilities. The major limitations are available resources and time. Some of the types of activities which can be part of such training are discussed below. Included are activities which must be initiated by the group, rather than opportunities for formal training, such as college or university courses which already exist for the individual counselor to utilize. Their organization into an integrated program is the task of the local committee.

1. *Individual conferences with a supervisor or consultant.* This is perhaps the most common activity which can be utilized in improving the competencies of a staff. It is a method which is adapted to meeting the needs of the individual. Kirk discusses a program utilizing this method, in which the conferences were entirely unstructured.[2] She reports that the counselors were not used to such permissiveness, and in the course of time the conferences developed into case discussions. While this approach pro-

[2] (1) Barbara A. Kirk. Techniques of in-service counselor training. *Personnel Guid. J.*, 1955, **34**, 204–207. (2) Barbara A. Kirk. Evaluation of in-service counselor training. *Educ. psychol. Measmt*, 1956, **16**, 527–537.

vides definite content, and may lead to the discussion of general problems, the individual conference should not be limited to discussion of specific cases.

Where cases are being discussed, there is no better method of knowing and understanding what the counselor does than by the use of tape recordings of his interviews. This method, which is now widely used in the supervised practice training of counselors in colleges and universities, is notable by its absence in other settings. Counselors (and often their supervisors!) are reluctant to expose themselves so openly. But the incompleteness and unreliability of memory, and even of written notes or records made during or immediately following counseling, are notorious. Counselors do not remember the verbatim remarks which they and their counselees make. What they remember is partial, and is their impression or interpretation of what occurred. For the purpose of training and learning, however, it is important that the counselor and the supervisor have available an accurate, complete record of what was said. Tape recordings provide this. If the counselor is really interested in learning and improving, he will recognize the necessity of exposing himself, both to himself and to a supervisor. This can be done only in a situation where the counselor feels secure. Such security is difficult to achieve where the purpose of the conference is the appraisal or evaluation of the counselor for purposes of personnel ratings or action such as promotion or salary increases. It can only occur where the purpose is to help the counselor to improve his functioning.

2. *Group conferences, or seminars.* A second major method of in-service training is the holding of regularly scheduled meetings or conferences of professional staff members. These may be weekly, biweekly, or monthly. Weekly meetings may be of shorter duration than monthly meetings—the former usually one to two hours, the latter a half or a whole day. Monthly meetings are perhaps better suited for bringing together staff members in a system, county, or district where distance may make weekly meetings inconvenient or difficult.

The content of these meetings should be related to the needs and interests of the counselors participating. Where the group has had relatively little training or preparation, a series of meetings may be set up to consider such topics as the philosophy of counseling, problems in the use of tests, using occupational information in counseling—in fact, any of the subjects making up the chapters in this and other texts in counseling and guidance.

Where the group is lacking in advanced training, or where it is large, lectures and formal presentations may be more useful than free or open discussion. Kirk[3] found that the group of counselors studied wanted more structuring than was provided. She felt too much had been assumed regarding their background, and that they were not ready to use the unstructured seminar approach. More advanced groups might be able to profit more from free interchange. However, even here more formal presentations by experts of topics such as statistics, research, and evaluation, and new theoretical developments would be of value.

Another type of activity for group meetings is the review of current or recent journal articles. Groups having this as their purpose are sometimes called journal clubs. Books may also be reviewed and discussed by members of the group.

Where it is desired to utilize a number of approaches or to cover a number of areas, two series of conferences or seminars may be conducted together, or on alternating weeks. The writer, as chairman of an in-service training committee for counselors in a large agency, developed a series of meetings on personal counseling and another on research and statistics. The two series were conducted together, but on alternate weeks.

These discussions and seminars should make use of available resources in the community or surrounding area as well as within the group itself. Staff members from nearby colleges and universities may be invited as guest speakers. Staff members of other community organizations, including the agencies discussed in the last chapter, such as the Employment Service, the Division of Vocational Rehabilitation, and mental hygiene clinics can contribute to the knowledge of counselors. Members of related professions, as well as representatives of industry, labor, and government make useful resource persons. In the kind of organized program being discussed here, it is important that the contributions of these resource people fit into the planned and progressive content of the conferences.

[3] *Ibid.*

Another source of relevant content may be found in film strips and motion pictures. Films are now available in many areas of interest to counselors—counseling procedures and techniques, mental health and mental hygiene, occupational information, job analysis, personnel practices, and in various areas of psychology.[4] Recordings, on discs or tapes, of counseling cases are also available.[5]

3. *Case conferences and demonstrations.* Another approach to in-service training is the use of actual cases, which the group discusses and analyzes. The main purpose here is teaching, rather than the staff discussion of cases as a basis for action. The latter situation is of course a learning experience for even experienced counselors. But the use of cases in in-service training is specifically for the purpose of training relatively new or inexperienced counselors. Cases are thus selected to illustrate and stimulate the discussion of particular kinds of problems or problem areas, or procedures.

In demonstrations an experienced and skilled counselor shows how a particular situation or problem should be handled. Test administration and interviewing techniques may be demonstrated. Subjects may be members of the group or other members of the school staff, or actual students or clients. In the latter case, the subject should be aware of the fact that he is being observed, and his permission obtained. Usually a one-way vision screen and a sound amplifier are used. Where the number of observers is small direct observation may be possible.

4. *Workshops and institutes.* In contrast to the conferences or seminars discussed above, which are relatively brief in duration but repeated over a period of weeks or months, workshops or institutes are concentrated in time, lasting from a day to two weeks. They are devoted to an intensive study of a particular area or problem. They usually involve special consultants or resource persons.

Such workshops or institutes are useful to bring together coun-

[4] Catalogues of films are available from several sources. See also Mary F. Harkheimer & J. W. Diffor (Eds.) *Educators guide to free films.* (20th ed.) Randolph, Wisc.: Educators Progress Service, 1960.

[5] For example: *The Case of Jim,* available from the American Guidance Service, Nashville, Tenn.

selors in an area or region for the study of a major or common problem area in which outside consultants can be of assistance. Since they require large blocks of time, scheduling is limited to times when the schools are not in session. A workshop just before the opening of school can be a useful way of orienting new counselors in a system, and preparing for inaugurating new services or procedures. Such workshops are becoming common for teachers.

5. *Visits to community institutions.* Counselors should have firsthand familiarity with the institutions of the communities in which they and their students live. Time taken to become acquainted with them, and with the people associated with them, is time well spent. Such institutions would include the social welfare agencies and organizations. The major industries of the community should be known by the counselor from observation based on visits. Special schools, technical institutes, and colleges should be personally known to the counselor. Visits to institutions such as schools for the mentally retarded, the mentally and emotionally disturbed, and the physically disabled will broaden the education and understanding of the counselor. All of life and living, in its various aspects, is pertinent for his background and will contribute in some measure to his competence as a counselor.

It is apparent that in-service training may take many forms, cover many areas, and utilize many techniques. The important factor is the presence of an organized, continuing program which will make it possible for counselors to maintain and improve their competence as counselors.

Research and Evaluation

Several reviews have been made of the results of research in the field of counseling and guidance. Some of these, together with a few references to single studies, will be found in the Suggested Readings at the end of this chapter. Some studies have been mentioned in Chapters 11 and 14. The *Review of Educational Research,* a publication of the American Educational Research Association, reviews research in counseling and guidance at three-year intervals, the most recent review appearing in April, 1960. Here we are interested in the nature and problems of research undertaken to evaluate the effects of counseling and guidance services, rather than in the results of such research.

It is not enough to set up a program of guidance and counseling services, and then to assume that nothing further need be done. Even with trained personnel, and a program of in-service training to maintain or improve their competence, we cannot assume that desirable results are being achieved. We need to look at the program critically, and make some efforts to determine what results it is having, whether it is producing the effects which are desired. Evaluation is the process of appraising existing programs and practices to judge whether they are achieving their goals or objectives.

There has been some confusion regarding evaluation and research. Evaluation is not research, but may involve research. Research is a method or technique of evaluation. Research methods may be used to determine whether or not certain results are achieved, or what results are achieved. It makes no judgment as to the desirability of these results. Evaluation has a value aspect. It has a connotation of goodness or badness. This goodness or badness may be in terms of success in reaching certain goals or objectives which are accepted as desirable or good. Rushong notes that "evaluation is the process of making a subjective judgment on the basis of objective evidence of the extent to which the objectives of the educational program are being achieved."[6] Research is neutral in respect to its methods and results, however.

Some kinds of evaluation do not involve research. They attempt a direct judgment of whether a program is good or bad, successful or unsuccessful. Sometimes objectives or goals are specified, sometimes not. But no measurement is involved, no data are collected regarding results or outcomes. The evaluation consists of judgments of experts, of administrators, of teachers, of parents, of counselors, or of students or clients as to whether the program is good, useful, worthwhile, or not. Another approach to evaluation which does not involve research is the use of check lists of the presence or absence of trained or professional

[6] H. D. Rushong. Present status and trends in the evaluation of counseling. *Educ. psychol. Measmt*, 1953, 13, 418–430. Reprinted in G. F. Farwell & H. J. Peters (Eds.) *Guidance readings for counselors*. Chicago: Rand McNally, 1960. Pp. 629–639.

personnel and kinds of services and activities, or the extent of services. Numerous such devices have been developed.[7]

Most people recognize that this is not sufficient as a basis for determining the effects of a program. It provides no suggestions for improving services. More detailed, more objective, more controlled analysis is necessary. Such analysis need not involve experimentation, or research under planned and controlled conditions. Experimental research is desirable and necessary for determining the effectiveness of new techniques or methods, and for comparing various methods or programs. But other research methods can be applied to assessing the results or effectiveness of existing programs. Experimental research attempts to obtain answers to predetermined, specific questions concerning the application of controlled practices or "treatments"—what is known as "survey" research attempts to answer the general question of what happened. Evaluation of existing programs utilizes survey research methods.

If evaluation is an appraisal of the success or effectiveness of achieving certain goals or objectives, then it is necessary to know what these objectives are. It has been suggested in Chapter 2 that the objectives of counseling and guidance are the same as those of education. While these objectives may be stated in various ways and in detail, the statement of the Educational Policies Commission is a succinct one: the basic aims of education are (1) self-realization, (2) good human relationships, (3) economic efficiency, and (4) civic responsibility.[8] The acceptance of these objectives meets the requirement that the objectives of student personnel work should be related to the educational objectives of the school.[9]

The goal of the counseling and guidance program which is related to the general objectives of education has often been stated

[7] (1) W. Coleman. Some criteria for evaluating elementary school guidance services, *Elem. Sch. J.*, 1955, **5**, 274–278. Reprinted in Farwell & Peters (Eds.), *op. cit.*, pp. 623–628. (2) D. C. Andrew & R. DeV. Willey. *Administration and organization of the guidance program.* New York: Harper, 1958. Chapter 13.

[8] Educational Policies Commission. *The purposes of education in American democracy.* Washington, D.C.: National Education Association and American Association of School Administrators, 1938.

[9] P. L. Dressel. Personnel services in high school and college. *Occup.*, 1951, **29**, 331–340. Reprinted in Farwell & Peters (Eds.), *op. cit.*, pp. 608–623.

as the optimum development of the individual's intellectual, emotional, social, and occupational capacities. Personal adjustment, social adjustment, and vocational adjustment have been mentioned as goals (see Chapter 12 for a discussion of the goals of counseling). Maturity, independence, responsibility (or a responsible independence), and self-actualization are frequently mentioned as objectives.

It is not enough to state such general objectives, however. They must be defined and stated in the form of observable criteria. The specific characteristics, events, or behavior which are to be accepted as evidence of the objectives must be stated and defined. These are the *criteria* for the achievement of the objectives. The specification of such criteria is a difficult task. Objectives are usually broad and general, sometimes vague, and resistant to reduction to observable criteria. The criteria which are developed or accepted may not actually be related to, or be valid evidence of, the goals or objectives, or may only partially represent them. There may not be general acceptance of certain criteria as evidence of the objectives. Some of the behaviors which are evidence of the objectives may not be easily defined, or may not appear immediately or soon enough to use in evaluation procedures. The problem of defining or setting up criteria is the most difficult problem of evaluative research. Froehlich in his review of attempts at evaluation of guidance activities noted that "the lack of suitable criteria has been the greatest single difficulty to date."[10] This has continued to be true to the present. One of the difficulties complicating the development of criteria in this area, as distinguished from the academic or intellectual outcomes of education, is the fact that we are interested in attitudes and

---

[10] C. R. Froehlich. *Evaluating guidance procedures: a review of the literature.* U.S. Office of Education, Federal Security Administration, Misc. 3310, 1949. See also the following: (1) E. J. Shoben, Jr. Some problems in evaluating criteria of effectiveness. *Personnel Guid. J.,* 1953, 31, 287–294. Reprinted in H. B. McDaniel, J. E. Lallas, J. A. Saum & J. L. Gilmore (Eds.) *Readings in guidance.* New York: Holt, 1959. Pp. 283–286. Also reprinted in Farwell & Peters (Eds.), *op. cit.,* pp. 574–580. (2) B. T. Jensen, G. Coles & Beatrice Nestor. The criterion problem in guidance research. *J. counsel. Psychol.,* 1955, 2, 58–61. (3) C. H. Patterson. Methodological problems in evaluation. *Personnel Guid. J.,* 1960, 39, 270–274.

behavior rather than knowledge, in personality characteristics rather than academic achievement per se.

Some of the criteria or evidences of the objectives of counseling and guidance services which have been proposed are the following: reduction in scholastic failures; improvement in grades; reduction in drop-outs or increased continuations to graduation; increased acceptance in college; success in college; participation in extracurricular activities; realism of occupational choice; success in obtaining employment; persistence on a job; satisfaction with the job; improved personal adjustment; reduction in disciplinary problems. Many of these criteria are relatively objective. But some may be questioned as to their relevance. Many are affected by many other factors than counseling and guidance, and are therefore not adequate as criteria. The list does represent the attempt to specify objective criteria of behavior. However, many of the most significant aspects of behavior are difficult to objectify. In addition, some of the criteria may not apply to specific individuals. Hatch and Stefflre discuss the defects of some of these commonly used criteria.[11]

Even when specific criteria are stated and defined, we are not yet ready or able to evaluate the success of our practices in achieving them. The criteria must be put into a form in which they can be measured in some way. Instruments must be discovered or developed which will yield measures or scores of the criterion variables. Some of the criteria listed above are used because they are easy to quantify or measure. The need for objectivity in observation and measurement has led to the acceptance of easily observed and measured criteria which are sometimes not entirely relevant or which are substitutes for other criteria, Immediate criteria are used instead of ultimate or long-term criteria. Participation in student activities, for example, may be used instead of civic activity in later years, without any evidence that they are actually related.

The next step in evaluation is the use of the criteria in such a

[11] R. Hatch & B. Stefflre. *Administration of guidance services.* Englewood Cliffs, N.J.: Prentice-Hall, 1958. Chapter 7. See also R. M. W. Travers. A critical review of techniques for evaluating guidance. *Educ. Psychol. Measmt.,* 1949, **9**, 211–225. Reprinted in Farwell & Peters (Eds.), *op. cit.,* pp. 640–651. Also reprinted in H. B. McDaniel, *et al., op. cit.,* pp. 383–389.

way that we can determine if scores on the criteria are related to counseling and guidance services. That is, we must determine if counseling and guidance services affect or influence measures of the criteria. This is not as simple as might appear. It requires a plan of study—or, as it is usually termed, a research design—which when followed will answer the question: Does the application of counseling and guidance services make a difference? Merely measuring criterion variables in a group of students exposed to such services is not sufficient. This will not tell us whether the scores obtained have any relationship to the services. There are two major methods of determining this. One is to obtain scores before exposure to the services, and compare them with scores obtained following the provision of services. The other is to compare two groups, one of which has had the services, and the other of which has not. It is necessary, however, to rule out, insofar as possible, the possibility that the results may have been due to factors other than the services provided. For example, comparing students before and after exposure to services may, if the time period is long, involve the results of normal growth and development. In the case of comparing two groups, the group which is exposed to counseling and guidance services may have more potential for change or improvement—they may be more intelligent, more highly motivated, more mature, etc., and thus might have shown greater change even without the services. It is therefore necessary to attempt to control such factors in studying the results of counseling and guidance services. One way of doing this is to equate or match the groups before the study, or to select the two groups in such a way that they can be considered equivalent. This is not always easy to do, however.[12]

The problem of evaluation of services is an important and difficult one. All that is attempted here is to point out its importance and to suggest the difficulties involved in such evaluation. We cannot continue doing what we are doing because we feel or believe it is helpful. We must appraise our activities in terms of the results, and be willing to change them if results are not achieved.

[12] The problems involved in such studies are discussed in the references cited in earlier footnotes. See also C. H. Patterson. Matching versus randomization in studies of counseling. *J. counsel. Psychol.*, 1956, 3, 262–271.

Evaluation by means of research enables us to check the effects of what we are doing. It is perhaps necessary to suggest caution, however. While it has not been demonstrated without question that counseling, for example, is highly effective, this does not mean that we should abandon it. The lack of evidence to date is to a great extent the result of the difficulties involved in such research. Few studies are adequate enough to encourage much confidence in their findings. While ultimately we must demand objective evidence of our efforts, there seems to be enough accumulated or subjective clinical evidence, with some research support, to feel that counseling does make a difference, that *most* clients (or students) obtain *some* benefit from the counseling process.

The Counselor's Role in Research

It is apparent from the foregoing brief discussion that research is difficult. It requires knowledge of research techniques and methods, and time and facilities for the collection and analysis of data. If electronic computers are not required, at least an automatic calculator is necessary. And the results of any single study in a single school are limited. What place has research in the work of the busy practicing counselor? We shall attempt to answer this question under two headings: (1) the counselor as a consumer of research, and (2) the counselor as a producer of research.

The counselor as a consumer of research. Practice, at least good practice, is based upon research. Research is the basis of professional activity, the source of the knowledge which is characteristic of a profession. A profession cannot operate upon the basis of common sense alone, nor of intuition or superstition. Magic is no longer an accepted basis of explanation; witch doctors are not currently accredited as professionals.

The counselor as a professional person must therefore base his practice, insofar as possible, upon accepted knowledge based upon research. It is apparent, therefore, that he must be familiar with the results of research. His education in counseling, and the in-service training discussed above have as their purpose the acquisition of the professional knowledge requisite for competence. Since the counselor must keep abreast of developments and advances in his field, and since these advances incorporate the results of research, it follows that the counselor is a consumer of research.

Unlike the consumers of most of the articles of our industrialized society, who need know little if anything of their development, construction, or mechanism, the counselor must know something about research if he is to use its results intelligently. While it would perhaps be desirable to have middlemen who would take the results of research, interpret them, and spell out their implications for application in practice, such a group does not exist. The practitioner must do this for himself. The counselor as a professional person has a responsibility, as do other professional persons such as the doctor, for keeping abreast of advances in his field. This responsibility has several aspects.

First, the counselor must expose himself to new developments, to reports of research. This is part of his personal responsibility, discussed above in connection with in-service training. He does this by subscribing to and reading the journals of his profession and current books and monographs reporting research, and by attendance at professional meetings where the results of recent research are reported.

Second, he must prepare himself to be able to understand what he reads. Practitioners often avoid reading research articles, and look for material of the "how-to-do-it" variety. The complaint is often made that research reports are dry, do not apply to the practical situation, are equivocal, or are too complicated to follow. Counselors sometimes seem to have a number phobia, and pass over articles with tables of figures. Since they are not especially trained in research, they feel inadequate in reading research reports, and may tend to avoid the responsibility of keeping up with research developments.

Now it is true that some, if not most, research reports are not entertaining reading, and some are difficult to understand. Few are definitive or earth-shaking as to their findings, and many are not immediately relevant or directly applicable to practice. Nevertheless, they are important. Progress is slow, and significant results accumulate by small increments. It takes imagination, intelligence, and caution to recognize or develop applications. But the counselor who is to grow and improve his competence must do this. He must read and understand what research is being done, if only to realize that there are no simple, sure, and final answers to the questions and problems with which he is faced in his practice. In some areas, such as the development and expansion of tests, change is rapid. The counselor cannot depend on others, such as publishers, to evaluate new tests for him. He must be able to read the manuals and reports critically and make his own decisions.

The counselor must, it is apparent, have a basic knowledge of statistics. An understanding of measurement is essential. It is not required that he be a statistician, however. The essential knowledge is relatively simple, or should be if the fear of statistics did not inhibit understanding, and if statistics is well taught. An understanding of the theory of statistical inference, of the significance of differences, of correlation and simple analysis of variance will enable the counselor to understand the majority of reports of published research. Good research is not necessarily statistically complex. Some of the best research has been quite simple in terms of the statistical techniques used.

The counselor as a producer of research. One of the best ways to understand research is to do it. This suggests that conducting a research project as part of an in-service training program would be useful. Such group research can help counselors understand research, as well as meet the responsibility of contributing to research.

The practitioner is in a particularly favorable position as a potential contributor to research. He faces problems every day, and is aware of problem areas, questions, and needs for information which research could supply. Research is essentially nothing more than a systematic, objective attempt to obtain answers to questions. An experiment is essentially a *controlled* experience. Research attempts to answer questions by collecting information that is objective, reliable, and valid, which is free from opinions, biases, prejudices, and the influence of extraneous factors. It involves a clear definition of the question or problem, and a specification of the conditions which will provide an answer, uninfluenced as far as possible by interfering factors or conditions.

Conducting research is not as formidable as it sounds. Research need not always be complex, extensive, or involve advanced statistical devices—again, good research is basically simple. It does not require a Ph.D. Perhaps the greatest obstacle to research being done by counselors, aside from their fear about its complexity, is the lack of time. A progressive administration will include research in the job description or job requirements of the counselor, and allocate time in which it can be done.

While extensive and intensive research projects are expensive in terms of time and money, there are many smaller studies or projects which can be undertaken by a counselor or a group of counselors. Many of the questions which arise in the counselor's mind may be answered, in part at least, by recourse to data which is available in the records and files. One of the basic reasons for keeping records is research, although too often records are not set up to facilitate their use for research. As a result it is often difficult to utilize data which are already available. Often they are incomplete. Nevertheless, there is still much that such data may yield to the imaginative counselor. Test records particularly are useful. There is a need for "do-it-yourself research" involving tests.[13] Local norms for tests are often useful. Publishers of tests welcome such data, and counselors can contribute to normative data on tests by sending it to the publishers.

Research is not limited to experimentation, as seems to be implied by some. If it were, there would be relatively little research in the human sciences. Counselors are sometimes discouraged because they cannot perform experiments. But there are other kinds of research,[14] and counselors can engage in such types. There is room for the contributions of counselors who are puzzled by questions, and who are stimulated to attempt to find answers —at least partial answers—to their questions. Research is a way in which curiosity can be satisfied, and every counselor, if he is alive and growing, should be curious, should question traditional ways of doing things, should be willing to test the effects of what he is doing and to try new approaches and evaluate them. This is re-

[13] (1) H. S. Dyer. The need for do-it-yourself prediction research in high school guidance. *Personnel Guid. J.*, 1957, **36**, 162–167. (2) Y. Y. Harris & A. A. Dole. A pilot study in local research with the Differential Aptitude Test battery. *Personnel Guid. J.*, 1960, **39**, 128–132.

[14] C. H. Patterson. Methodological problems in evaluation, *op. cit.*

search, and it is something that should be part of the duty and responsibility of every counselor.

Follow-up studies of graduates are frequently emphasized as an area of research activities of counselors. What happens to graduates of the school? Are the predictions of the counselor borne out? Do those whom he feels are not college material, but who go on to college anyway, succeed or fail? Are the tests used in the counseling and guidance program related to success or achievement after graduation? These are only a few of the questions which follow-up studies may help to answer.

Summary

It is important that consideration be given to the improvement of services if a counseling and guidance program is to maintain its effectiveness. Two aspects of this concern are the development of professional competence in the individual and the development of the program on the basis of research.

The counselor has a responsibility to himself, his clients, and his profession to maintain and increase his professional competence. Methods of doing this include personal reading and study, affiliation with and participation in professional organizations and their activities, and attending regular and special courses of training, including participation in in-service training programs. Suggestions were made concerning the nature and content of in-service training programs.

Counselors should be concerned about research in two ways. First, as consumers of research they should know enough about research methods and techniques to be able to understand and utilize research reported in the literature. Second, they should be, to some extent at least, producers of research. It is not necessary that the counselor be trained to the doctoral level in research and statistics to contribute to research. As a practitioner he is faced with many problems and questions which are important, to others as well as to himself. Almost every counselor is, or should be, in a position to provide at least some tentative answers to some of his questions. Searching for such answers, in as objective a way as possible, is research. Research is thus something which is not beyond the counselor as a practitioner, but is a natural reaction to the facing of questions met in everyday practice.

SUGGESTED READINGS

Benson, A. L. (Ed.) *Criteria for evaluating guidance programs in secondary schools.* U.S. Office of Education, Federal Security Agency, Misc. 3317. Washington, D.C.: Government Printing Office, 1949. A detailed statement of criteria of various kinds, but mainly of the nature and extent of services provided and the qualifications and competence of staff.

Benson, A. L. (Ed.) *How to use the criteria for evaluating guidance programs in secondary schools.* U.S. Office of Education, Federal Security Agency, Misc. 3317a. Washington, D.C.: Government Printing Office, 1949. A companion to the reference above. The procedure involves a combination of self-evaluation and evaluation by outside experts against the criteria.

Caravello, S. J. Effectiveness of high school guidance services. *Personnel Guid. J.,* 1958, **36,** 323–325. Results indicate that a full-time counselor specialist was more effective than teacher counselors.

Dressel, P. L. Personnel services in high school and college. *Occup.,* 1951, **29,** 331–340. Reprinted in Farwell, G. F., & Peters, H. J. (Eds.) *Guidance Readings for Counselors.* Chicago: Rand McNally, 1960. Pp. 608–623. This is a good, brief discussion of the problems of evaluation of student personnel services.

Hatch, R. & Stefflre, B. *Administration of guidance services.* Englewood Cliffs, N.J.: Prentice-Hall, 1958. Chapter 7 is an excellent discussion of the evaluation of guidance services.

Merenda, P. F. & Rothney, J. W. M. Evaluating the effects of counseling—eight years after. *J. counsel. Psychol.,* 1958, **5,** 163–168. A more detailed report of an aspect of the study reported in the book by Rothney (see below).

O'Dea, J. D. & Zeran, F. R. Evaluating effects of counseling. *Personnel Guid. J.,* 1953, **31,** 241–244. A critical review of eighty studies related to the evaluation of counseling.

Rothney, J. W. M. *Guidance practices and results.* New York: Harper, 1958. A report of one of the most extensive evaluations of counseling at the high-school level, involving a five-year follow-up.

Samler, J. Professional training: end goal—or kick-off point? *Personnel Guid. J.,* 1952, **31,** 15–19. Emphasizes the importance of in-service training for maintaining professional growth and competence in counseling, and suggests some subjects or areas for training.

APPENDIXES

APPENDIX I

Counseling and Guidance

Provisions of the National

Defense Education Act of

1958 (Public Law 85-864)

TITLE V—GUIDANCE, COUNSELING, AND TESTING; IDENTIFICATION AND ENCOURAGEMENT OF ABLE STUDENTS

Part A—State Programs
Appropriations Authorized

SEC. 501.   There are hereby authorized to be appropriated $15,000,-000 for the fiscal year ending June 30, 1959, and for each of the three succeeding fiscal years, for making grants to State educational agencies under this part to assist them to establish and maintain programs of testing and guidance and counseling.

Allotments to States

SEC. 502.   From the sums appropriated pursuant to section 501 for any fiscal year the Commissioner shall reserve such amount, but not in excess of 2 per centum thereof, as he may determine for allotment as provided in section 1008. From the remainder of such sums the Commissioner shall allot to each State an amount which bears the same ratio to the amount of such remainder as the school-age populations of such State bears to the total of the school-age populations of all of the States. The amount allotted to any State under the preceding sentence for any fiscal year which is less than $20,000 shall be increased to $20,000, the total of increases thereby required being derived by proportionately reducing the amount allotted to each of the remaining States under the preceding sentence, but with such adjustments as may be necessary to prevent the allotment of any such remaining States from being thereby reduced to less than $20,000.

State Plans

SEC. 503. (a) Any State which desires to receive payments under this part shall submit to the Commissioner, through its State educational agency, a State plan which meets the requirements of section 1004 (a) and sets forth—

(1) a program for testing students in the public secondary schools, and if authorized by law in other secondary schools, of such State to identify students with outstanding aptitudes and ability, and the means of testing which will be utilized in carrying out such program; and

(2) a program of guidance and counseling in the public secondary schools of such State (A) to advise students of courses of study best suited to their ability, aptitudes, and skills, and (B) to encourage students with outstanding aptitude and ability to complete their secondary school education, take the necessary courses for admission to institutions of higher education, and enter such institutions.

(b) The Commissioner shall approve any State plan and any modification thereof which complies with the provisions of sub-section (a).

Payments to States

SEC. 504. (a) Payment under this part shall be made to those State educational agencies which administer plans approved under section 503. For the fiscal year ending June 30, 1959, such payments shall equal the amount expended by the State in carrying out its State plan, and for the fiscal year ending June 30, 1960, and for each of the two succeeding fiscal years, such payments shall equal one-half of the amount so expended; except that no State educational agency shall receive payment under this part for any fiscal year in excess of that State's allotment for that fiscal year as determined under section 502.

(b) In any State which has a State plan approved under section 503 and in which the State educational agency is not authorized by law to make payments to cover the cost of testing students in any one or more secondary schools in such State to determine student abilities and aptitudes, the Commissioner shall arrange for the testing of such students and shall pay the cost thereof for the fiscal year ending June 30, 1959, and one-half of the cost thereof for any of the three succeeding fiscal years out of such State's allotment. Testing of students pursuant to this subsection shall, so far as practicable, be comparable to, and be done at the same grade levels and under the same conditions as in the case of, testing of students in public schools under the State plan.

Part B—Counseling and Guidance Training Institutes

Authorization

SEC. 511. There are hereby authorized to be appropriated $6,250,-000 for the fiscal year ending June 30, 1959, and $7,250,000 for each of the three succeeding fiscal years, to enable the Commissioner to arrange, by contracts with institutions of higher education, for the operation by them of short-term or regular session institutes for the provision of training to improve the qualifications of personnel engaged in counseling and guidance of students in secondary schools, or teachers in such schools preparing to engage in such counseling and guidance. Each individual, engaged, or preparing to engage, in counseling and guidance in a public secondary school, who attends an institute operated under the provisions of this part shall be eligible (after application therefor) to receive a stipend at the rate of $75 per week for the period of his attendance at such institute, and each such individual with one or more dependents shall receive an additional stipend at the rate of $15 per week for each such dependent for the period of such attendance.

APPENDIX II

1960 White House Conference on Children and Youth: Resolutions Relating to Guidance Services in Schools[1]

That coordinated programs of pupil personal services, adequately staffed with professional personnel, be established in these areas: attendance, guidance, health, psychological, and social work. (187)[2] That guidance and counseling programs be strengthened, expanded, and coordinated at all levels; and that the role of the guidance and counseling program be clearly defined. (190)

That guidance and counseling begin in the elementary school with educational and vocational planning based on early, continuous, and expanded testing and diagnostic appraisal of each child, in order to identify abilities, weaknesses and problems, mental, physical, and emotional. (191)

That every secondary school have sufficient trained professional counselors to deal with adolescent problems; that each adolescent be counseled throughout the secondary years by the same staff adviser, acceptable to him; that school planning for adolescents be based on awareness of individual differences in skills and capacities; that community counseling services be made more widely available to youth

[1] From *Conference Proceedings: Golden Anniversary White House Conference on Children and Youth, March 27–April 2, 1960.* Washington, D.C.: Golden Anniversary White House Conference on Children and Youth, 1960.
[2] Numbers in parentheses are the numbers of the recommendations in the Composite Forum Recommendations.

and their parents; and that coordination between school and community services be emphasized. (192)

That school resources for identification and guidance of the gifted, limited, and otherwise exceptional child, as well as for the average and normal youth, be expanded and improved. (193)

That vocational counseling and guidance programs be provided with adequate financial support from Federal, State, and local sources; that school personnel, boards, and parents interpret to taxpayers the need for increased and improved guidance services; and that these services cooperate closely with Government, employment services, industries, labor unions, armed services, trade and service organizations, higher educational institutions, and other community groups. (194)

That the qualified professional staff (of every school system) include educational and vocational guidance counselors, job placement counselors, physical health personnel, psychologists to assist in diagnosis and continued study of the children, and school social workers or visiting teachers to assist in the treatment of children with special problems. (195)

That the ratio of students to elementary school counselors be 600 to 1. (196)

That the number of students per counselor in secondary schools be decreased from the present ratio of 625 to 1, to 250 to 1. (197)

That more adequate psychological and psychiatric services be provided for all school-age youth in a ratio of 1 specialist to 2,000 pupils. (198)

That all States require the certification of guidance counselors and other specialized personnel. (199)

That the qualifications for certification be continually reviewed and strengthened, in accordance with the latest research findings in the field; and that they recognize and give credit to appropriate training and work experience in lieu of classroom teaching. (200)

That the training of guidance and counseling personnel for elementary and secondary schools, colleges, and community and professional agencies be intensified and improved to meet the demand; and that Federal funds for the education of school counselors be given only to institutions with professionally approved counselor education programs. (201)

That all local school units encourage in-service education programs in guidance and counseling; and that rural teachers take in-service training geared to rural area learning needs. (206)

That vocational guidance and placement services be strengthened and expanded, with more qualified, professional counselors, in schools and in State and private employment agencies; that communication and cooperation among these groups be increased; and that detailed studies be made of occupational trends and requirements, in order to provide youth with full, up-to-date information on job opportunities in general and the outlook in specific occupations. (253)

That training of guidance counselors include knowledge of physical and mental demands of job and placement opportunities. (254)

That guidance services give more attention to potential dropouts at all levels, and that counselors stress the importance of education, motivate their ambition, and encourage them to remain in school so that they will be better prepared for work. (178)

That parents be brought in to participate in educational and vocational planning with a qualified counselor at the time their children drop out. (179)

That joint action be initiated among schools, parents, employers, unions, and State and community agencies, starting at the elementary level, to find solutions to the problems of "dropouts," minority youth, and others with special employment difficulties. (263)

That local programs for gifted children and youth provide for—
    . . . broader and more sensitive tools for identification, including means of uncovering latent talents in handicapped, culturally deprived, and emotionally disturbed children; guidance by able and sympathetic adults with high values, of parents and teachers as well as the gifted themselves. . . . (166)

That dynamic programs of instruction and services be provided for the slow-learning child, to stimulate him to make the most of his potentialities, including—
    . . . definite preparation for vocational and social life; work experience; educational guidance for child and parents to remove obstacles to full utilization of his capabilities. . . . (172)

That schools or other agencies provide counseling services with sufficient numbers of qualified, specialized personnel for individual guidance to handicapped children and their families from the time the handicap is first recognized to adult years, in order to help the children understand their own capabilities and limitations; identify children who will need special vocational training; help the family to understand and deal with the handicapped child's needs. (559)

That the schools develop liaison with public and voluntary agencies serving the handicapped, to help the transition of handicapped youth from school to work. (562)

That all schools provide multidiscipline services for identification of mental handicaps at the start of a child's school experience, with evaluation throughout his education. (592)

That the provisions of the National Defense Education Act be expanded to assist communities in establishing psychological and guidance services in elementary schools. (411)

INDEXES

INDEX OF NAMES

INDEX OF SUBJECTS